HOW I PHOTOGRAPH WILDLIFE AND NATURE

Leonard Lee Rue III

World Almanac Publications
New York, New York

All photographs by Leonard Lee Rue III unless otherwise noted.

Book design by Thomas P. Ruis
Cover design by Jay J. Smith

First published in paperback in 1985.

Distributed in the United States by Ballantine Books, a division of Random House, Inc. and in
Canada by Random House of Canada, Ltd.

Library of Congress Catalog Card Number
Newspaper Enterprise Association ISBN: 0-94818-51-0
Ballantine Books ISBN: 0-345-32624-5

Printed in the United States of America

World Almanac Publications
Newspaper Enterprise Association
A division of United Media Enterprises
A Scripps Howard company
200 Park Avenue
New York, NY 10166

10 9 8 7 6 5 4 3 2 1

CONTENTS

With love to Irene Vandermolen,
with whom I have spent
some of the very best years of my life.

FOREWORD

Wildlife photography is a rather new profession. Indeed some outdoor enthusiasts—naturalists for the most part—have been taking bird and mammal pictures ever since cameras became portable enough to carry into the field. Some of their fading wildlife studies, buried deep in archives and attics, are remarkable, given the immense limitations of early equipment and technology. Some names come to mind.

Jim Corbett, the legendary stalker of man-eating Bengal tigers, eventually put his rifles aside and ended his career by just filming the big cats. He was the first person to succeed in doing so. Carl Ackeley shot splendid photos of African big game before he was fatally injured by one of his subjects, an elephant. George Shiras pioneered photographing North American big game; his night pictures by flash of the Wyoming moose (named *Alces shirasi* after him) are still outstanding.

But today thousands of professional photographers are roaming wild lands around the world, and many are producing astonishingly good work. Of all these, one name, Leonard Lee Rue III, is far more widely known than all the rest. That isn't any wonder.

Pick up almost any publication that ever uses natural history illustrations and you will find Rue's credit line on the most striking of the wildlife photos. Stated as simply as possible, more of his nature photographs have been printed and reprinted than those of any other cameraman, past or present. It is difficult to comprehend how one man has accomplished so much. The truth is that no one is better qualified to write about wildlife photography than Lennie Rue. The pictures and advice in this book well illustrate what I mean.

It is easily possible, I'm convinced, to pick out Rue's pictures from those of his contemporaries. Technically they are perfect. They are made by someone who understands (and uses properly) all of his equipment. But there are qualities harder to define evident in his raccoons and vireos, in his weasels and whitetail deer.

To begin, you simply do not shoot such fine pictures of creatures without being an animal behaviorist as well as being totally at home in your "laboratory"—the outdoors. You must be patient and possessed of equanimity. Most of all you must be young and enthusiastic, no matter how old you are. At 57, Lennie Rue slogs the swamps and steepest slopes, slapping at mosquitoes, like someone half his age. Or so it seems to someone who just may be his oldest admirer.

When anyone asks me (as they often do) how to become a successful wildlife photographer, I always advise them to follow the example of Lennie Rue.

Erwin A. Bauer
Teton Village, Wyoming

ACKNOWLEDGMENTS

Art Wilkens really got me started in photography, many years ago. I had taken photographs with a box camera as a kid, but Art's interest in photography rubbed off on me and prompted me to get my first 35 mm camera when I was nineteen. Ed Bates helped me understand the basics of cameras and helped with equipment selection. Evelyn Serfass taught me how to develop rolls of film, and Graham Wilson taught me how to print black and white photographs.

Over the years I have been helped by many, many people. It is one reason why I try to help others. I still ask help from others; none of us ever gets to know it all.

Here, alphabetically, are a few of the people who stand out in my mind. I want to thank them, and unnamed thousands, from the bottom of my heart: Pat and Le Roy Bauer, Nell Bolen, Harry Darrow, Phil Dotson, Bob Elman, Roy Guinsler, Charlie Heidecker, Cleve Hickman, John Holmes and sons, Nick Hromiak, George Johnson, Marie and Ray Kirkland, Gary Knepp, Debbie and Roger Marcum, Ed Miller, Ollie Nehland, Mike Quinton, Bill Shipley, Ralph, Fred, and Eric Space, Rita and Charlie Summers, Joe Taylor, Ruth and Charlie Travers, Danita and Glenn Wampler, Larry West, Floyd Wolfarth, Betty and Jim Woodford, and Wally Wrede.

Thanks also to Bob Kapke, my agent, to Jane D. Flatt, my publisher, and to Patricia Fisher, my editor, all of whom were as excited as I was about this book.

My heartfelt thanks go to my sister, Evelyn Rue Guthrie, for again taking time from her extremely busy schedule to decipher my handwriting and turn it into this manuscript. And to her husband, Bill, for reading it. My oldest son, Leonard Lee Rue IV, goes by the professional name of Len Rue, Jr., so that editors and publishers can distinguish between us. Lenny is a better technical photographer than I will ever be. People can recognize my style of photography, but they cannot distinguish between my photos and the photos of those whom I have taught: Len Rue, Jr., Tim Lewis Rue, James Keith Rue, and Irene Vandermolen. A special thanks to Irene for all the miles, all the smiles, all the memories, and all the photographs.

God be with all of them and you.

Leonard Lee Rue III
Blairstown, New Jersey

INTRODUCTION

... I will teach you the good and the right way.
                                    —I Samuel 12:23

A recent survey by the U.S. Fish and Wildlife Service revealed that one of every two Americans over the age of sixteen participated in some form of outdoor activity involving fish and wildlife during 1980. Among the nearly 100 million people engaged in these activities were 83 million who observed and photographed wildlife.

Those statistics have to make wildlife photography the number one outdoor participant activity in the nation. Unlike most sports, where the bulk of the public are merely viewers, in photography we are all participants.

I am deluged with letters and constantly meeting people who say that they envy my being out-of-doors all the time, photographing wildlife. They want to know how one goes about becoming a wildlife photographer. A classic letter in my files consists of just three questions: "How do I get to be a wildlife photographer? Where do I find the wildlife? Where do I sell my pictures and for how much?" Obviously I cannot reduce a lifetime of experience and knowledge into a letter. But that is what I attempt to do in this book.

I have always been interested in wildlife; it has been the pivotal point in my life. I started taking notes on wildlife and their behavior when I was eight years old. At the age of fourteen I delivered an oral report in school on my stated goal of becoming a wildlife photographer. Everything I have done in my life has been directed toward that goal.

The single most important aspect of wildlife photography is knowing about wildlife. You have to love wildlife to really understand it, and it requires lots of time and effort to gain the needed knowledge. It will be time enjoyably spent. You must learn about wildlife traits, habits, and habitats; you must know where the wildlife is, where it is going to be at certain times of the year and day, and why it will be there.

I make no apologies for the fact that I am a professional naturalist and wildlife photographer today because I was a trapper as a kid. I was raised on a small mountain farm during the Great Depression, and no farm kid at that time ever had spending money. A man working on a farm earned a dollar a day. Fur prices were not high, but a few dollars could be made by trapping.

I loved wildlife of all kinds, and every minute I could spare, and some that I could not, I was out studying wildlife. I knew every inch of the woods, fields, brooks, and rivers in my area. I learned what creatures of the wild eat, where they find their food, when food is available to them, and what time they usually eat it. I found the dens of woodchucks, skunks, raccoons, and foxes; muskrats' bank dens and their houses; pheasants' nests; and owls' roosting sites. I learned to read signs; I was constantly on the lookout for tracks, droppings, hair or fur, gnawings on wood or bone, and any other indication of what wild creature lived where and why. I have not trapped in years, but the knowledge I gained about wildlife stood me in good stead when I began to photograph wildlife. And I am still learning about wildlife today.

Obviously most folks cannot learn about wildlife the way I did; only 2.5 percent of our entire population lives on farms or ranches today. Although nothing will ever take the place of studying wild creatures in the field, there are many other ways to learn about wildlife.

A tremendous amount of knowledge can be gained by reading some of the thousands of excellent books written on wildlife. My personal library has over 7500 reference books. And I hope you will read some of the 18 books I have written on the subject.

I also suggest that you join your local Audubon Society bird club. Many Audubon members are experts on all kinds of wildlife and know where it can be found at almost any given time. Go to Audubon camps, on Sierra Club trail trips, or to your local museums, and walk their nature trails. Your local hunting club probably has many hunters willing to share a knowledge of wildlife acquired from countless seasons spent afield. The biologists and game protectors of your state's Fish and Wildlife Division are also excellent sources of the whereabouts of almost any species of wildlife found in your immediate area.

No full-time schools specialize in the teaching of wildlife photography, but the basic photographic knowledge that schools of photography do teach is essential and can be adapted to photographing wildlife. Classes are available in wildlife photography, and I have opened a school of my own.

If you cannot afford the time or money for a school or special courses, I suggest that you join your local camera club, particularly the Photographic Society of America Camera Club's nature division. There are many excellent naturalists who are superb photographers in that division, and I have great respect for their work. These people are much more likely to share their knowledge and techniques with you than are some of the pros.

As a beginning wildlife photographer you should not plan exotic trips abroad. Start in your own backyard. I take a lot of excellent wildlife photographs from the windows of my home. Don't shoot through the glass; it can be done, but it shouldn't be. Open the window. I have several drapes in my home made out of camouflage material (although this is not essential) that serve as a blind.

Most wildlife photographs are taken in state or national parks, refuges, and sanctuaries, or on private or public preserves, because the wildlife in these areas is not as wary as it is in places where it is hunted. Only where the wildlife is completely protected does it gets old enough to become the fully mature, magnificent specimens that you see gracing magazines and books.

Before I go any further, I want to make one point that I cannot emphasize too strongly. As a wildlife photographer you have a moral obligation to the wild creatures you are photographing: You must not cause harm because of your activities. If you start to feed birds in the fall, you must continue throughout the winter months, until their natural foods are again available in the spring. When photographing nesting birds, do not keep the female off the nest for so long a time that the heat of the sun, or the cold, kills the eggs or chicks. If you work with baby wild animals, do not touch them; your scent on their bodies may cause their mother to abandon them. Do not subject reptiles and amphibians to excessive sun or heat because their skin will dry and they will die. Do not force wildlife to do something contrary to its nature. All wild creatures are constantly beset by natural forces and predators; do not sacrifice their lives for your photographs.

They say that "patience is a virtue." I certainly hope that you are virtuous, because no one can be a successful wildlife photographer without having the patience of Job. You cannot hurry wildlife; it has all the time in the world. Wildlife makes no appointments, it doesn't have to eat or sleep at a specified time. Many times, while the photographer is waiting at a den for

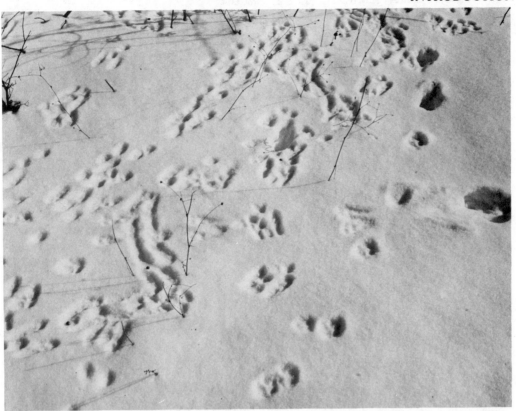

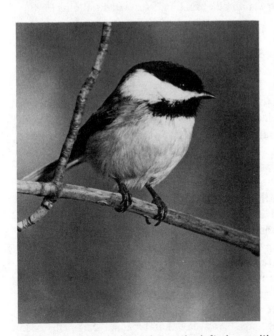

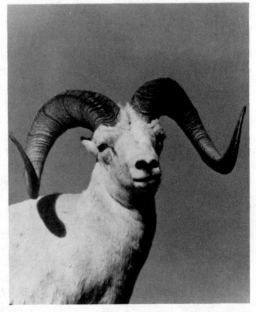

Top Cottontail rabbit tracks on the left along with tracks of the gray fox that caught the rabbit making the tracks.
Bottom left A black-capped chickadee photographed from my window.
Bottom right You have to photograph in protected areas to get close to beautiful mature animals like this Dall's sheep ram. Photo by Tim Lewis Rue

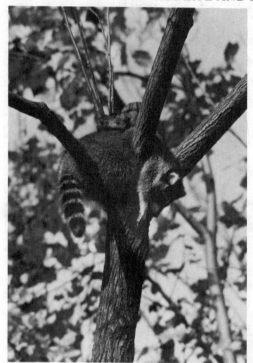
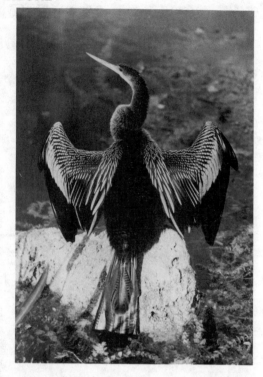

Left You cannot hurry wildlife; if a creature wants to sleep, it sleeps—as this raccoon is doing.
Photo by Irene Vandermolen
Right This anhinga was photographed from the trail named after it, in Everglades National Park,
Florida. Photo by Irene Vandermolen

an animal to reappear, the animal simply curls up inside and goes to sleep. Or he is waiting at a
feeding area, and the wildlife simply does not show up—because it has discovered the photographer or simply because it has found better food elsewhere. I love photographing from a
blind because even when I am not taking photographs, I am observing everything about me
and taking copious notes to be used in future lectures and books. I always say that I have all
the patience in the world, but because of my many commitments, I just don't have the time to
use it.

The kind of wildlife photography you do is largely determined by your own physical condition. But if you are able to be up and around at all, you can be a wildlife photographer. One of
my favorite spots for photographing is the Anhinga Trail in the Everglades National Park.
Many people negotiate this beautiful, paved trail in a wheelchair. Many excellent photographs
are taken from automobiles in state and national parks and at refuges. Most African animal
photographs are taken this way. People who are restricted to their homes, even those who live
in cities, may be able to photograph birds at a feeder from their windows, as I do. Aquariums,
terrariums, and small stages can be set up and photographed anywhere inside the home.

Photography under adverse conditions does require good physical conditioning. Don't ever
attempt to climb in our western mountains after elk, wild sheep, and goats without precondi-
tioning. You must exercise, you must stay in shape. Any day that I cannot carry 25 to 35
pounds of equipment up in the mountains I am out of business. And, be the good Lord willing,
I hope to photograph wildlife till the day I die. You can, too. This book can help you realize
that goal.

BASICS OF PHOTOGRAPHY AND EQUIPMENT

*The best pictures are recorded in your mind
and heart, not on film.*
— L. L. Rue III

Photography is the capturing of reflected light forming an image on a chemical emulsion. In its simplest form, a photograph can be taken through an uncovered pinhole allowing light to be projected on a piece of film at the rear of any light-tight box. Modern cameras are greatly advanced refinements of this basic premise; light enters through a lens, recording an image on film held flat at the rear of the camera body.

Joseph Nicephore Niepce made the first crude photograph in France in 1826. In 1837 Louis Jacques-Mande Daguerre perfected his daguerreotype by which he recorded fantastic photographic details on silvered copper plates. In England, William Henry Fox Talbot introduced his photogenic process in 1835. Talbot made paper light-sensitive with a solution of salt and silver nitrate. The major difference between the two systems was that with the daguerreotype there was a single metal, fine-detailed, image; with the paper photogenic system, hundreds of duplicate impressions could be made, although fine detail was lacking.

Combining the best of both techniques, Frederick Scott Archer of England developed the collodion, or wet glass plate system. This allowed for a negative, with fine detail, to be made on glass plates from which hundreds of reproductions could be made. The major drawback was that the plates had to be coated, used as soon as possible, and developed at once. In 1855 Roger Fenton photographed the Crimean War, and in 1862 Matthew Brady photographed the Civil War. Both men used a portable darkroom on the battlefields and wet plates. Timothy H. O'Sullivan and William Henry Jackson immortalized the scenic grandeur of our western states using wet plates.

In 1880 the dry glass plate was perfected; it could be prepared ahead of time, exposed and processed at a much later date. George Eastman brought out a film in 1888 that had a gelatin layer on a paper base. This was refined further to the basic film that we use today of an emulsion on a plastic base. From then on, photography belonged to the masses. Greater emulsion speeds, coupled with finer detail, have been the goal ever since with both black and white as well as color photography.

George Shiras III is the "father of wildlife photography." Shiras took his first photographs of deer in 1889 at Whitefish Lake, Michigan. His list of credentials is most impressive, and many of his photographs, made in the 1890s, cannot be topped today even with the most modern equipment.

Shiras was the first to photograph wildlife from a canoe in daylight, the first to get wild animals to take their own pictures, the first to use a remote release, the first to photograph wildlife with a flash at night from a canoe, the first to have wild animals take their own flash pictures at night, the first to use two sets of flashes and two cameras to get before-and-after shots of wildlife, and the first to use a camera as a gun on flying birds. People throughout the world were impressed by his work. He was awarded a gold medal at the Paris Exposition of 1900 and the Grand Prize at the St. Louis Exposition of 1904.

Shiras's contemporaries—photographers A. Radclyffe Dugmore, W. E. Carlin, E. D. Warren, C. William Beebe, W. H. Nash, Edward J. Davison, Charles Rice, Enos A. Mills, A. L. Preneehorn, and William L. Finley—were also pioneers in wildlife photography. All did truly outstanding work before 1900. What is even more amazing than the photographs they took is that they did it in spite of the equipment and film they had to use. The emulsion speed of the film was exceedingly slow, the lens aperture was slow, and cameras were bulky and heavy.

Seeing Photographs

A most important aspect of photography is the ability to "see" a photograph. Not everything that we see makes a good photograph, but even the most commonplace subject can be depicted advantageously by one who has the eye of an artist. And good photography is art.

What is a good photograph? Anything that pleases the eye of the beholder. What is a good, salable photograph? Any subject that is correctly exposed, composed, and focused and that the beholder, or photographic editor, wants or needs. Although a known photographer's work will be looked at more readily than that of an unknown, the beginner's work will sell if it is exactly what is wanted or needed. This crass commercial fact keeps the doors to photographic sales open to everyone.

I am primarily an animal portraitist. I attempt to capture a creature at its best because I love all creatures. I try to photograph wildlife when it is most attentive, when it is most alert. I try to capture a highlight in the eyes, to make the subject look "alive." I try to get the creature in its most characteristic pose when it is "doing its own thing." I try to capture tension or tenseness in body position and limb placement because implied action enhances the photograph. I try to be at the creature's own level, eyeball to eyeball; I want it to be seen as others of its kind would see it. Or I photograph it from slightly below; if possible, I try to silhouette it against a clear blue sky to simplify the background and strengthen the subject. This is my style, a style instantly recognized by thousands of people, even before they see the credit line.

Basic Composition

The human eye is seldom, if ever, at rest while the observer is looking at anything. It darts rapidly from one point of interest to another, focusing at different planes if a three-dimensional object is being viewed. And usually the observer is unaware that this is happening.

Artists, including photographers, have always been cognizant of this rapid eye motion. Deliberately, even subliminally, they direct the eye to focus on the object they wish to emphasize.

One basic fact must be remembered: The human eye sees selectively, or subjectively; the camera sees objectively. The camera records three dimensions as two—height and width; depth can only be implied. Still cameras take still photographs; motion is lacking, although it can be suggested. The emphasis must be supplied; the viewer must be forced to see what the photographer wants him to see.

This emphasis is achieved through subject placement, lighting, shading, framing, simplifying, perspective, scale, motion direction, repetition, balance, form and selective focusing.

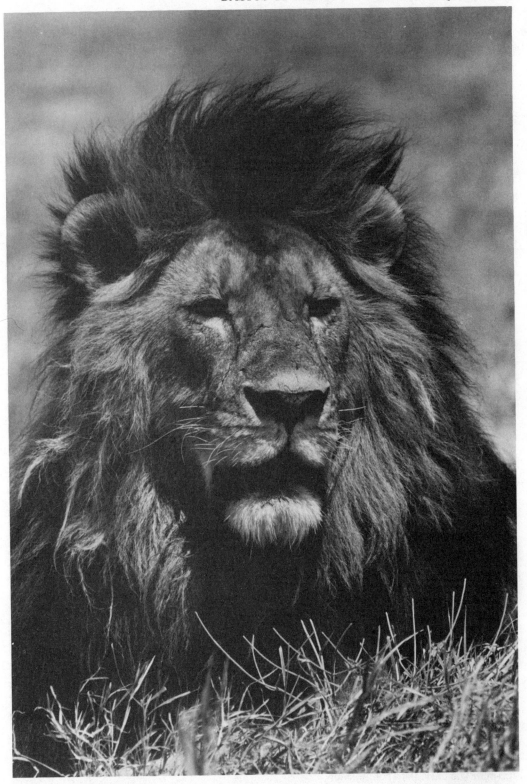

I am best known for the superb animal portraits that I take. This male African lion is one of the finest specimens I have ever seen.

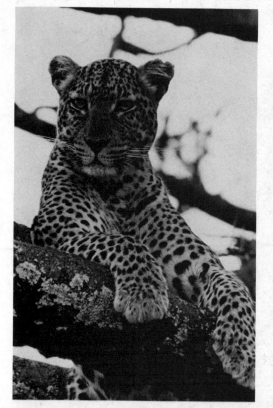
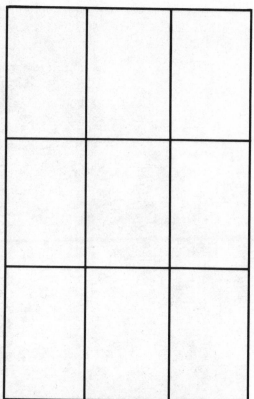
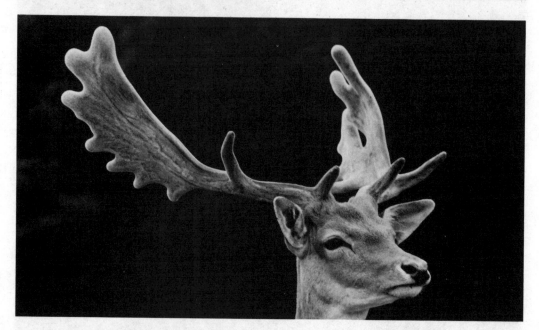

Top left In my portraits I try to present each creature at its best. From this photograph, the viewer knows exactly what an African leopard looks like.
Top right The basic third composition.
Bottom The positioning of this fallow deer in the print reflects the strong points of the rule of thirds. Photo by Irene Vandermolen

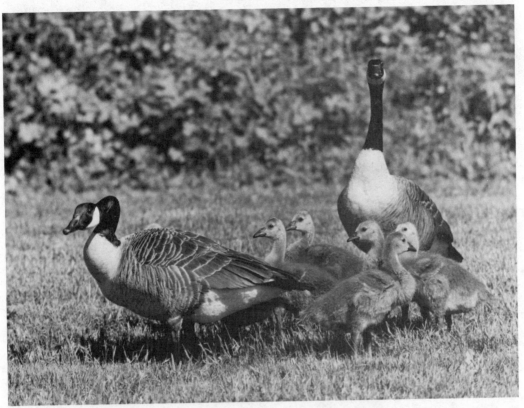

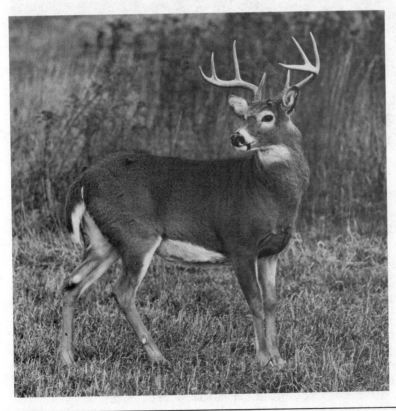

Top This portrait of a Canada goose family follows the rule of thirds. Photo by Irene Vandermolen

Bottom Your attention is focused on this white-tailed buck's eye in response to the intersection of the third lines. Photo by Irene Vandermolen

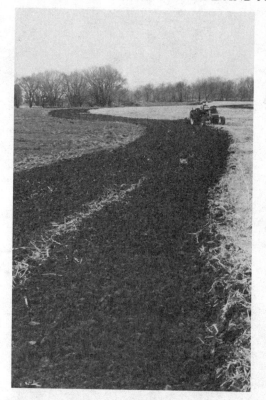

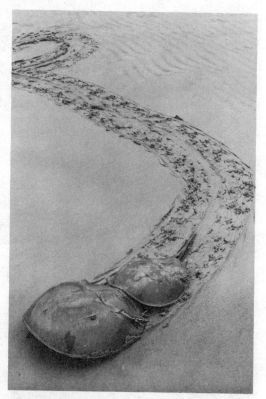

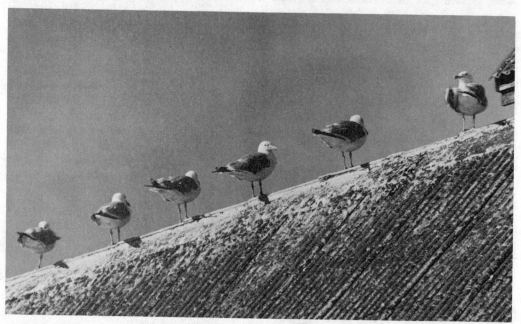

Top left The S-curve in composition pulls the viewer's eye to the tractor as the main subject and then follows the sweeping curve to the horizon.

Top right With this interrupted S-curve your eye starts at the horeshoe crabs, goes up to the circle, and back to the crabs.

Bottom The spacing of these herring gulls is showing territorialism biologically. In composition it is showing the use of diagonal lines and repetitiveness in the spacing of the gulls.

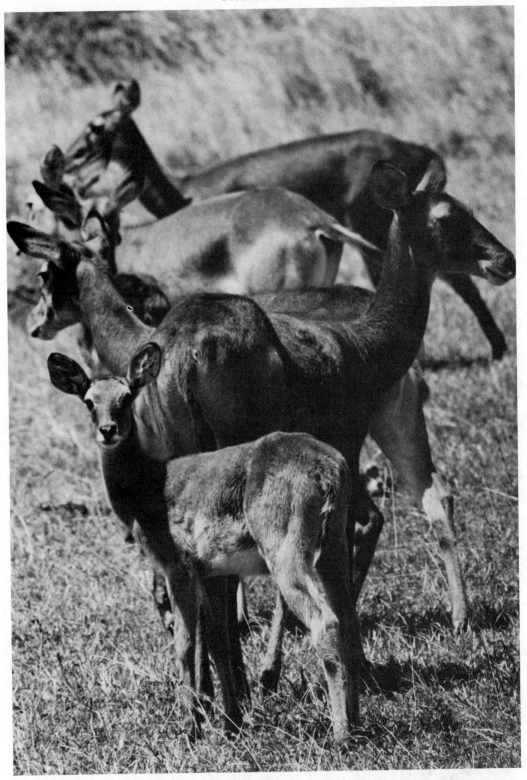

The wedge form in composition is very strong. This photo depicts female Uganda kob and their young.

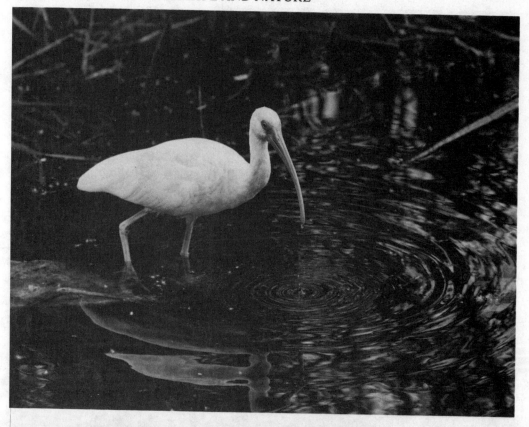

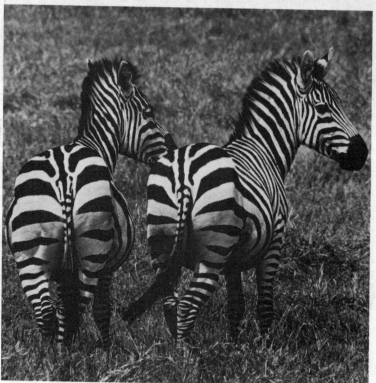

Top Circles form powerful compositions. Although the white ibis is the main subject, your eye is pulled automatically to the center of the circle. Photo by Irene Vandermolen *Bottom* This photo of Burchell's zebras follows the rule of thirds as well as the composition of striking patterns.

Probably the most basic rule of composition is the rule of thirds. Photographs are usually much more pleasing if the subject is not directly centered. It does not matter whether you are using a 2¼ square or 35 mm or larger rectangular format. Simply divide both the horizontal and vertical dimensions into thirds. The four points where the horizontal and vertical lines intersect are usually the points of strongest interest. Remember, however, that all rules are made to be broken, and on occasion a subject may be centered to strengthen a point. Still, most artists and photographers follow the rule of thirds.

The accompanying photographs and their captions illustrate the basics of composition without belaboring the point.

Cameras

When I became serious about wildlife photography 35 years ago, the camera used then by most professionals was the Super D Graphflex single lens reflex using 4 × 5 sheet film. I had every intention of buying one, but I settled instead on a single lens reflex (SLR) 35 mm. Later I switched almost entirely to a 2¼ SLR, but I have since changed back. I'll tell you why in a moment, but first let's discuss cameras and lenses.

Basically, a camera is a light-tight box containing a viewing system, mechanisms for holding and advancing the film, and usually a focal plane shutter that controls the speed at which the photograph will be taken. Today there are the miniature cameras taking half-frame pictures equal to 16 mm film. There are 35 mm rangefinder and SLR cameras, 2¼ or 120 mm SLR and 2¼ twin lens reflex cameras, 4 × 5 view cameras, and instant development cameras put out by Polaroid and Kodak.

Although wildlife can be photographed with all these cameras, the only two practical systems for wildlife photography are the 35 mm and the 2¼ SLR cameras. The SLR is preferred because the subject is viewed and focused directly through the lens. What you see is exactly what you record on film. Rangefinder cameras use two optically split images that line up when the focus is perfect. These cameras work well under low light conditions and when there are strong vertical lines. Because you are not viewing through the taking lens, however, you may not be recording exactly what you see through the viewfinder. The better SLR cameras of both formats incorporate the rangefinder principle on the ground glass of the through-the-lens viewfinder.

Most 35 mm SLR cameras have a focal plane shutter at the rear of the camera that consists of a cloth or titanium curtain that has slits in it of various widths. The speed at which the slit passes in front of the film and the width of the slit determines the amount of light reaching the film, hence the speed at which the photograph is taken. The top speed of the focal plane shutter is usually 1/1000 of a second, although better ones have 1/2000 and the new Nikon FM2 has a shutter speed of 1/4000. This is a lot faster than the average photographer needs, but coupled with a fast lens and fast film, it may prove a boon to wildlife photographers.

Most 35 mm cameras have a viewfinder that is parallel to the ground so that the camera is held at eye level. All cameras using eye-level viewfinders today have a pentaprism, a five-sided optical device, so that the object being photographed is right side up and the left and right sides are properly placed. Waist-level viewfinders have the right and left sides reversed, making it almost impossible to follow a moving subject. The standard eye-level viewfinder is ideal for about 95 percent of the situations being photographed.

There are times when it is extremely helpful to be able to look straight down into the viewfinder. This is particularly true when photographing flowers, reptiles, amphibians or small mammals from or at ground level. Many of the better cameras offer a right-angle viewfinder, or the regular viewfinder can be removed and replaced with one for viewing straight down. I carry the latter viewfinder with me most of the time.

Inside the viewfinder are different focusing grids that can be interchanged according to the preference of the photographer. Some grids have fine screens, some very coarse screens for fast focusing, some incorporate a rangefinder focusing system and some have a clear spot for microscope focusing.

A rubber eyecup should be used, not only to protect the eye against impact and prevent touching the metal in extremely cold weather, but also to shield out extraneous light that may affect the internal metering system.

For those who need them, prescription eyepieces may also be purchased and screwed onto the viewer eyepiece as an aid to accurate focusing. And the Early Winters Company of Seattle, Washington, has a product called Vision, which is an excellent solution to the fogging of the eyepiece of your viewfinder in cold weather.

Ordinarily, the film is advanced manually by cocking the film advance lever, and this system is sufficient for most amateurs. Professional photographers, who have to take a great many photos, because livelihood depends on it, usually use a motor drive. A disadvantage is that the motor drive and battery pack to run it usually weigh more than the camera and are expensive. But there are many advantages to using a motor drive. Sequential action shots can be recorded with it. A number of shots of even a stationary subject can be taken in a short period of time because motor drives take three to seven frames per second, according to the system being used. The rewind feature is also very desirable; it enables you to get the spent roll out of the camera and a new roll into it in the shortest possible time. It often seems that the best action shots and the most alert poses occur when the camera is out of film. An additional advantage to me, as a biologist, is that by using a motor drive and knowing the number of frames per second, I can accurately record the speed of wildlife activities.

There is usually less camera "shake" when a motor drive is used than when the shutter is released manually because the shutter is tripped electronically. The motor drive also allows an entire roll of film to be shot by remote control.

A final advantage of the motor drive is that some cameras using a motor drive draw power from the large battery pack for light metering, saving the small battery provided for this purpose. This is especially desirable in extremely cold weather when the small battery is much more prone to failure.

A camera used for wildlife photography must have a shutter speed of at least 1/500 of a second and preferably 1/1000 or 1/2000. It must have interchangeable lenses, and the more lenses available in the system the better. It should be an SLR, although some rangefinder cameras can be used. It should have a built-in metering system because taking readings with a hand-held meter is too time-consuming, causing pictures to be lost. It is desirable to be able to attach a motor drive or have one built in.

The miniature half-frame cameras are novelty items. The film size is much too small to be projected. It is also next to impossible to get suitable enlargements made, and so photographs taken with these cameras are not salable.

The 35 mm camera is the most versatile system. The better systems have hundreds of components and allow you to meet the needs of practically any situation. A disadvantage is that you usually need two camera bodies—to shoot black and white and color—or else you have to roll the film back into the canister. The new Rolli 35 mm SL2000 does have interchangeable backs.

The 2¼ or 120 camera is heavier and bulkier than the 35 mm, and most of the lenses do not focus as close as those of the 35 mm unless you use supplementary lenses, tubes, or bellows. The weight is a disadvantage if you have to carry it for long distances, but it is an advantage while shooting because the heavier camera can be held more steadily. With most 2¼ SLR cameras, the lenses are also much more expensive than those for the 35 mm because most of them have leaf shutters in the barrels. The leaf shutter, although slower than most focal plane shutters, has the advantage of being able to synchronize with electronic flash at any shutter

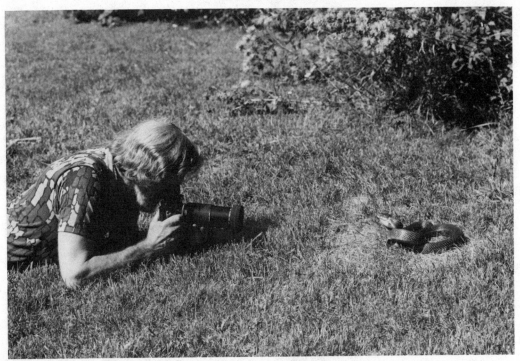

L. L. Rue III using a top viewfinder on camera to get a lower viewing angle on the pilot black snake. Photo by Charlie Heidecker

speed. A major disadvantage to the large lenses of the 2¼ SLR camera is that they are also slower lenses—and many have 5.6 as their largest opening. This means that they are difficult to focus because they are darker and harder to see through than the 35 mm.

A major advantage to the 2¼ SLR cameras is that most of them have interchangeable backs or magazines; the photographer can carry a half dozen different backs and film types. The square format lets cropping and composing be done in the darkroom instead of at the instant the photo is taken. The larger film size makes for easy enlargements of black and white photos. A disadvantage to the large film size is that Kodachrome is not made in this size, although it easily could be. Transparencies of Kodachrome and Fujichrome are preferred by most publications over the Ektachrome film. Kodachrome must be processed by a laboratory, whereas Ektachrome can be done at home.

Many professional photographers have both cameras, using the 2¼ for black and white photography and the 35 mm for color. If I am actually carrying the cameras on my back, however, I use only the 35 mm.

The 4 × 5, 5 × 7, or even the 8 × 10 camera is almost never used on wildlife, although it is the workhorse of scenic photographers. It is just too bulky, too heavy, and too slow to operate for wildlife photography, and the film is just too expensive.

Underwater photography may be done with either 35 mm or 2¼ format cameras. A wide variety of watertight housings are made by camera manufacturers or independents. Today, several underwater cameras are waterproof in themselves; Nikonos is the best known and probably the most successful. Underwater flashguns, electronic flash, and underwater meters are also available.

The instant development cameras can be used to test a lighting setup, but they are not suitable for wildlife.

Most of the techniques I discuss, and most of the methods I reveal, can also be used by the

This sequence of a white-tailed deer bounding in deep snow could only be captured with a camera having a motor drive.

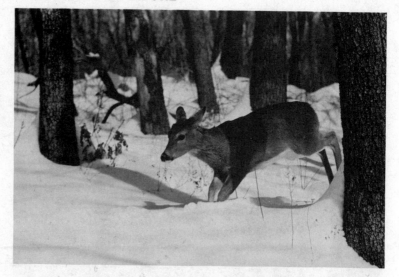

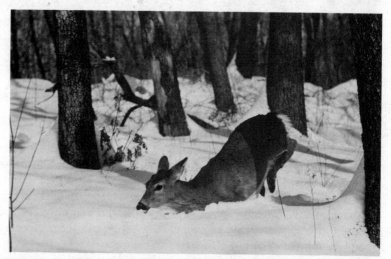

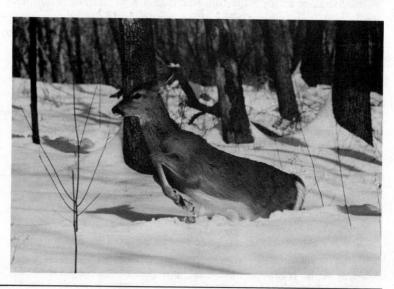

cinephotographer. I do not intend to discuss movie making because I don't do it. I used to, and I have thousands of feet of film. But you cannot shoot stills and movies at the same time and do a good job. I found that every time I was using one camera, I wished I had the other. Although really successful cinephotographers can make big bucks if a film they make gets on television, I make a good living from selling still photographs to be used in publications, to illustrate my own books, or to accompany my lectures.

Lenses

The lens consists of a set of glass elements and a diaphragm controlling the light entering the lens. In addition, some lenses contain a leaf shutter controlling the speed.

The lens is the heart of any camera system. The better the lens, the higher the resolution (or fine detail) that can be recorded. Usually, the faster the lens, the larger and heavier it is, thus making it more expensive. In most cases faster lenses are desirable, but this is not always the case. I'll explain why in a moment.

Most lenses are exceedingly complex with from two to ten glass elements inside the barrel. Usually, the more elements in the lens, the sharper the image recorded. The larger the anterior end of the lens, the more light it admits to the film, thus qualifying it as a "fast" lens. However, an $f/3.5$ 400 mm lens is an exceedingly fast lens, whereas an $f/3.5$ 50 mm would be an exceedingly slow lens. Since the f number is the ratio of focal length to the aperture, a lens having a large focal length has to have a large diameter in order to have a fast f number. Such a large diameter makes it more costly and heavy; therefore, it is common for large focal length lenses to have high f numbers. The focal length of the lens is the distance measured from the optical center of the lens to the film. This length may be given in either inches or millimeters; for example, a 50 mm lens is considered a 2-inch lens. The 50 mm lens is considered the normal or standard lens for a 35 mm camera because it takes a lens of that length to cover the diagonal measurement of the film. The 80 mm lens is the normal lens for the 120 or 2¼ camera because that is the diagonal measurement of that film.

A lens of any given focal length has only the magnification of that length, no matter the size of the film upon which the image is being recorded. It is customary to divide the length of the normal lens of the camera you are using into the length of a larger telephoto to come up with the increased magnification. When you divide 50 mm into 500 mm you say the magnification is ten times. Someone using a 2¼ camera would divide 80 mm into 500 and would say the magnification is six times. With a half-frame or a 16 mm movie camera, the division of 25 mm into 500 mm would be 20. In each case the magnification equation would be correct, yet the image delivered to the film would be exactly the same, regardless of the size of all three formats. All lenses set at the same f stop, regardless of focal length, when used on the same subject and under the same light conditions, yield the same image brightness on film of the same ASA (American Standard Association) or ISO (International Standard Organization) rating. In an attempt to standardize film ratings throughout the world, the ISO (International Standard Organization) will be the one used in the future.

Engraved on the barrel of the lens will be a series of f stops with the lowest number being the largest aperture. A typical series of numbers might be $f/2$, $f/2.8$, $f/4$, $f/5.6$, $f/8$, $f/11$, $f/16$, $f/22$. Each sequential designation allows twice as much light to reach the film as the next highest number. Conversely, each designation allows only half as much light to reach the film as the lower number.

In addition to the basic numbers, you may see such numbers as $f/3.5$, $f/4.9$, and $f/6.9$. These are half stops. Even if these numbers are not engraved on the barrel, there may be click stops on the aperture ring showing where they are. With or without the click stops, most lenses can be set anywhere between the designated numbers. East of the Mississippi River on a bright, sunny day, using Kodachrome ASA 64/ISO 64 will give you a meter reading of 1/125 of a second at $f/9.8$ for a normal subject outdoors. The stop $f/9.8$ is seldom engraved, but if you merely put the aperture indicator halfway between $f/8$ and $f/11$, the exposure will be correct.

In addition to controlling the amount of light entering the camera, the diaphragm also controls the depth of field. The higher the f stop number, the smaller the aperture opening, and the greater distance that is registered in sharp focus. A law of optics states that for any object that is in critically sharp focus, the distance for ⅓ in front of the object but ⅔ behind the object will also be sharp, the exact distance being determined by the f stop and the distance between the camera and the subject. Another inherent characteristic of most lenses is that they achieve their maximum sharpness between two to five stops from their largest aperture. For example, an $f/2.8$ lens is sharpest at $f/5.6$, $f/8$ and $f/11$.

Lenses made for other than a focal plane shutter have a leaf shutter built into the barrel of the lens. Lenses without the shutter, when they are of equal quality, are much more inexpensive than those with the shutter. A top speed for most leaf shutters is about 1/500 of a second; focal plane shutters are four to eight times faster. A disadvantage to the focal plane is that it is usually synchronized with electronic flash at speeds of one-sixtieth or one-eightieth of a second. When used in daylight, "ghost" images may appear on the film. Leaf shutters can be synchronized at any speed, eliminating this problem.

Camera lenses come in a bewildering array of focal lengths. The 50 mm is the normal lens for the 35 mm camera, and the 80 mm is normal for the 2¼. The normal lens for each format is usually the fastest lens available in the entire system. Anything less than those lengths for either camera is referred to as a wide angle, whereas lenses longer than normal are referred to as telephotos.

Each lens, according to its focal length, covers a different horizontal angle of coverage. The 50 mm lens covers 39 degrees of a circle. The wide-angle lenses cover more; the 35 mm covers 54 degrees, the 28 mm covers 65 degrees and the 24 mm covers 74 degrees. Lenses with a shorter focal length than 18 mm are usually referred to as "fisheye lenses" because they generally provide a round photo with a straight line distorted to curves.

The 85 mm lenses cover 24 degrees, the 105 mm lenses cover 19 degrees, and the 135 mm 15 degrees. These lenses are referred to as medium telephotos and are excellent for making a large image on the film of a subject nearby without distortion of the features. The long telephoto lens of 200 mm, 300 mm, 400 mm, 500 mm, and 600 mm cover approximately 10, 6, 5, 4, and 3 degrees respectively. These lenses are used when a subject cannot be approached closely or when it is dangerous to get too close.

One of the greatest innovations in lenses was the introduction of zoom lenses that allowed various focal lengths to be incorporated in one lens. The early models were not good; they would be sharp at one or two focal lengths and have all sorts of aberrations at others. The best of the new zoom lenses have solved this problem admirably; the lens is critically sharp at all focal lengths and at all apertures.

Teleconverters, doublers, or extenders have greatly expanded the usefulness of any lens to which they can be fitted. The early models were a disaster as they vignetted the edge of the photograph. There are still some poor ones on the market. When the better lenses are paired up with teleconverters made explicitly for a particular lens by the same company, the results are excellent.

In most things in life, you get what you pay for. This is particularly true of lenses. Competition is so keen between the many companies manufacturing lenses that their prices are competitive for equal products. The sharper, and faster, the lens, the higher the price of that particular lens. I buy the fastest lens I can get in the telephotos because each increase in an f stop allows me to work perhaps half an hour earlier in the morning or later in the day, the times when wildlife is most active! Or, it allows me to shoot at a higher shutter speed at any time.

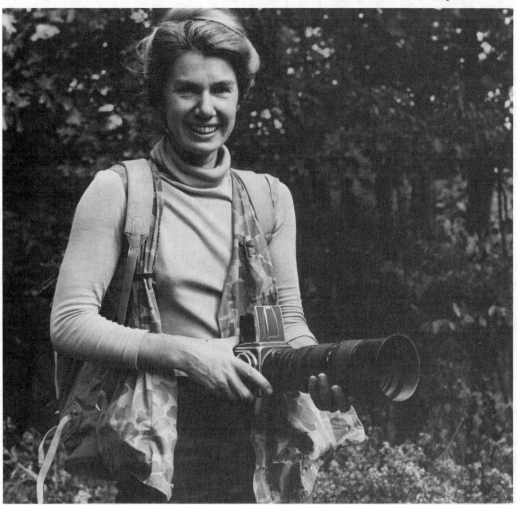

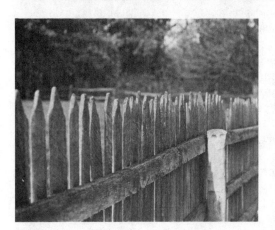

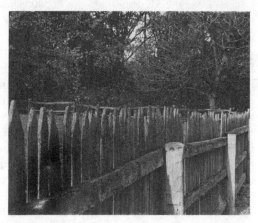

Top Irene Vandermolen using a Hasselblad 2¼ format camera and a zoom lens.
Bottom left The shallow depth of field, or limited sharpness, results from the lens being set wide open at *f*/3.5.
Bottom right Every picket on this fence is sharp resulting from the same lens being closed down to *f*/22.

Film

The actual sharpness of the photograph depends to a large degree on the speed of the film.

Black and white film has a layer of silver halide crystals in an emulsion on an acetate film base. Color film has a layer of dyes of the primary colors. The greater the thickness of the emulsion, the higher the ISO/ASA rating of the film. The higher rated, or faster, films are said to have more latitude, which means that they can record the greatest range of tones from pure white to jet black. The depth of the emulsion determines the sharpness of the image recorded.

Thin emulsion films have the lowest ISO/ASA rating but produce the sharpest images. They have little latitude and cannot be used under poor light conditions. Because they have so little latitude, the films must be exposed properly.

The depth of the emulsion of high-speed films shows up as larger grains of silver in the black and white films and as dye clumpage in the color films. This so-called grain does not allow for the sharpest recording of an image, but it does enable the film to be used under adverse lighting conditions. High-speed films are also more tolerant of exposure error.

The proper exposure of any film is determined by the amount of light, either available natural light or light from a flash, and the ISO/ASA speed of the film. The decision is up to the photographer whether he wants to stop action or if he needs great depth of field.

One of the most popular films is ISO/ASA Kodachrome 64. I prefer more color saturation, and so I slightly underexpose this film by using a guide number of ISO/ASA 80/150 instead of 64, or I use Fujichrome ISO/ASA 100 at ISO/ASA 125. A bright, sunny day will yield about 4000 footcandles of light in the eastern United States, no matter what metering system is used. Extrapolated on a metering scale, you will find that 1/125 of a second shutter speed and a lens aperture of $f/9.8$ to $f/11$ gives you a properly exposed photograph with these films. If you want greater depth of field, you have to have a higher aperture number; to stop action, you need a faster shutter speed. However, all the combinations that follow allow an equal amount of light to reach the film: 1/15 of a second shutter speed at $f/32$, 1/30 at $f/22$, 1/60 at $f/16$, 1/125 at $f/11$, 1/250 at $f/8$, 1/500 at 5.6, 1/1000 at $f/4$, and 1/2000 at $f/2.8$. Extremely long exposures, taken under low light conditions, require additional time to compensate for the film's lessening ability to record an image. This is known as reciprocity failure.

Please note that to utilize this complete range depends also on the speed of the lens. Telephotos in the 400 mm or 600 mm range usually do not have $f/2.8$ apertures, only the Canon 400 mm 2.8L does—and the 1/2000 shutter speed cannot be used. Most of them do not have $f/4$ either. Fast 50 mm lenses that have a maximum aperture of $f/1.2$ or $f/2$ don't close down to $f/22$ or $f/32$.

For years I used nothing but Kodak films. They are still among the best, although today I find that Fujichrome does a very fine job. Kodachrome 25 (KR 25) is one of the best films for fine details and is the standard against which most films are judged. It gives good whites and greens and reproduces skin tones very well, although with a slightly blue tinge. I do not use this film because of its slow ISO/ASA rating.

The bulk of my color transparencies have been taken with Kodachrome 64 (KR 64) with an ISO/ASA rating of 80. This is an excellent film with slightly warmer, reddish tones than the KR 25, and the higher ISO/ASA rating allows for more color saturation. I have given as many as 200 lectures per year using transparencies and the KR 64 gives brilliant slides. Although the dye clumpage is greater in KR 64 than in KR 25, the difference in fine detail is not readily apparent. The extra one and one-half stop increase in the ISO/ASA rating allows me to stop more action or get greater depth of field.

Fujichrome 100 is a happy compromise between two films. The detail is as sharp as KR 25, its color responses are natural and good, and it has a higher ISO/ASA rating than KR 64. Fuji's stated goal is to capture 15 percent of the American film market, and with film of this quality, they will probably better that goal.

With no Kodachromes available in sizes larger than 35 mm, the 2¼ cameras have to use Ektachrome. Ektachrome 64 is a very good film but, like KR 25, leans toward the blue end of the spectrum. If equal-quality photographs are taken with Kodachromes and Ektachromes of the same subject, the Kodachromes will be the ones bought, because of the finer detail. Ektachrome's great advantage is that it can be processed at home as soon as you get done shooting, whereas Kodachromes must be factory processed. Fujichrome can also be processed at home, but better results are obtained when the film is processed in Fuji chemicals in their Anaheim, California plant.

I use high-speed films only when I am forced to. Then I will choose Ektachrome 400 over Ektachrome 200 because it is, in my opinion, much the better of the two films and offers a more faithful rendition of color values. I am more apt to use Ektachrome 400 on bright, sunny days to stop action than I am to use it under low light conditions. Color is a reflection and refraction of light. Without light, you don't have color, so I don't shoot it. Instead, I switch to black and white films.

My favorite black and white film is Kodak's Plus X Pan Professional that has an ISO/ASA rating of 125. I always process this film in Accufine developer, however, which allows me to up the ISO/ASA rating to 320. This film has good, fine grain and a wide tone of grays from pure white to jet black.

I don't use the Panatomic films for the same reason I don't use KR 25. The ISO/ASA rating is too slow.

For high-speed film, I prefer Kodak's Tri X with an ISO/ASA of 320. Using Accufine development, I get a good, fine grain, a wide range of tonal contrasts, and an ISO/ASA rating of 1200.

A remarkable new black and white film is Ilford's XPI. This film has a variable ISO/ASA rating of from 50 to 1600. I use this in my lowest natural light conditions, and it renders an image when all else fails. Because of its tremendous latitude, it is practically a "mistake-proof" film. When testing the film, I set my camera shutter speed at 1/250 of a second and made the exposures at apertures of from $f/3.8$ to $f/22$. All negatives were of good printable quality.

I do not use color print film because I do not make color prints. You cannot sell prints to any publishing house; they all want transparencies. When I submit, I send in my original transparencies because I want the editors to see the finest quality that I am capable of producing.

I realize that many other fine films and developers are available, but these are my choices. I heartily recommend that when you find a good film, or a good film and developer combination, you stick with them. Too many photographers have to try every new film that comes on the market; they are forever testing, and so they never achieve the consistency that is mandatory for good results. I have had the best results with color film when it is processed by its manufacturer.

Don't try to economize on film. If you take ten photos, you have ten photos to choose from; if you take 100 photos, you have 100 to choose from. I often take 20 rolls of 36 exposure 35 mm film on a good shooting day. The law of averages is on your side if you shoot, shoot, shoot.

How to Properly Expose Your Film

Any object or subject can be seen only by the light reflected from it or emitted by it. In the absence of light, snow appears black. The proper exposure of your film can be done only if you calculate or meter the light reflecting from your subject. More photographs are ruined by improper exposure than by improper focusing.

The manufacturers of film generally enclose a sheet of exposure guides to help ensure that you get good results with that particular film. They list conditions from bright sun to deep shade, and if you do not have an exposure meter, these tables will generally suffice.

A basic photographic rule for exposure states that in bright sunlight, with your camera set at

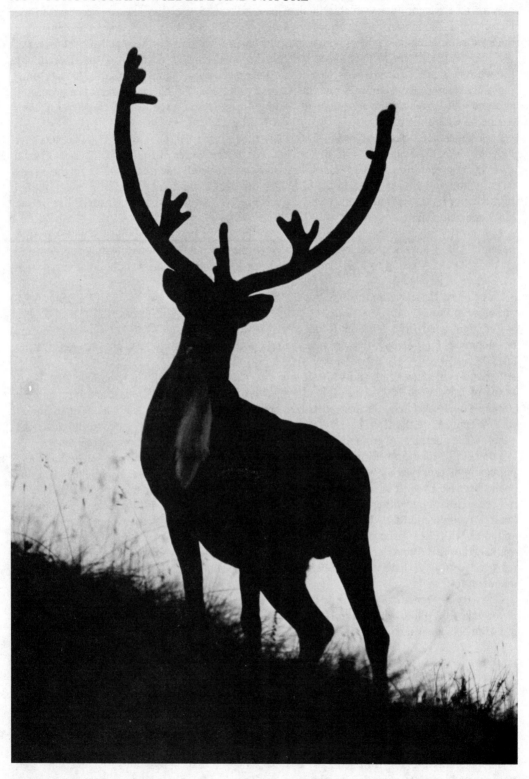

Silhouette shots result when the meter reading is taken from the bright sky instead of from the dark caribou.

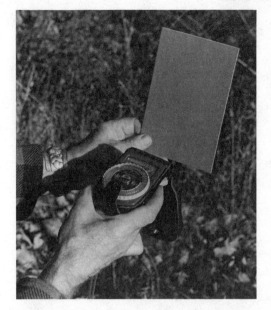 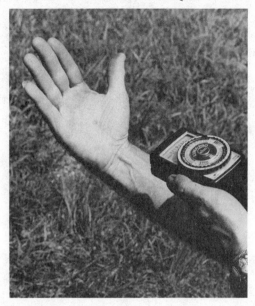

Left When metering a gray card, be careful of both shadow and glare which can affect the reading. Photo by Irene Vandermolen
Right You can meter your hand and open your lens one stop for the proper exposure of an average scene. Photo by Charlie Heidecker

$f/16$, your shutter speed can be set at the ISO/ASA speed of the film. Kodachrome 64 would give you a setting of $f/16$ at 1/60 of a second, or an equivalent setting based on those numbers. In general, I have found that these settings underexpose my film by one-half to one stop, making it too dark; but it does serve as an emergency guide.

It also helps to know that if the day is hazy, instead of bright sun, the lens must be opened one stop; if the day is cloudy, it must be opened three stops. Even on a bright day, the sun must be behind you to get the maximum reading. If you take a photo at right angles to the sun, the lens must be opened up one stop. If your subject has the sun to its back, and you are shooting into the light, you must open the lens two and a half to three stops. If you shoot into the sun at the same setting as with the sun behind you, your subject will be silhouetted and black.

Most photographers use a meter to measure the amount of light falling on, or reflecting from, their subject. Meters may either be held in the hand or built in as an integral part of the camera. Some cameras are completely automated as to exposure so all the photographer does is focus, compose, and shoot. These cameras are not satisfactory for wildlife photography because they properly expose for only average subjects against average backgrounds.

Meters do not have the ability to think; you have to do that. Only you know what is the most important feature in any scene that you photograph.

In nature you seldom find pure black or pure white. It has been determined by scientific metering that snow reflects about 90 percent of all light falling on it, whereas an average scene reflects 18 percent. Light meters may work on reflected or incidental light, but they both attempt to average out any reading at 18 percent.

The focal length of the lens being used also affects the area being metered. For example, a 200 mm lens covers 10 degrees, a 400 mm lens covers a little more than 5 degrees, and a 600 mm lens covers a little over 3 degrees. In effect, the lenses turn the camera into a spot meter.

I often use a Honeywell-Pentax 1-degree spot meter for precise metering of specific subjects that contrast with their surroundings when I cannot approach more closely.

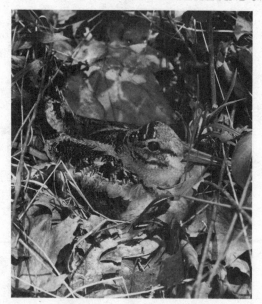 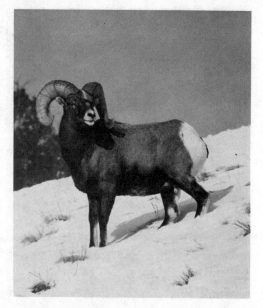

Left Many wild creatures, such as this woodcock, are colored the same as their surroundings so that they are hidden by their camouflage.
Right A spot meter reading directly from this bighorn ram's body will give you a correct exposure.

An incident light meter records the amount of light falling on the subject, giving you an average reading. An advantage to the incident meter is that you need not be near your subject to take a reading. However, you must be sure that the angle of light falling on the meter's sphere is exactly the same as that falling on the subject. The major disadvantage to using the incident meter is that it always averages the light falling on a general scene and not on a specific subject. I would say that 99 percent of all photographs taken are exposed by the metering of reflected light.

Many cameras offer automatic exposure with either aperture or shutter control and with manual override. With aperture control, you set the lens aperture, and the meter adjusts the camera's shutter speed. With shutter control, you set the shutter speed, and the meter adjusts the lens aperture.

Most of the time I do not use these automatic features because the meter is averaging all scenes. When the subject is lighter or darker than the background, compensation must be made, and only you can do the compensating.

There are also times when you want to take an average reading and cannot do so because of light or dark backgrounds. If you get close to your subject, you can meter the lightest area and the darkest area and average out the exposure. With a spot meter, you can do the same thing from a distance. An incident meter will give you the average, or you can use a "gray card."

You can buy a gray card at any photographic supply shop. The card has 18 percent reflectancy on the gray side and 90 percent on the white side. The card can be used with either a hand-held or built-in meter. In low light, the reading can be taken from the white side, but you must open up your lens two and one-half stops to to get the proper exposure. The white side reflects five times as much light as the gray side does.

When using a gray card, make sure that it is getting the same angle of light as your subject. Turn the card so that it does not reflect glare, and don't let your body cast a shadow on it.

Skin tones are approximately two times as bright as the average scene, and so you can take a meter reading off your hand instead of using a gray card. Compensate by opening your lens one full stop for proper exposure.

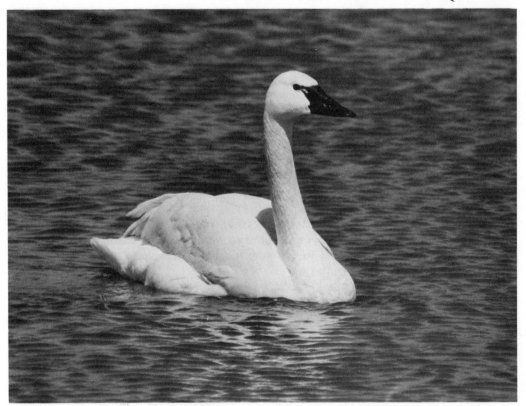

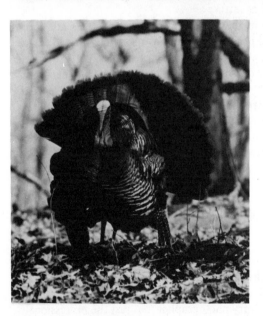

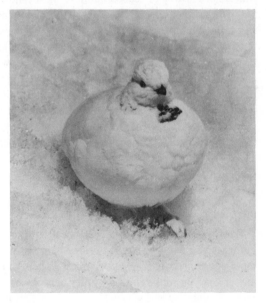

Top Unless the background is very dark, I would meter the water to get the correct exposure for this whistling swan.
Bottom left To correctly expose this very dark wild turkey, I metered its surroundings and shot.
Bottom right To meter white on white, meter either the snow or the ptarmigan and shoot. If any dark background is to be included, you would have to open your lens 1½-2 stops to render detail in the dark areas. Photo by Irene Vandermolen

If a person is your main subject, you need not move in close to meter his or her face. Instead, meter your hand. If the person is only part of an average scene, meter your hand but open your lens one stop for the proper exposure.

Black and white film has more latitude than color film. When shooting color, you meter both the highlights and the shadow areas and make your setting halfway between. With black and white film, you also meter the high and low areas, but split your exposure ⅓ to ⅔, favoring the exposure for the shadows. In very low light conditions for black and white, you not only underexpose for the shadows but also increase development time to capture the light areas. You can make this correction if you process your own film, or tell the lab to do it for you.

Most wildlife is basically colored the same as its surroundings. With some animals, their camouflage is so good that we do not see them at all. Nature planned it that way for their survival. Shades of brown, from light sandy tan to dark umber, are dominant colors with most mammals. Birds, despite being more colorful, still approximate their background. The proper exposure can be gotten from either the creature or its background.

When photographing an average creature against snow, take a meter reading from the snow and open your lens one and one-half to two stops. Or use a spot meter to take the reading directly from the creature and then shoot.

Unless the background is very dark, I usually meter the background and expose for it and then the subject is exposed properly. If the background is very dark and the subject is pure white, I meter the highlights and shadow and average it out. A gray card can do the averaging for you, or you can meter your hand and open up the lens one stop for an average reading.

When photographing a dark subject on a dark background, meter either and then shoot.

When photographing a white subject on a white background in bright sunlight, such as a ptarmigan on snow, take a meter reading of either and then shoot. If you are using Kodachrome 64, however, set your exposure at 1/125 at f/16 no matter what your meter reads; the film is not capable of recording more light than that setting allows.

If you are not absolutely sure of the exposure, make the best calculation you can and then shoot. To be on the safe side, "bracket" your exposure. Bracketing means taking additional photos at different settings than the one calculated. Leaving the shutter speed set the same, take additional photos with your lens closed down one-half to one full stop and then opened up one-half to one full stop. Don't use bracketing as an excuse not to learn how to expose your film correctly, but if the shot is important, don't try to save on film. All pros bracket when the chips are down. Film is still the cheapest part of any photo trip.

I cannot overstate the importance of knowing how to expose your film properly under even adverse conditions. The accompanying photos serve as examples.

My Equipment

As a professional wildlife photographer, the question I am asked most frequently is, "What kind of equipment do you use?"

I always advise buying the very best equipment you can afford because in photography you get what you pay for. Higher-priced cameras are usually more rugged, more reliable, and have more accessories than cheaper ones. When you have a good, reliable camera, you know that any errors you make in taking photographs are likely to be yours, not the fault of the equipment. Reliability and versatility are important to every photographer, not just the professional.

Most SLR 35 mm cameras come with a normal 50 mm lens that has a speed in the vicinity of f/2. I don't recommend that lens. I always get a 55 mm macro lens for my normal lens, even though its largest aperture is about f/2.8. This is an instance when lens speed is not of paramount importance. Most normal 50 mm lenses do not focus any closer than about 18 inches. The 50 mm and 55 mm lenses are not normally used in wildlife work except for close-ups, and with the normal 50 mm you cannot get close enough to your subject. Macro lenses

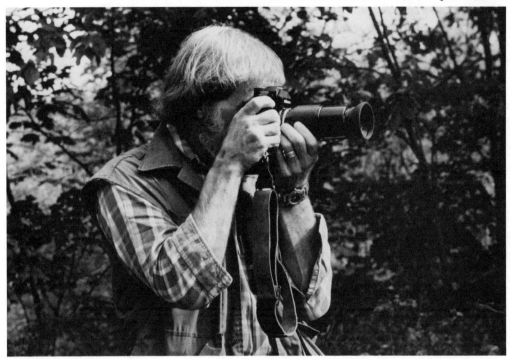

This Nikon 80-200 zoom lens is one of my favorite lenses. Photo by Irene Vandermolen

have built-in extension tubes, you don't have to add anything, and you can focus down to about 7 inches. With this lens, you can photograph flowers and small reptiles and amphibians close up and really do a good job.

The slightly slower lens is not a great drawback because the lens is usually used outdoors where the amount of light is not a problem. Macro photographers customarily use a small electronic flash with these lenses even if good light is available because of action-stopping properties of the light and the great depth of field that using such a light allows.

For years the 135 mm was my most important lens for nesting birds and small mammals. Although I still have a 135 mm, I don't use it. Another lens in my kit is the 70 to 210 mm zoom, which incorporates the 135 mm. This is one of the two most important lenses I carry and is ideal for large subjects at distances up to 100 feet or smaller subjects that are much closer.

Most zoom lenses of this category are $f/3.8$ to $f/4.5$ and are light enough and still short enough to be hand-held. A basic rule of thumb states that a lens should not be hand-held when the shutter speed is slower than the focal length of the camera. With a 70 to 210 mm zoom, it is supposed to be okay to shoot the 70 mm at 1/60 of a second; but when using the lens at 210 mm, the shutter speed should be 1/250. I customarily shoot the lens at 1/125 no matter what focal length is being used.

My favorite long telephoto lens is the 400 mm. According to the rules, this lens could be hand-held if the camera shutter was set at 1/500 of a second. Only under optimum conditions would there be enough light to use a 400 mm lens and Kodachrome film at 1/500.

I started in photography when Kodachrome had an ASA rating of 10. The lenses were slower then, and every photograph had to be taken with a tripod. I use any lens larger than a 300 mm on a tripod. Many photographers claim that they can hand-hold a 400 mm lens and get needle-sharp photographs. I can't, and most photographers can't either. I fully realize that if a gunstock or other device is used, holding the heavy lens is possible.

HOW I PHOTOGRAPH WILDLIFE AND NATURE

Many wildlife photographers swear by their 500 mm mirror lenses because they are compact and light and because some photographers can hold them steady with a gunstock. Such lenses are great for capturing action. I do not like mirror lenses because they have a fixed aperture, usually $f/8$, which means they can be used with color film only in good light. Because the aperture cannot be changed, your only control is in changing your shutter speed. My biggest objection to the mirror lens is that any reflective surface, such as dew or raindrops on the vegetation, or sparkling water, photographs with a halo around each and every dot. I have a 500 mm mirror lens but carry it only as a spare in case something happens to my 400 mm telephoto.

I also use the Novoflex system, which is unique because it is the fastest-focusing system in the world. Nothing can compare to it for photographing action. Instead of turning a focusing ring around the barrel of the lens, you just squeeze a pistol grip to focus. A locking ring allows for the very fast interchanging of the 240 mm, 400 mm, and 600 mm lens heads. In addition, a set of bellows can be permanently installed, an integral part of the latest model, and allows the 400 mmm to be close-focused down to 8 feet. These lenses are amazingly sharp. I use them frequently to photograph small birds and mammals at close distances of 8 to 20 feet.

To work even closer on small creatures, I use the 105 mm and the 200 mm macro lenses. Although these two lenses give me about the same image size on my film, when focused at their closest range, as the 55 mm macro lens does, they allow me to be two and four times as far away from my subject. This extra distance is often desirable to prevent scaring the subject. It also provides an extra margin of safety when photographing poisonous creatures up close.

These are the lenses I use and why. Fully 75 percent of the photographs I take are taken with the 55 mm, 80 to 200 mm, and 400 mm lenses. I also carry the 1.4X and the 2X teleconverters, which when used on the 400 mm lens makes it a 600 mm and 800 mm respectively. A drawback to using teleconverters is that while they double the focal length of the lens, they also double the amount of light needed for exposure.

The wide-angle lens that I prefer is the 24 mm because it most closely depicts what I see with my eyes, not counting peripheral vision. A human being has about 180-degree vision, but only if the eyes are moved from side to side. One of the greatest disappointments is to photograph a scene and not be able to encompass what the eye is beholding. Naturally, the shorter the focal length of the lens, the greater distortion to all verticals, if the lens is not held perfectly horizontal to the ground.

Of course, I have other lenses that I use that are more specialized. My 600 mm lens is an excellent one but is too heavy to carry in the mountains. It is ideal where it does not have to be carried too far, say, across the road in national parks. The 600 mm with the 2X teleconverter, making it a 1200 mm lens, helps me do superb work on birds and large mammals at a distance. Many times, even when a creature lets the photographer get closer, better pictures can be taken with a big lens at a greater distance because the creature does not feel threatened and behaves in a more normal fashion.

I do a lot of work from a photographer's blind and find the best lens to be my 50 to 300 mm zoom. Once photographers are concealed in the blind, they cannot move closer to, or get farther away from, the subject. When doing work from a blind, the photographer usually knows about where the animal will be in the area. The trouble is that the creature doesn't know where you think it should be, and it may appear very close or at a greater distance than anticipated. When your lens is protruding through the wall of the blind, and the creature is in view, you cannot change lenses without scaring the wildlife. A good zoom lens takes care of such contingencies easily.

The aforementioned outfit is the one I carry under most circumstances. With it, I can photograph everything from flowers close up to big game at long distances. I state again that better equipment betters your chances of taking the best photographs. I also want to stress that although the equipment helps the photographer get the photo, it is the photographer who makes the photograph. It's like asking an author what kind of typewriter he uses.

One final suggestion: if possible, test a lens for sharpness before you buy it, or test it as soon as possible after you buy it. Many photographers use a lens testing chart, which is excellent. Equally good results can be gotten by photographing a newspaper page of type. Because I intend to use my lenses on wildlife, I test it by taking photographs, in color, of animal skins and mounted bird specimens. If I get the detail that I want in the fur and in the filaments of the feathers, I'm satisfied. Lens testing is very important because each lens is an individual. There is always a slight variation in lenses made by the same manufacturer under identical conditions. Testing will see that you get one of the best of the batch.

Flash

I do not like to use flash because it always introduces an artificial aspect into the photograph. Under most conditions, it makes photos appear as if they were taken at night, which is fine for animals but not for birds. Multiple lights produce multiple highlights in the creature's eyes, whereas the sun produces only one. Two highlights in the eye may be caused by two lights in the out-of-doors. Three to five highlights tell everyone that the creature was photographed indoors in a studio setup. Many excellent photographs are taken this way, but I just don't like to do it.

I don't know of any pro who uses flashbulbs today; it is far cheaper and more convenient to use electronic flash. The old-time flashbulbs did pack a lot of power however, and did allow a lens to be closed down, giving tremendous depth of field.

The flash units that I use fall into three general categories. The smallest unit is for close-ups of flowers and insects, at 12 to 18 inches. It has no automation or thyristors.

The units I use most often are the small Vivitar and Sunpak models. These are for fill-in flash, synchro-sunlight, and subjects that are 2 to 8 feet away. These can be used automatically; they have thyristors for fast recycling and electric eyes to monitor light output.

My big flash units are made by Metz. These units can be used with regular house current at 110 volts or with a battery power pack. I have three light heads that can be triggered directly by cable from the power source or by slave units. They can be used manually or automatically. These are my workhorse units and the ones I use when I expect to have to leave the power pack turned on for 6 to 8 hours at a time.

I have one small ringlight that I seldom use because the lighting is so flat that I don't care for the results. It is fine for flowers. It is not suitable for wildlife because the circular ringlight is mirrored in the creature's eye as a white donut.

Filters

Some photographers ridicule the idea of using filters, claiming that it is ridiculous to put a cheap piece of glass in front of a lens that cost hundreds or even thousands of dollars. Others go to extremes, using filters to create conditions that do not exist in nature.

I have skylight filters on all my lenses to reduce the bluish or cold cast to much of the natural lighting. Their main purpose, however, is to act as a protective shield for the expensive lens. I feel that if you buy high-quality filters, they do not detract from your photographic quality.

I also carry a pola filter, which polarizes light, to enhance scenics by increasing the contrast of the blue sky and the fluffy whiteness of cumulus clouds. I don't use this filter often because, as I said, I usually up my ISO/ASA rating slightly, which underexposes my film slightly, giving me this same effect without making it too apparent. The pola filter is also very useful

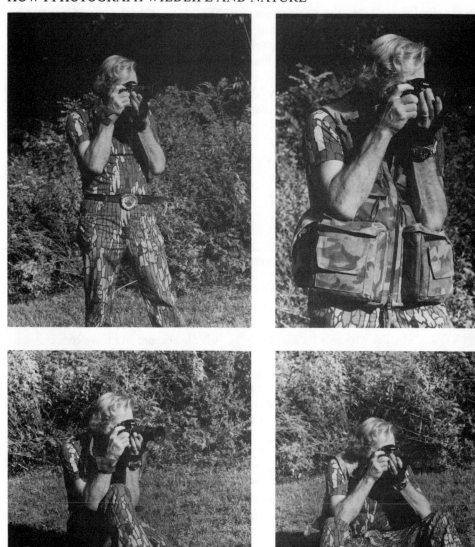

Top left I can hold my camera steady horizontally by bracing my elbows against my body, bracing my forehead against the camera, and keeping the camera straps tight around my wrist and neck. Photo by Charlie Heidecker

Top right Bracing my elbows on the top of the pockets of my Ultimate Photo Vest permits me to hold a camera exceptionally steady. Photo by Charlie Heidecker

Bottom left Kneeling and bracing my elbows against my knees also enables me to hold my camera very steady. Photo by Charlie Heidecker

Bottom right Sitting allows the camera to be held even more securely. You may wish to hold your knees high for support. Photo by Charlie Heidecker

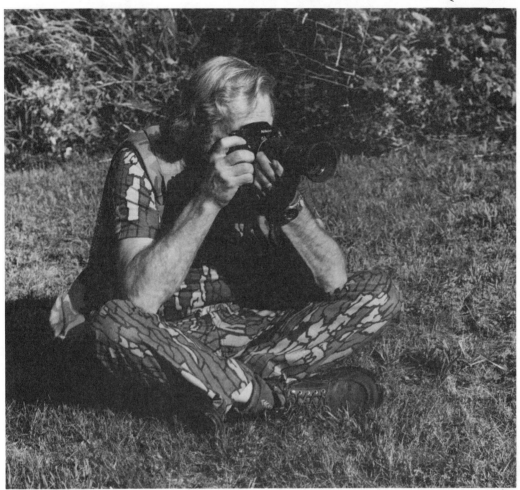

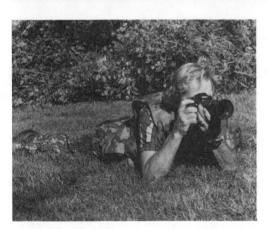 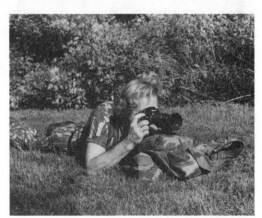

Top Or you may wish to sit and brace your elbows on the inside of your knees. Photo by Charlie Heidecker

Bottom left If conditions allow you to lie down, this position will allow you to hold your camera exceptionally steady. Photo by Charlie Heidecker

Bottom right Whenever possible brace your camera upon some support. Such bracing is almost as steady as a tripod. Photo by Charlie Heidecker

for reducing glare from water, ice, glass, or any other smooth, shining, reflective surface.

I do not use any special filter in doing normal black and white photography of wildlife, and I don't know of any wildlife photographers who do.

Camera Handling

The best camera and the finest lens will not produce a good photograph if the camera is not held steady. Because 85 percent of the populace is right-handed, the shutter release controls are on the right side of the camera. People generally find it most comfortable to support the camera's weight in the palm of the left hand, while the fingers of the left hand focus the lens. The three fingers of the right hand and the thumb grip the right side of the camera, while the index finger pushes the release button. The camera is pulled back against the face so that the viewfinder eyecup is steadied against the forehead. Both arms are braced against the body.

Just before I release the shutter, I take a deep breath and hold it. This is the same breath control needed for rifle shooting. Occasionally I am not able to get the expression, pose, or action I want, and I'm still holding my breath. I then have to let out the breath, grab a couple of deep breaths, hold it, and squeeze the release button. Don't jab at it, squeeze gently.

If you are standing while taking the photograph, point your left foot at the subject, while your right foot is back about a foot and pointed slightly to the right. Relax. Don't hold your body rigid, or the tension will cause you and the camera to shake.

Lean against any solid support you can find. Kneel if conditions allow you to do so. Sitting with your legs folded in front of you is even better because you can then prop an elbow on each knee.

I often lie down if the ground is dry and a low angle will be satisfactory. With your two elbows braced on the ground and the camera braced against your forehead, you have about as steady a position as you can get.

I can comfortably hand-hold a 250 mm lens shooting at shutter speeds of 1/125 of a second, even though the rule of thumb says I should use 1/250. Occasionally I hand-hold a camera at 1/60. I have to brace the camera against some rock-solid object if I have to shoot at 1/30. Anything slower requires a tripod.

Tripods and Other Camera Supports

I use a tripod or other support for most of my photographs. I know that I miss some action shots because it takes a little longer to get into action. I also know that more of my photos are needle sharp and thus more salable than photos taken without support.

Tripods come in many sizes and shapes, and unfortunately many of them are tripods in name only. Do not get the lightest tripod you can find because it probably will not be rigid enough to do the job properly. Buy a sturdy tripod, even though it is heavier. I use Gitzo and Husky tripods, and with a ball head, they weigh between 11 and 12 pounds; my largest Gitzo weighs 14 pounds. Even when I climb in the mountains, I carry my tripod with the legs fully extended. It is awkward, cumbersome, and tiresome, especially when the going is very steep, but I can get into action more easily, and the pictures I take are sharp. That factor makes all the extra effort worthwhile.

I prefer the ball head over all other heads because if you put your tripod down on a very uneven surface, a twist of just one knob has your camera level.

Of course, as I climb a slope, I automatically shorten one leg of the tripod to match the steepness of the slope in anticipation of having to use the tripod quickly. In climbing very steep mountain sides, with the camera and telephoto on the tripod and the legs extended, I have often had to reach overhead and hang the outfit on some rocky outcropping, then scram-

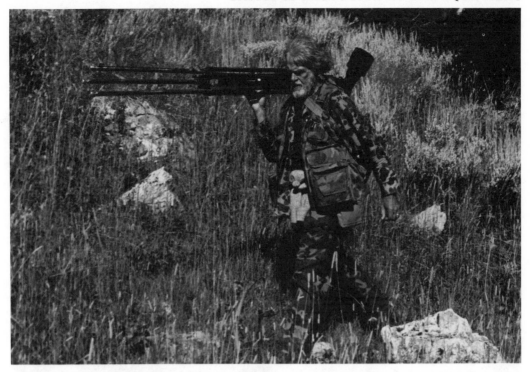

Top When working in the field, I customarily carry my tripod with the legs fully extended to facilitate getting into action fast. Photo by Len Rue, Jr.

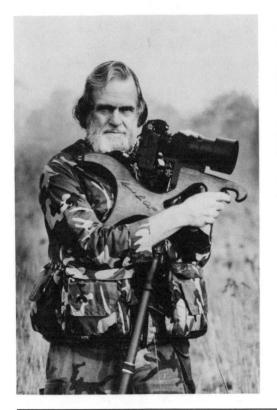

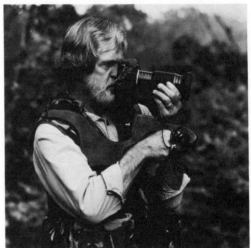

Left The Gitzo unipod used with the L.L. Rue III photo gunstock gives it good support. Photo by Len Rue Jr.
Above The L.L. Rue III shoulder pod is exceptionally well designed and allows me to hold lenses up to 300 mm very steady. Photo by Len Rue Jr.

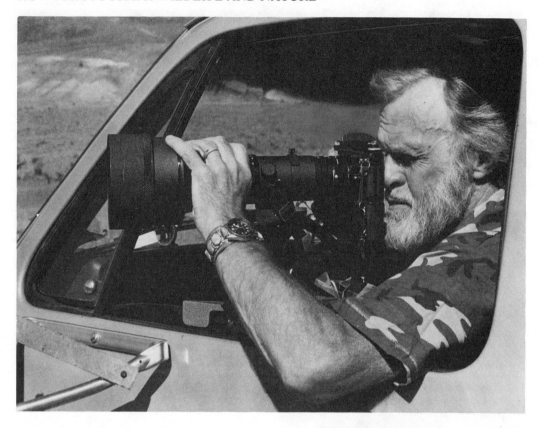

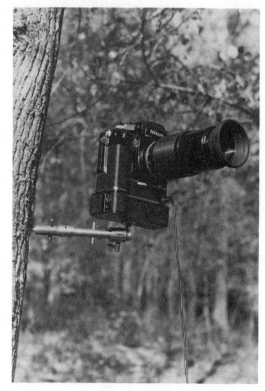

Top The Gitzo window pod allows me to shoot from a vehicle and holds my camera as steady as would a tripod. Photo by Len Rue, Jr. *Right* A homemade wood screw device and ball head holds my camera for remote work. Photo by Irene Vandermolen

ble up and move it up again. If I know I won't be using the camera during the climb, I dismantle it and put the camera and lens in my backpack and tie the tripod to the side of the pack in the vertical position. Don't place the tripod crossways across the top of the pack and secure it with the pack flap. Being crosswise, the tripod may catch on the rocks as you climb, causing you to lose your balance and throwing you off the cliff.

Gitzo tripods are also to be recommended because their Safari models are the only tripods that come in anodized, drab olive color. Any wildlife photographer who uses a bright, shiny tripod is handicapping himself because the reflective glare of the metal will alert, if not greatly alarm, creatures that are miles away. If your tripod is bright aluminum, use a spray can, not a brush, to paint it a flat black. Brush painting the legs will put on too thick a coat of paint, and this may prevent the proper telescoping of the legs.

When I cannot use a tripod, or when I know the action will be fast, I use a unipod. The one I use is the Gitzo because it is the only unipod that also incorporates a shoulder brace. A regular unipod prevents the camera from wavering up and down but does nothing to prevent it from moving in a 360-degree circle. Using a unipod with a shoulder brace, your two legs become the other two legs of a tripod. To further steady the unipod, some photographers shorten the single leg and then sit down, bracing the unipod further with their legs and body. The unipod also becomes a good walking staff when climbing a mountainside or fording a fast-moving stream.

A number of photographers get really good results with lenses up to 400 mm mounted on a gunstock. Although I am a rifle instructor and know about controlled breathing and pulse rate, I just cannot hold a lens of that size satisfactorily, although I do use one occasionally on flight shots. I do use the Leitz gunstock on my 80 to 200 lens.

Many times, you will be able to approach wildlife more closely in a vehicle than you would on foot. Many creatures have become accustomed to cars and trucks and do not consider them a potential danger. Almost all of the photographs taken in Africa, in the game parks, are taken from a vehicle because it is against the law to wander about on foot.

The most stable window pod is also made by Gitzo and requires no clamping, which greatly facilitates the use or removal of the pod. A wide, cushioned base is placed over the lowered window, and the weight of the camera and lens is supported by a short leg that rests against the inside of the car door. I also mount a ball head on my window pod. The window can then be raised or lowered to the proper eye level.

In an emergency, a bean bag, cushion, folded blanket, or jacket can be placed over the lowered window to help steady the lens. The drawback is that with no supporting leg, the camera has a tendency to rock on the fulcrum contact point. When shooting from a flat surface, such as from the roof hatch of a Land Rover, from a large rock, or from the ground, any of these items work very well. Wherever possible, however, and if the telephoto lens is not too big, I prefer short-legged (4 to 6 inches), wide-stance tripods, such as the R & B and Rowi.

I carry in my vehicle a number of clamps, such as C-clamps or Vice-Grip pliers, with the standard ¼- or ⅜-inch camera attachment threads welded to them. These can be clamped on branches, tables, angle irons such as bumpers, and they work well. I also have had some large woodscrews welded with a cross tee of iron and fitted with a small camera ball head attachment. These can be screwed into wood or trees, and I often use them for remote work. They can be unscrewed when the job is finished.

Metallized Products has just brought out a brand new product called a Space Rescue Blanket. It is meant to be used as an emergency body-heat-retaining blanket. The material is a waffled aluminum, and it makes a fantastic photographic reflector. As soon as I got one I cut a 35″ x 36″ piece out of its 69″ x 72″. This piece weighs about 1½ ounces and can be folded 4″ x 4″ x ¼″. With this in the pocket of my photo vest I never expect to be without a reflector for fill-in light again. You can have someone hold it; you can drape it over a bush, high grass, or weeds; or you can make a frame for it. You can sit on it on wet ground, use it as an umbrella, wrap it around your shoulders for warmth, or use it as a signaling panel if you get lost.

ADDITIONAL EQUIPMENT

*I never say I've got a photo till I have the film
developed and hold the results in my hand;
till that time, I have only taken the photo.*
                    —L. L. Rue III

Photo Vests or Jackets

A photographer never has enough pockets in which to store his film, spare lenses, lens caps, and so on. For years I have worn an L. L. Bean Warden's jacket for photography because it is lightweight, durable, and has lots of pockets. In warm weather I use one with the sleeves removed.

I have tried several commercial photo vests, but they all leave a lot to be desired. Obviously the people producing them are not using them. The Ultimate Photo Vest shown here, which I designed, meets all the requirements of such a garment. A photo vest or jacket is a must.

Clothing

A wildlife photographer must be out in all kinds of weather and must dress accordingly. During the summer, regular blue jeans and lightweight chambray work shirts are satisfactory. There is no place in the out-of-doors for short pants and short-sleeved shirts. Long pants and sleeves provide a measure of protection against sunburn, scratches from brush and briars, poison ivy, insect bites, and scrapes from kneeling or lying on the ground. If the weather is hot, both the pants and the sleeves can be rolled up.

Raingear should always be carried if you are going to be away from shelter. I prefer a rainsuit made of Gore-tex because excessive perspiration passes out through the material while keeping you dry from the rain.

A hat should be worn for protection from the sun and rain. I prefer a soft, water-repellent hat with a 1 to 1½-inch brim. A wide brim gets in the way when you want to look through your camera viewfinder.

Your feet are always your main means of transportation, and so good shoes are a must, as are Vibrim lug soles. Many injuries occur in the out-of-doors from slipping, and lug soles often prevent this from happening. Shoes should cover the ankles for maximum protection. Danner Gore-tex boots are the lightest weight good boot on the market today and are absolutely waterproof. Heavy wool socks, reinforced with nylon, should be worn to protect and cushion your feet.

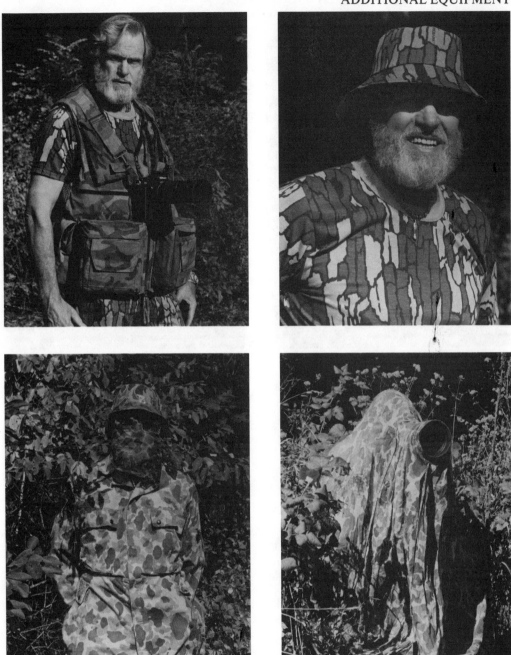

Top left A good photo vest is a must. My Ultimate Photo Vest allows the photographer to carry 4 lenses, 60 rolls of film, and has straps to hold the camera. Photo by Charlie Heidecker
Top right I like a soft hat that can be folded up, but with a small brim to shade the eyes. Photo by Charlie Heidecker
Bottom left I prefer to wear camouflage whenever possible to be as inconspicuous as possible. A mesh face mask and gloves really help. Photo by Irene Vandermolen
Bottom right My Pocketblind weighs about one pound and is actually worn. The photographer and the camera become the supports. In about two minutes you are ready. Photo by Irene Vandermolen

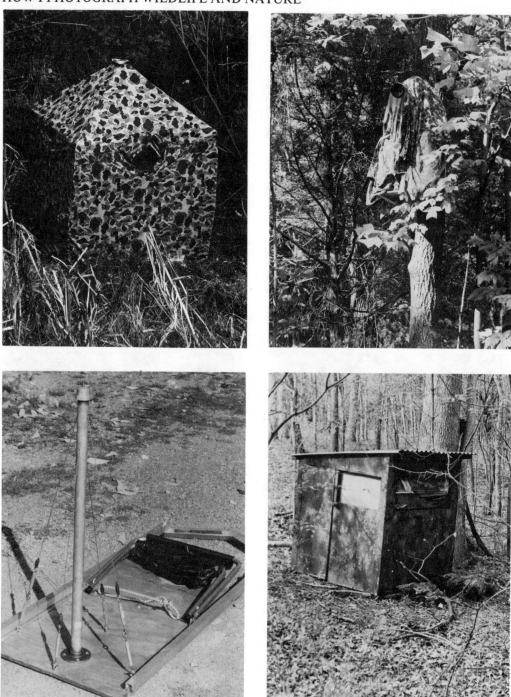

Top left My Simplex Blind consists of spring steel poles and roof supports and is covered with a camouflaged, waterproof material.
Top right The Baker climbing tree stand and L. L. Rue's Pocketblind in use. Photo by Irene Vandermolen
Bottom left The adaptations needed to allow the use of the Baker tree stand as a photographic platform. Photo by Irene Vandermolen
Bottom right A small permanent photographic blind made out of plywood.

I have worked in temperatures of -39 degrees with the wind-chill factor making it -80 to -90 degrees. In cold weather, you should dress in layers that can be removed or added as needed, according to the weather and your activity.

Polypropalene long underwear is one of the newest materials. It is fantastic; it whisks perspiration away from the body and keeps you dry and warm. If it is exceptionally cold, I wear thermal long johns, the waffle weave, over the poly.

Wool trousers go on next, and they can be gotten in different weights. L. L. Bean puts out the heaviest I know of.

I wear a wool shirt, a light insulated jacket, and, if it's very cold, a down jacket over the top. If I am walking, I always carry the outer layers till I get to where I may be inactive. Sweating can kill you in the winter; walk cool to stay dry.

I prefer a knitted wool balaclava with a slight brim for winter headgear. When walking, I tuck the hat under my belt; yet I have it to wear when I need the protection. Forty percent of your body heat can be lost through your head. Keep your head warm, and your body will be warm. A knitted hat also allows perspiration to escape.

I usually put rubbing alcohol on my feet before I go out in cold weather as it stimulates the flow of blood. Then I put on pure silk socks, a pair of poly or wick socks, then the best heavy wool and nylon socks I can buy. I wear insulated Danner boots or felt-lined shoe pacs with lug soles. If I am going to be in a blind or inactive, I wear surplus army mukluks, which have two or three layers of felt boot inside. I do not like or recommend any footwear that depends on perspiration for warmth. I want my feet dry to keep them toughened.

I have tried hundreds of combinations for hand warmth. The warmest I have found is pure silk gloves with a pair of long wool wristlets over the gloves. The wristlets protect your arteries and veins from cooling down and act as mittens by keeping your fingers together. Your fingertips, sticking out at the ends, are covered with silk, which allows you to operate your camera and touch the metal parts without sticking to the metal. If it is extremely cold, I also use large, loose, sheepskin mittens held on with tie strings so that they are not lost when I remove them to actually take pictures.

In cold weather, do not take your cameras into a warm room; keep them cool so that condensation does not cause them to malfunction. In the field, cameras can be kept from getting too cold by being worn under your outer layer of clothing. In extremely cold weather, I fasten a hand warmer with elastic bands to the back of the camera and over the motor drive. That adds just enough warmth to allow usage under the most severe conditions.

Whenever possible, I prefer clothing in camouflage colors. I always carry a light, mesh face mask of camouflage material. Although it is not usually needed, I prefer to blend in with my surroundings whenever possible. Many articles of camouflaged clothing have a hard surface that makes noise when it rubs against brush. This alerts the wildlife. I prefer soft-napped clothing, like wool, or like that put out by the Winona Knitting Mills or by Trebark.

Protecting Your Gear

Cameras and lenses must be given maximum protection. The first and most important protection you can have is to take out camera insurance. Reliable companies offer special policies at $1 or $2 per $100 of insured value. Most policies have a $100 or $200 deductible clause so that you pay for minor repairs or losses yourself. The insurance covers against major losses through theft or accident.

In the back of my photo vest, I always carry two large plastic garbage bags for emergency use. If a sudden shower comes up, I can put one bag over me for a poncho and the other over my camera and gear. They weigh almost nothing and are inexpensive.

When shipping or storing my camera gear, I have found that the Pelican Company plastic

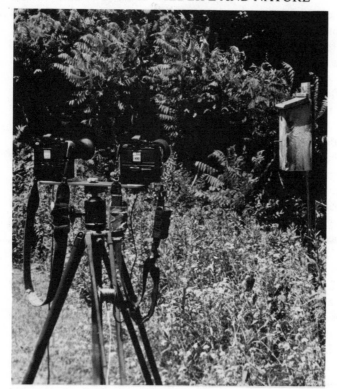

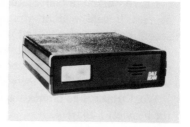

Left Two 35 mm cameras, one having color film, the other black and white, are being tripped simultaneously by remote control.
Above The Dale Beam photographic tripper.

cases are the strongest and most waterproof; they also give excellent protection against dust. If a waterproof and dustproof soft sack is needed, the best I have found are the Drysack by Coleman and the Super Sack by Early Winters. These items are great protection when you are canoeing or rafting. If your camera does get wet, keep it submerged till you can get it to a repairman. Water doesn't rust the camera, but oxidation by air does.

To carry my basic lenses and cameras in the mountains, I use a Lowe-Pro soft backpack with a foam liner, or I use the soft pack and drop the lenses and cameras in special sheepskin cases from the Made to Order Company. I also carry the Lowe-Pro when I travel by plane and send only my spare equipment and larger, lesser-used lenses as luggage. Too often, my luggage and I have not arrived at the same destination at the same time. By carrying my basic unit and a stock of film with me at all times, I am ready to work. The Lowe-Pro, Temba, and Orvis camera bags work very well in plane travel.

To carry the maximum of equipment back in, I use a rigid pack frame such as the Kelty, Alpenlite, or Coleman.

Blinds

Blinds can be as simple as a piece of camouflage material thrown over you and your camera or as elaborate as the building of a permanent structure.

Many companies, including Baker, sell long pieces of camouflage material and four rods to support it. This works great with animals because it conceals your outline; but because it lacks a top, it is not suitable for birds.

A semipermanent blind can be made from a piece of light chicken wire with natural grasses or brush woven through the mesh. The main drawback to using natural materials is that it is strictly forbidden in national parks and refuges, and that is where a lot of your photography will have to be done.

I have a very lightweight Pocketblind on the market that can be carried and worn when needed. My larger Ultimate Blind and my Simplex Blind will also be available. These blinds have evolved from my years of working with blinds.

A rigid blind is easily constructed. The accompanying photos show how to make one. Small tents also make good blinds, and if you are going to have to get up very early in the morning to photograph at dawn, you might want to sleep in the tent overnight.

Any blind must be rigid or taut enough so that it does not flap or blow about in the wind. This kind of action panics wildlife. An emergency blind can be made from the large cardboard cartons refrigerators are shipped in.

To photograph water birds or animals, a blind can be built on a rowboat or flat-bottomed skiff. The boat must be securely anchored while being used, however, to prevent it from drifting or rocking.

Steel scaffolding can be used to raise a blind high enough to work on tree-nesting birds. Just make sure the scaffold is securely anchored.

I frequently use a Baker tree stand to climb the tree and then serve as a base for a blind. The photo on page 46 shows how this is done.

To be effective, blinds should be left in place for extended periods so that the wildlife becomes accustomed to them and ignores them. The drawback to leaving blinds out, unfortunately, is that today they are often stolen.

I have a small wooden blind that has been in place for 14 years. It is covered with vines and is an integral part of the landscape. From it, I have taken some of my best deer photos.

I love working from a blind because even when I am not taking photographs, I am studying wildlife and taking copious notes that I will use in my books and lectures. Once wild creatures become accustomed to a blind, they carry on their daily activities in a completely normal fashion.

Remote Releases

Occasionally it is not practical to set up a blind, either because of terrain, habitat, or time. That is when a remote release comes into its own. The camera can be set up and focused on a nest, den hole, or feeding station. The shutter can then be activated by the photographer, who is hidden some distance away.

If the distance between the photographer and his camera is not more than 50 feet, the shutter can be activated by using an air bulb and a long length of tubing, such as the Rowi release. Squeezing the air bulb sends a surge of air through the tube, activating a plunger that has been screwed into the camera's cable release socket.

If your camera has a motor drive and battery pack, you can trip it with an electric remote cord. Most of the cords supplied by manufacturers are no more than 10 feet in length, and that's not long enough. Cut the electric cord in the middle, and you can splice in up to 200 feet of lightweight stereo speaker wire. Solder the connections before taping the splice to ensure good conduction.

The newest device for the remote releasing of the camera's shutter is Nikon's ML-1 transmitter and receiver. The receiver is mounted on the camera's hotshoe or taped to the strobe that is using the hotshoe. It is then connected with a cord to the camera's remote release socket and turned on. The transmitter is pointed at the "eye" on the rear of the receiver. When a button is pushed on the transmitter, a beam of red light is picked up by the receiver and activates the shutter.

Although the receiver can be set for either a single shot or continuous shooting, there is no way to shut off the continuous button until the entire roll of film is used.

Both transmitter and receiver have two channels. If you have one camera loaded with color film and one camera loaded with black and white, set the two receivers on different channels,

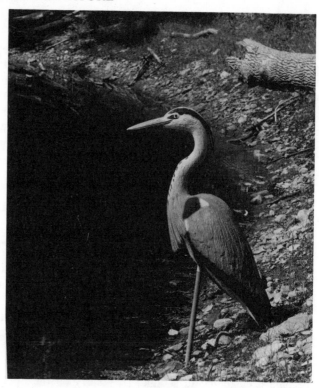

A Cabela great blue heron confidence decoy. Photo by Charlie Heidecker

and by flipping the switch on the transmitter, you can direct either camera to shoot. By using two receivers and two transmitters set on different channels, you can shoot both cameras simultaneously. The transmitter will work up to 180 feet, but there must be no intervening vegetation.

A number of companies offer radio-control remote releases. These devices are much more expensive than transmitters but can be used at much greater distances. And there are no wires to mess with.

When I first started in photography, I made a simple triggering device that allowed an animal to take its own picture. It was good for only one shot. With the advent of motor drives and electronic flash, I built a treadle that trips each time it is stepped on—and that's good for an entire roll of photos. I used to encase my camera in a waterproof box and leave it out overnight. I wouldn't think of leaving equipment out overnight now, unless I was in a very remote area. It is a sad commentary on our times that anything, anywhere, left unguarded may be stolen. It was not that way in the out-of-doors just a few years ago.

The ultimate remote release is an electric eye. When the subject breaks a beam of light, it activates a solenoid, which triggers the camera's shutter and flash. Most of these devices are bulky and use 110 watts, which tethers you to an electric power source.

A young fellow by the name of Greg Dale has just put on the market a lightweight electric eye/acoustical photographic triggering device that he calls the Dale Beam. The Dale Beam trigger emits a pulsed beam of infrared light, which is reflected off a small reflector back to the built-in receiver. Interrupting the beam triggers the camera or electronic flash. The trigger can also be switched to "sound"; the outputs are activated by a built-in microphone.

The unit weighs a mere 26 ounces, has a range of 26 feet, and can be operated with 110 AC current or by rechargeable ni-cod batteries. This means that the unit can be used anywhere. The sensitivity of both the light and the sound activation can be controlled. I predict that we will soon be seeing even more spectacular wildlife photos as serious nature photographers find out what doors this device will open for them.

The main advantage to using the electric eye is that when it is used in conjunction with high-speed flash, tremendous action photos can be taken at bird feeders and nests. Everyone's reaction time is different, but I know that I miss many photos when triggering a camera by hand. It does take a great deal of experimentation when using the electric eye to calculate where the subject will be, so that the focus can be predetermined, after it has broken the light beam.

The main disadvantage to using any remote device is that the camera has to be focused on a specific, predetermined spot. If the subject does not occupy that exact spot, it cannot be photographed. That is the main reason I prefer using a blind. When I am in a blind, I am behind the camera and can move the camera as the subject moves.

Small Items to Be Carried

To photograph wild creatures, you must go where they are or bring them to where you want them to be. All species have a natural habitat to which they have adapted through evolution. Very often they cannot live outside that habitat. Within the habitat, most creatures have a home range where they spend their lives. Within that home range are areas frequented more often than others and at specific times. Such focal points are nest or den sites, singing perches, lookout sites, watering holes, food sources, protective cover or roosting areas, and sleeping and breeding spots.

You cannot force a creature to come to a spot that is not natural to it, but you can entice it to a specific spot in a natural area. To do so, you must appeal to its basic instincts: survival, sex, food, and water. Although this is the usual order of importance, the ranking may change according to circumstance. For example, in desert areas, water always takes priority over food; where water is plentiful, it does not.

Ordinarily there is not much you can do about the survival factor except to remember that you cannot entice or lure a wild creature away from protective cover. People who build new homes and have wide expanses of lawn often wonder why birds do not come to their feeders. The answer is simple. There are no shrubs for protection. If you are going to bait birds or animals in order to photograph them, do it along the edge of woods or have brush rows or other protective cover nearby.

I often use scents to appeal to an animal's sex or food instincts. Decoys either attract members of the opposite sex, act as a challenge to members of the same sex, or allay the fears of an entirely different species.

Calls of many kinds are also used. A swisssshhing sound, made with your mouth, may attract small birds to come nearer. Imitating the call of an owl may do the same thing. The little wooden Audubon bird caller works great. Duck, goose, and turkey calls bring these birds in closer. Predator calls alert many birds and animals.

Aids to Bringing in Wildlife

For 17 summers I guided wilderness canoe trips in Quebec, Canada. I was often 200 miles or more from the nearest town. I am an Eagle Scout and their motto, Be Prepared, is one that every person venturing into the out-of-doors should live by.

Wildlife photography often requires that you work in wilderness areas. Be prepared, and you will come back out.

The following are items I wear or carry both at home and in the woods:

1. A 6-inch Randall sheath knife—a working tool.
2. A 28-blade Swiss Army knife—a portable toolkit.

3. A Bic lighter in case I need to build a fire.

4. A 6-foot piece of nylon parachute shroud cord.

5. A tube of Chapstick.

6. A ¼-inch-wide 10-foot Stanley tape for record measurements.

7. A "lipstick" case camel's hair photo brush for cleaning lenses.

8. In warm weather, a Cutter compact snakebite kit.

9. In warm weather, a bottle of Cutter insect repellent.

10. A packet of toilet paper in a plastic bag.

If I'm going to be off the beaten path, I carry a survival pouch on my belt. It contains the following:

1. Emergency space blanket of mylar to prevent hypothermia.

2. The Acme Thunderer whistle for signaling.

3. A couple of safety pins—handy around blinds.

4. Potable Aqua tablets for water purification—strong enough to kill *giardia lamblia*.

5. A small, strong plastic bag to contain water or other substances.

6. A few assorted nails.

7. An emergency fishing kit.

8. Cortaid for poison ivy and insect bites.

9. Mycitracin as an antiseptic for cuts.

10. Band-aids.

11. Percogesic tablets (stronger than aspirin).

12. Snare wire.

13. 20 feet of thin, strong nylon cord.

14. Change for a phone call, if needed when you get out.

15. A small piece of duct tape for patching anything from pants to canoes.

In my photo vest I always carry the following:

1. Orvis Bite Light—handy when working in a blind.

2. Air bulb camel's-hair brush.

3. Lens cleaner and tissue.

4. Cable release or electronic shutter release.

5. Granola food bars.

6. Dried raisins, apples, etc.

7. Dried jerky meat.

Take along a small canteen, flask, or plastic bottle of water. Don't drink water from brooks and streams, even in the wilderness. The species *giardia lamblia* protozoa is now found in many wilderness areas and can cause sickness. I add Gookinaid to the water to boost energy and prevent cramps or muscle spasms. It contains glucose and electrolytes. If you are active, you must drink water. Never venture in a desert area without ample water.

Getting Off the Road to Take Photographs

Most wildlife photography is done on the basis of a day trip. I usually work out of my home for the day and come back at night. I am very fortunate in having good friends living in some of the general areas that I want to photograph throughout the country and the world, and I am often able to work from their homes. I sometimes fly to an area and stay in a motel and use a rented car to get out in the field. On extended trips, I live in my trailer and go to work each day in my truck. My truck has a small camper on the back in which I can sleep if I want to drive into areas where I cannot take the trailer.

I drive to the desired area and continue to drive as I scout for the wildlife I hope to photograph. Or I drive to a specific area where the wildlife should be found and hike in.

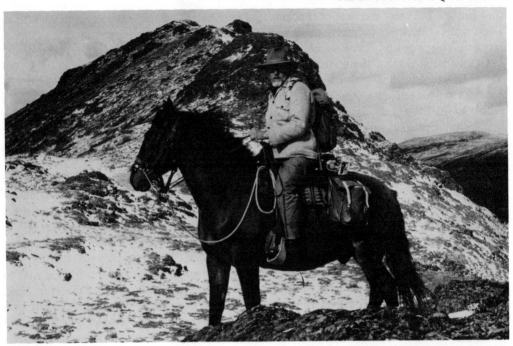

I advise carrying your cameras and small lenses in a backpack, even while using a horse, as I am doing in this photo.

Whenever I am going to be away from the road, I make sure that I carry the emergency gear I described above. Not to be prepared is sheer stupidity. I shoot all day, or until I lose either the light or the wildlife, then I hike back out. This is how I do 90 percent of my photography.

If the animal I want to photograph is too far from a path or trail to be able to walk in, photograph it, and walk back out, then I plan to stay the night. My Early Winters Sleep Inn, the waterproof sleeping bag shelter, a 1-kilo bag, and a Therm-a-rest mattress weigh a shade over 5 pounds. With that gear I can spend a very comfortable night even if the temperature drops slightly below freezing. I do not carry a stove; I do no cooking if I am going to be out for a couple of days. Natural-grain cereal bars provide the carbohydrates I need for energy, and jerked venison provides the protein. I use Gookinaid in my water to replace the electrolytes lost by walking. And I carry vitamin tablets.

For a total weight of less than 8 pounds, not counting the water, I'm all set for two or three days if need be. My biggest problem is to carry enough film to shoot as much as I like. There is a definite limit to how far you can walk to do photography. Anything over three days becomes an expedition and must be planned that way. Then I carry an MSR-X-GK stove, a couple of pots, extra food, and my Katadyn water filter, and I'm all set. I prefer the MSR-X-GK stove over all others because it burns any liquid fuel.

In the 17 years I guided those canoe trips in Canada, I paddled a minimum of a 1000 miles each year. A canoe is still one of the best ways to get a lot of gear into otherwise inaccessible areas. A canoe is no good if you plan to photograph sheep and goats, but it is great for ducks, geese, moose, beaver, and black bear. Make sure that you carry your gear in heavy-duty waterproof plastic bags. I use the Coleman Drysack for large items and the Early Winters Super Sacks for smaller gear.

I do not like fiberglass or aluminum canoes. The early fiberglass models striated and peeled. I cannot speak for the latest models. Aluminum canoes are rugged, but they are not well designed. They are far too noisy and conduct the cold of the water through to the paddler, and they become hot from the heat of the sun. It is hard to get camouflaged paint to stick to an aluminum canoe. I am currently using a 17-foot Old Town Tripper canoe made of Oltonar Royalex. This is an unsinkable canoe; air bubbles are built into the material. The Royalex also has a "memory" so that the material will spring back to its original shape after an impact. I have painted my canoe with a flat, dead-grass-colored paint inside and out. It is relatively noiseless in even choppy water. It has a good shape for handling on lakes, a low bow and stern profile so that it does not catch wind, and being keelless, it responds well in rapids. I have put in an extra Canadian thwart halfway between the center thwart and the rear seat, where I kneel when I paddle alone. This canoe will comfortably hold three people and their gear and is capable of carrying a ton in calm water.

Most trips into the back country have to be done with a guide and packhorses. If your trip can be planned prior to the hunting season, the cost for such an outfit is much more reasonable. Most hunting seasons are only one month to six weeks in length, and all good outfitters are booked solid a year in advance. Some outfitters guide to national parks and areas where hunting is not permitted. These guides can be hired to go whenever you want to be there, but again, the earlier you get your reservations in, the better chance you have of getting your preferred time slot. These outfitters know where the best spots are for the animals you wish to photograph and where the animals will probably be at any particular time of the year. Most outfitters supply all the gear and food you will need. You might want to take your own personal sleeping bag of a weight heavy enough for the anticipated weather. The guide will provide panniers, a fitted cargo box that is fastened on a packhorse, for your camera gear. These boxes are a must because the horses often bang into trees as they go through the forest. I made several horse packing trips into British Columbia for stone sheep and mountain caribou. I used saddlebags but carried my main lenses in a small backpack. I did it mainly to be sure no accident befell the equipment I was counting on.

If you plan such a trip, I suggest you get in shape by riding a bit before you leave home. You are then less likely to get saddle sore the first two days on the trail. If you cannot do any preparatory riding, then on your first two days you should alternately walk a while and ride a while.

I have flown in every imaginable aircraft to get into an area I wanted to photograph. Going to Ungava after caribou, I flew in four different kinds of planes in one day, each one getting successively smaller. I have used planes in combination with other transportation after being dropped off. You can seldom do worthwhile photography from a plane, so you have to use a boat or a horse, or you have to walk after getting back into the wild. In remote areas most planes are on pontoons, and they can drop you off in any area that has a lake or river large enough for the plane to land on.

The ultimate in wilderness air travel is a helicopter. Helicopters can drop you on lakes, beaches, mountaintops, or any clearing that is large enough for them to land in. The cost of such aircraft is so prohibitively expensive, however, that it is beyond the reach of all except staff photographers working for a big company or publication. I'd love to use helicopters more often, but I just cannot justify the expense for the pictures produced.

Photographing Overseas

I have been blessed with having been able to spend three summers in Africa and to have had three trips to Europe, two to South America, and one to Asia for wildlife photographs. I hope to be able to go to many more areas because there are so many places I haven't been and so many species I haven't photographed. But I'll have to hurry.

In most parts of the world, it is getting much more difficult with each passing year to get good wildlife photos. As the world's human population continues to explode, the confrontation between wildlife and humans is accelerated because people need the land that the wildlife lives on. When people destroy the habitat, they remove the wildlife from the area forever.

Although I am an eternal optimist, I am also a realist. There will never be peace in the world, and wildlife is forever caught in the middle of conflicts. In many areas the wildlife has been, or is being, decimated. In many areas it is no longer safe to try to photograph wildlife. Diplomatic or ideological differences make it impossible to get to many places. Still, there are fantastic lands to go to and fantastic wildlife to be seen and photographed. I plan to get to as many of these areas as soon as it is possible for me to do so.

The most economical and hassle-free way to travel to overseas game areas is to go on a package tour. The tour people take care of customs, vehicles, travel permits, documents, hired help, guides, food, and lodging. Foreign governments treat tour groups better because they need tourists' dollars, and groups of tourists bring in big batches of much needed currency. Your air fare also is cheaper if it is a group fare. In many foreign countries, petrol (gasoline) is rationed and expensive; tour groups take care of the petrol situation. Many tour guides are very knowledgeable about wildlife. They have traveled in the same area repeatedly, and they know exactly where, and what, species will be available at almost any given time.

One disadvantage to a tour group is that you have to travel as a group, and so everything is geared to a group. I prefer to get up early and work late. Tour groups have to go at a more leisurely pace because most tourists demand it. It is difficult to do really good photography when traveling in a minibus with six or eight other people, and they all want to take pictures of the same animal at the same time. It is just as difficult to get that many people to hold still at one time so that your cameras can be held steady. In African game parks it is against the law for anyone to get out of a vehicle while in a park. And there are just not enough window spaces or open roof-hatch space for the number of people that the bus usually holds. Tour groups must adhere to a schedule, and I always work according to the subject and available light.

I have been most fortunate to come up with a happy compromise. I usually get a tour outfit to set up an individual safari for me, with them supplying what is needed but geared to where I want to go and how long I want to stay. On several occasions I traveled to my destination with a larger group to get the lower air fare, and then split off on my own after I got there. I have listed several very reliable outfitters in the appendix.

In Africa I traveled in both a Land Rover and a Toyota four-wheel drive. These worked out especially well because both had roof hatches that could be thrown back and the camera bedded down on the roof for good steady shots. Although I couldn't do it with rented vehicles, if the vehicles had been mine, I would have stripped out all the back seats and set up the tripod on the floor. Some photographers clamp a ball head onto the vehicle frame. The disadvantage in this is that you cannot shoot to the side or backward. By using a tripod centered in the hatch hole, you can walk around the tripod and quickly shoot in any direction without moving the vehicle.

With these vehicles we drove over any terrain to follow or get close to the action. That is permissible in Africa; vehicles are not allowed off the road in our national parks.

In Nepal we worked on rhinocerous on foot the first day. That was idiotic. The elephant grass was 15 feet high, and so it was almost impossible to find the game. When we did find the rhinos, it was hard to photograph them because of the grass. Also, there were tigers and leopards in that high grass, and there would have been absolutely no protection if one had charged. That's not the way to do it, although it was how most people tried to do it.

We then rented an elephant, and this worked out very well. When we located a rhino, it could be herded into the open. We could see much farther and better from the height of the elephant's back. We could cover a lot more territory because elephants walk with a 9-foot stride. Although sitting on an elephant's back was not the steadiest platform for taking photographs, sitting up there was sure a lot safer than being on the ground.

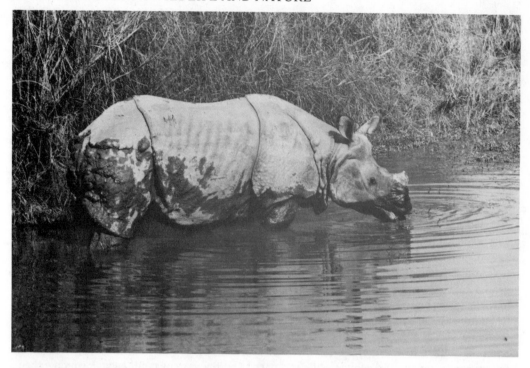

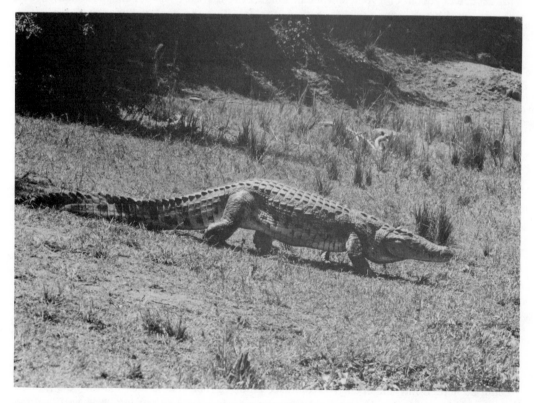

Top We photographed this one-horned rhinoceros in Nepal from the back of our elephant. Photo by Irene Vandermolen
Bottom Crocodiles can move amazingly fast on land for a short distance.

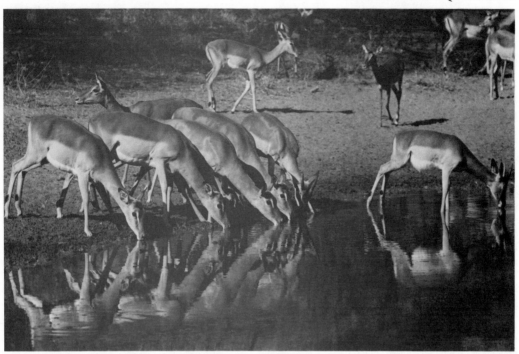

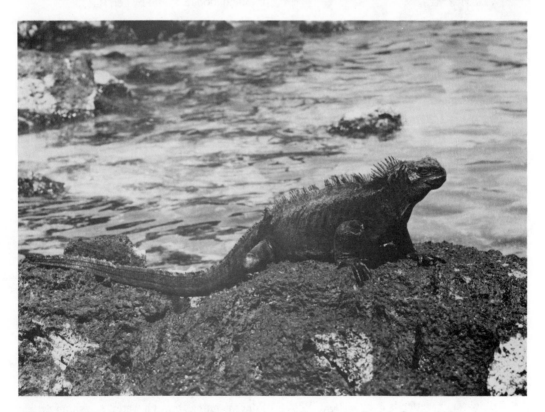

Top Impala drinking at one of only two waterholes in Mkuzi Game Park in South Africa.
Bottom Most of the wildlife, like this marine iguana, are easily photographed on the Galapagos Islands as they have no fear of man. Photo by Irene Vandermolen

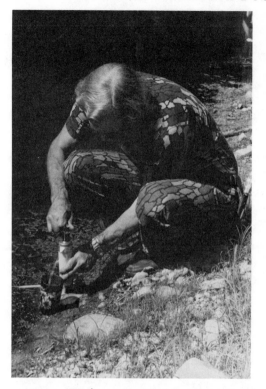

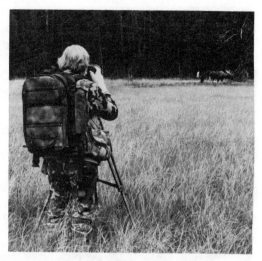

Left With this Katadyn water filter, I can remove all bacteriological material from any water, making it drinkable. Photo by Charlie Heidecker

Above The Lowe-Pro Quantum II is my favorite pack, which I am wearing here while photographing moose. Photo by Len Rue, Jr.

Tours, safaris, and trips vary greatly in cost, according to the accommodations that you expect. Most of my trips are camping trips, which are much less expensive than those booked into lodges and hotels. I have camped all my life, so this is no hardship for me. In fact, even camping safaris are a luxury because I do not have to do all the physical work. When I was guiding my wilderness canoe trips in Canada, I had to take care of everyone else.

I have worked from small powerboats in both East and South Africa to get close to some water species. I got some excellent crocodile photographs on the Nile. In the swamps of South Africa it was not safe to get out of the boat because these rapacious lizards can travel at amazing speeds for short distances on land. The guide said that anything that stepped out on land in the swamp was automatically booked on the croc's luncheon menu.

I went by rented car to Mkuzi Game Park in South Africa. I know of no other spot in the entire world that offers so many photographic possibilities. In Mkuzi, the government has built photographic pavilions in the middle of the only two waterholes in 100 square miles of dry scrubland. All the wildlife has to come to these waterholes to drink. From dawn to dusk there is an unending parade of impala, nyalla, kudu, baboons, warthogs, zebras, and other game animals and birds. This is an absolute must for every wildlife photographer.

I toured the Galapagos with a friend of mine, Dr. Cleve Hickman, who runs guided tours to the islands for college students. We toured most of the islands from the luxury of a yacht, the *Beagle II*. The Galapagos Islands are also a photographer's paradise because none of the wildlife fears humans. Although you are restricted to certain paths, you suffer no hardship because the paths go through the birds' nesting colonies. Telephoto lenses are seldom needed, except for the occasional portrait shot of some subject that is 40 or 50 feet away.

In some areas, such as the Everglades or the bayous of Louisiana, the best way to get into the shallow-water wetlands is by airboat. Photos of deer running through water, splashing up a storm, are taken in this manner. The boats can be throttled down to the precise speed of the deer so that you do not have to pan the camera. Just shoot at a shutter speed fast enough to stop the action of the deer and freeze the water droplets in the air.

Before leaving on a trip to any part of the world, you will have to have your passport in order. For many countries you will need various medical shots. Get them well in advance of your planned departure date because some shots may cause adverse reactions.

I strongly urge everyone about to travel overseas to join the International Health Care Service at 525 East 68th Street in New York City. The service can provide health suggestions before you go overseas, can give you inoculations, and can diagnose and treat any ailments you might contract while you are overseas—ailments your local doctor may have no knowledge of.

Everyone knows enough not to drink the water in any of the developing countries unless it has been boiled or treated. Now it has been discovered that you should not drink any untreated water in wilderness areas on the North American continent. For years I drank the water from virgin wilderness lakes and streams. I always said, "No people, no pollution." That's not true. I learned this lesson the hard way in British Columbia when I became deathly sick with salmonella poisoning. I drank water from a clear mountain stream that had evidently been contaminated by salmon dying upstream, after spawning. And any stream that has a beaver dam on it will have infectious *giardia lamblia*.

I won't have that problem again because I'll never take that chance again. Now, wherever I travel, I carry a Katadyn pocket filter with me. This device is a little larger than a flashlight. It is a hand-pumped filtration device that will absolutely remove every waterborne disease-carrying organism. With it you can make safe any water, anywhere, without chemical treatment or boiling.

Be careful not only of the water you drink but also the water you use for cleaning your teeth, bathing, or swimming. Pump your wash water through the Katadyn filter too. And don't swim in freshwater rivers or lakes overseas.

In 1970 I took a quick dip in the Nile in Uganda. I was in the water no more than five minutes, but that was long enough for me to be infested with schistosomiasis (snail fever). I did not realize I harbored the parasite until it was the cause of my developing a cancerous tumor. This was when I learned of the International Health Group. Dr. Ward Johnson treated me for the schistosomiasis. Over 600 million people worldwide have this disease.

Do not go swimming, and do not wade in the water while doing photography. Wear hip boots or waders, or stay out of the water. No photographs are worth the risks involved.

Make sure that you check with the consulates or the United Nations missions of the countries you plan to visit to find out what regulations they have. Many countries have restrictions on the number of cameras, types of cameras, and amount of film that you can take into the country. Many now are charging fees on your photographic equipment and film, and some require special permits, particularly if you do cinematography.

I strongly advise you to buy all your film in this country and take it with you. Chapter 11, "Selling Your Photos," tells you how to best protect your film and cameras while traveling.

My favorite backpack for my camera and lenses is my Lowe Quantum II sack. This protects my essential equipment with generous foam layering, and it fits under an airline seat. I always carry my basic lenses, several cameras and motor drives, and some film on board the plane and keep it with me at all times. When I went to Nepal, my luggage ended up going to Hong Kong and then back to London before finally being delivered, two and a half weeks later, to Katmandu. Thankfully, I had all my basic gear with me, and although I was hampered by not having my tripods, I rented one. I could work.

PHOTOGRAPHING SCENICS

Every day of my life I thank God for my eyes
that allow me to behold the natural beauty
that He has created.

L. L. Rue III

Except for people taking photographs of family and friends, more photos are taken of scenics than of any other subject. The great advantage of photography is that, through it, you can share the beauty you have seen with others. I use scenics to enhance my lectures. A photo featuring a creature is a portrait; a photo in which the creature is a small part of the scene is a scenic.

Equipment for Scenics

Some scenics are taken with the normal 50 or 55 mm lens because at times the use of a wide-angle lens dwarfs the subject by encompassing too much of the scene. Wide-angle lenses of various lengths are generally used for scenics because they more accurately record the breadth of what the human eye is seeing. I prefer the 24 mm wide-angle lens. Wide-angle lenses must be held absolutely parallel to the ground, or vertical lines will converge. Lenses of less than 18 mm are called "fisheye lenses" and are strictly for special effects as they converge all but the lines at the center of the photo, even when held parallel.

To avoid convergence, the pros use the large-format view cameras. By being able to tilt both the lens carrier and the film back, all lines can be rendered absolutely vertical and horizontal. Also, the greatest depth of field can be gotten through the tilting of the lens. Perspective-control lenses also enable the 35 mm camera photographer to have some control over convergence.

Scenics, to be done properly, should not be snap shot. A tripod is a must for viewcameras, but it should be used with all cameras because greater depth of field can be gotten by using a slow shutter speed and a smaller lens aperture.

Using a tripod tends to ensure that the photographer takes the time to compose the scene from the best vantage point. A cable release or electronic shutter release should be used to minimize camera vibration while the shot is taken. Tripping the camera with the self-timer release will also minimize camera vibration. Some cameras allow the mirror to be locked up to reduce the number of mechanical steps needed to take the photograph and reduce possible movement.

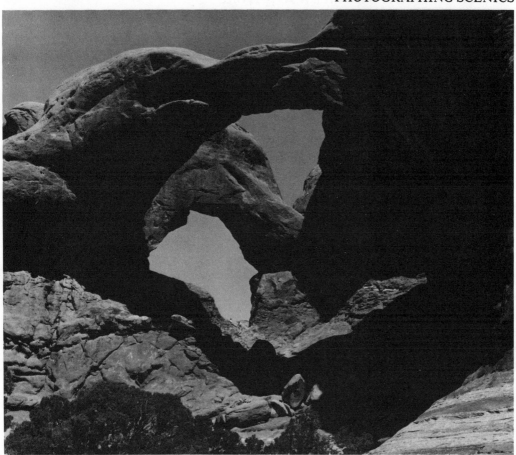

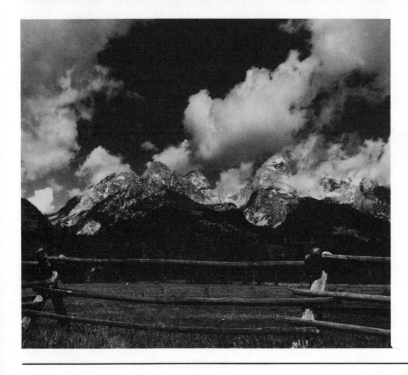

Top My son had to make several trips to get the most favorable lighting on these arches in Utah. A tripod also was used to allow for the needed depth of field. Photo by Len Rue, Jr.

Left I used the fence as framing to give the illusion of depth, I used a tripod so I could close the lens down for the exceedingly great depth of field, and I used a polarizing filter to darken the sky and enhance the clouds.

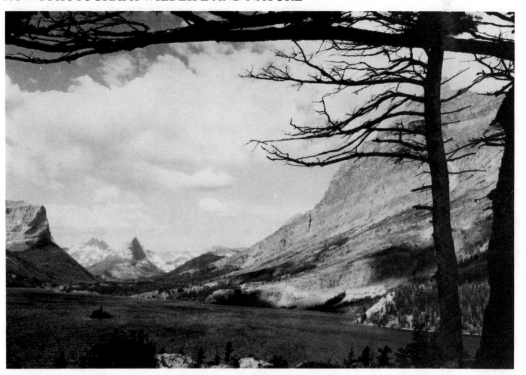

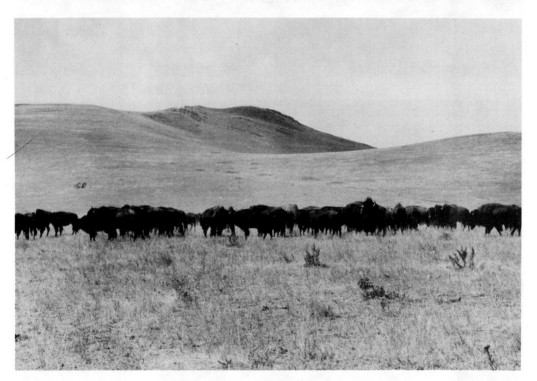

Top By including the rock ledge and the tree trunk and branches in the foreground, I added the dimension of depth to this photograph.
Bottom Shooting this bison herd from eye level produced a narrow black streak of the animals across the photo.

A great deal of time and work goes into taking a truly fine scenic photograph. A number of trips may be made to the same area to see what it looks like at different times of the day, under different lighting conditions, and at different seasons of the year. The angle of the sun not only changes hourly but with the passing of each season. Midday produces the harshest shadows.

Filters are used frequently in photographing scenics, either to enhance the natural tonal values or add desired warming, cooling, or additional tones. The polarizing filter dramatically darkens the sky, enhances the clouds, and also cuts the glare of light reflecting from water, ice, or glass.

Framing and Perspective

The proper framing of a photograph allows a two-dimensional picture to assume the property of the third dimension: depth. The frame in most outdoor photos is usually done by shooting through tree branches or other foreground foliage, through rustic fences, or through cave or tunnel entrances. If there is no foliage to shoot through exactly where I want it, I often have an assistant hold a branch where one is needed.

Framing is also done by the inclusion or introduction of some object into the foreground. Rocks, ripples in the sand, and foreground vegetation add depth. Picturesque pieces of driftwood can enhance seascapes. Shooting through icicles, snow cornices, or snow-draped branches enhances snow scenes. The inclusion of a statuesque cactus or the introduction of a weathered tree branch works well in desert areas. The limits to what you can use are imposed only by your imagination.

Occasionally a scenic is best shot from either a high or a low angle, which entirely changes the ordinary perspective. Low angles are good for enhancing depth, vastness, emptiness, aloneness. This is true whether the sky or the foreground has been given two-thirds of the frame. The low angle tends to make human accomplishments pale. High angles tend to shorten perspective, crowding the subject but also being particularly good when depicting flocks of birds or herds of animals. A herd of animals photographed at eye level appears as a dark line of single animals. Photographed from a high angle, the herd is distributed across the film as individual animals. It is for this reason that I have a platform built on top of the truck I use for photography. Just being 12 feet above the ground makes the subject appear as a flock or herd, instead of a line. A great angle is 45 degrees. Even when going to the extreme and photographing from an airplane, you should photograph animals at a 45-degree angle instead of straight down. The perspective of straight down shows the animals as they are seldom seen, and they may not be recognized. If the sun is extremely low, and the animals are standing or running parallel to the sun, their shadows may give a clue as to their identification.

It is in photographing scenics that the rule of thirds is stressed. Except in unusual circumstances, the horizon should not split a photograph in half. When the sky is allotted just the top third of a photo, the vastness or importance of the foreground is emphasized. When the foreground is allotted just the bottom third of the photo, the sky becomes dominant.

When making panoramic views, it is important that the camera be perfectly level. A panoramic head on the tripod is calibrated so that the camera is moved precisely so many degrees after each shot to make a continuous, 360-degree photo. Without such a head, the photographer has to make note of some feature within each exposure to act as a guide for the number of degrees the camera should be turned after each photo. It is best to overlap each shot slightly rather than miss a piece of the scene.

Times of the Day and Year

Scenics can be shot at any time of the day or year. The camera should not be shelved because

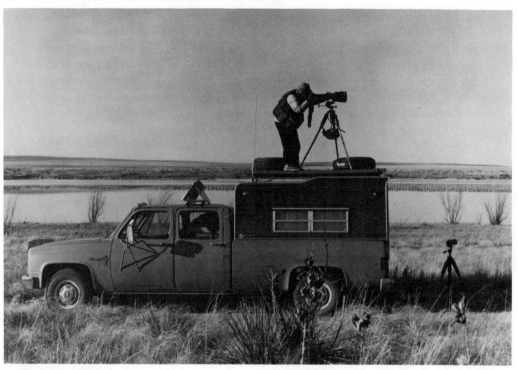

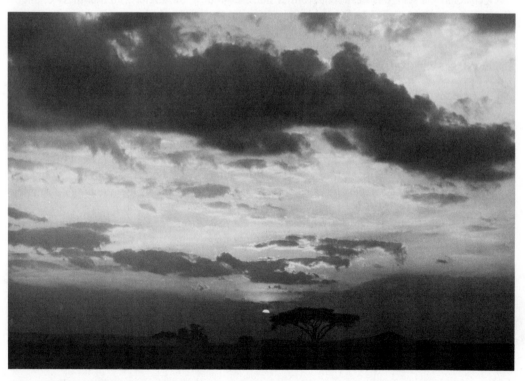

Top I added the ladder and platform to my truck so that I can use the height to give me that perspective when I need it. Photo by Irene Vandermolen
Bottom I discarded the third lines in order to emphasize the clouds and sky in this African sunset. The low horizon also denotes great expanse.

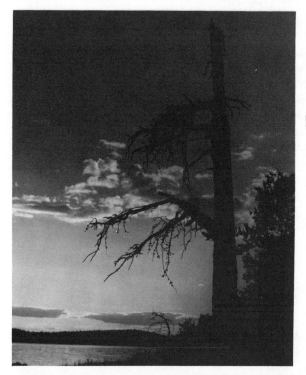

Left Following the rule of thirds emphasized this old dead pine silhouetted against a Canadian sunset. *Below* The inclusion of my canoe in the foreground adds scale to this photo because the canoe is a known object. The use of the canoe and the pine branches also serve as framing giving the photo the illusion of depth.

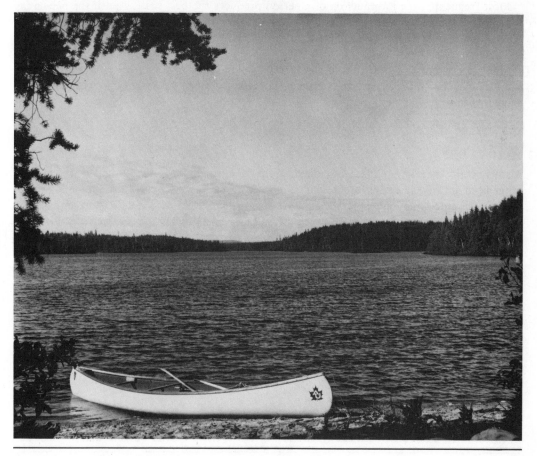

the weather is cold or because the sun is not shining. Many beautiful, soft mood photos can be taken when mist has softened the contours of the landscape or shrouded certain features in fog. If your camera is protected by an umbrella or a plastic cover, or if it is an underwater camera, photos can be taken in the rain or in a snowstorm.

Sunrises and sunsets are perennial favorites because of the chalky beauty of the color tones. Attention should be given to composition drama by adding foreground framing or subject focalization (some object or subject silhouetted against the sunset) as well as capturing the color. Unless the sun is muted by atmospheric haze or clouds, which produce the fantastic coloring, it must be hidden behind a tree or other object in the scene or under the horizon. Do not look at a bright sun through your camera—you may damage your eyes. With the sun hidden, metering is done directly from the brightest part of the sky. You may want to bracket the exposure slightly for different tones because there will be times when either underexposure or overexposure will produce a more pleasing photo than the actual metered reading.

The low-light angles, occurring early and late in the day, combined with shooting at an angle to the sun will produce dramatic texturing of sand, snow, rocks, and so forth.

Scale

Many scenics are enhanced by framing, but the actual size of the object used for framing may be unknown to the eventual viewer. You, as the photographer, know, but the inclusion or introduction of some common object of a known size will provide a scale by which the size may be judged.

Most frequently, the introduction of a person produces the best scale. And if the person is wearing a bright red or blue windbreaker, a spot of strong color is also added and enhances the photograph even further. I often include my truck and trailer in a scene because, again, they add a known dimension.

Many of my scenics feature a wild creature. The inclusion of a domesticated animal is good and may even be better if the size is primary because more people are familiar with domestic animals than with wild creatures.

Reflections

Many beautiful scenics are made by reflecting the background into a foreground of water. The water need not fill the entire foreground; it may be a small pond or even just a puddle. If the water is absolutely motionless, it will create a mirror image, and in that case an exact halving of the photo is suggested. Great interest is always shown in a photograph in which it is difficult to know which is right side up.

If the water is rippled, it is best to go back to the rule of thirds, letting the water dominate the foreground. Now the distorted reflection suggests energy and motion.

Shooting into the water at approximately a 45-degree angle not only reflects the clouds and the sky but is great for photographing floating leaves, water plants, and occasionally frogs. Close-up photography of large water droplets can also be used to reflect scenery. This is also good for miniature self-portraiture because the photographer and his camera will also be seen in the droplet.

Rhythm

Moving water may be depicted in different ways to denote different moods in scenics. A waterfall in an open area on a sunny day, using KR 64 or Fujichrome 100, may be shot at

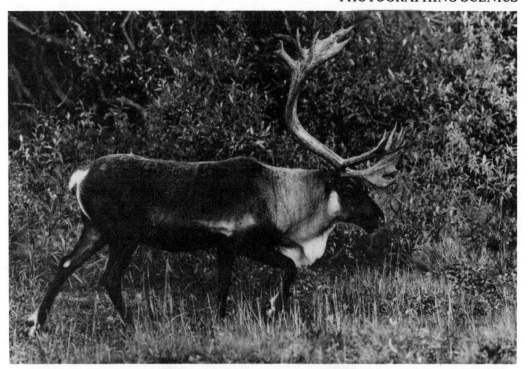

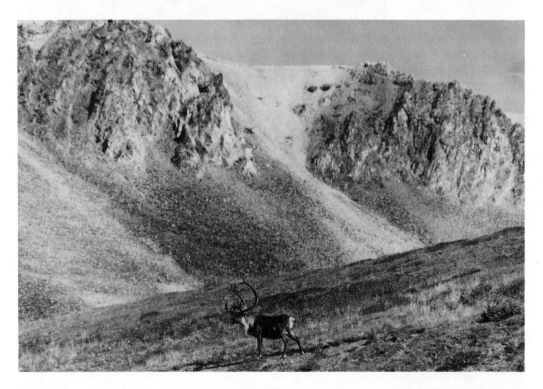

Top This is a fine photo of a caribou bull; the animal dominates the photograph. Photo by Len Rue, Jr.
Bottom In this scenic photo the caribou is used to give scale to the grandeur of the mountain Photo by Tim Lewis Rue

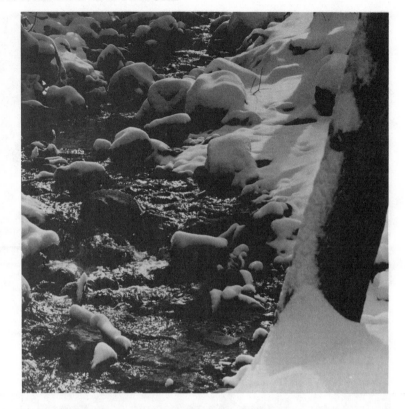

Top A slow shutter speed blurred the water in this stream while the corresponding high *f* stop allowed for exceptional depth of field. *Bottom* The power of this crashing surf was best captured by using a fast shutter speed freezing the water droplets in midair. Photo by Irene Vandermolen

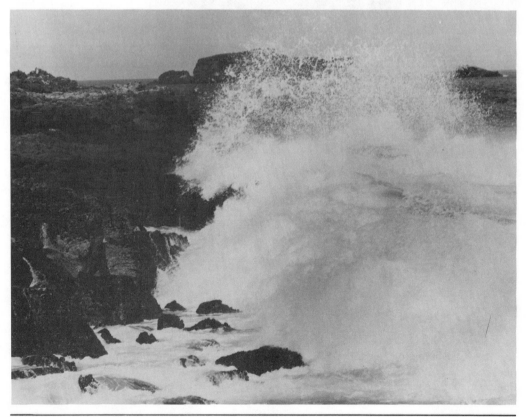

1/125 of a second at $f/9$ or $f/11$ respectively. To stop the action of the water, the shutter speed has to be set at 1/250 or 1/500 of a second. To get these speeds the lens must be opened up one or two stops. This shortens the depth of field, more or less isolating and freezing the action of the falling water, but imparting strength and kinetic energy.

To blur the water, the camera speed is set at 1/30 or 1/15 of a second, and the lens is closed down to $f/18$ or $f/28$. Although the blurring of the water shows motion, the great depth of field makes the overall photo less active, suggesting a more peaceful, tranquil mood.

The same holds true for photographing waves crashing up on a rock-bound coast. We all know the power and force of the waves; there has to be power and force or the water would not pound, it would gently lap. The freezing of the action denotes the greatest power.

Photographing Natural Phenomena

Some of the most dramatic scenics can be taken either just before or after a thunderstorm while the sky is black as night and the sun is shining under the edge of the cloud. Although the sunlight is not brighter than normal at this time, it appears to be much brighter by comparison with the dark sky. This is one of my favorite light conditions.

Any time the sun shines after a storm or even during it, rainbows are produced. People are awed by the beauty and are reminded that the rainbow is the sign of God's covenant with all living creatures on the earth. Rainbows are easily captured on film by metering the rainbow itself. Rainbows created by the mist from waterfalls can be metered the same way, but be sure you meter the rainbow and not the white, tumbling water.

Cloud photography can produce very dramatic photographs. The metering should be done from the clouds if they are lighter than the sky or from the sky if it is lighter than the clouds. Be sure to include at least a portion of the horizon to give a reference point to the clouds and a scale. Use whatever focal length lens allows you to capture the cloud formation you want and a portion of the horizon.

Lightning is easy to capture on film if the photograph is taken at night. The lightning becomes the light source. Put your camera on a tripod or aim it at a spot where flashes have just been seen, set your lens on infinity, open the lens to the largest aperture, and set your shutter on bulb. Open the shutter and hold it open until the lightning flashes, then close it. If you hold the shutter open for a longer period of time, you may capture a series of flashes, A shorter than normal lens makes it more likely that the flash will be in the area aimed at. Try to get a piece of the horizon in the photo to tie the lightning into the proper perspective with the earth. Foreground objects can often be silhouetted, with luck, against the lightning flashes. This kind of photograph is more successful in desert areas because more lightning occurs there. In the desert there is also less likelihood of encountering lights of man-made origin, which would detract from the lightning.

Scenics are among the least salable of photographs because of the competition from the pros who specialize in this particular field.

PHOTOGRAPHING WILDFLOWERS

*My reason for being is to make others aware,
through words and photographs, of the beauty with which our Lord has surrounded us.*
                    —L. L. Rue III

More people take photographs of flowers than of any other subject in nature. Photographs of wildflowers are easy to take because the flowers don't run away. Please note I did not say that they hold still. Good wildflower photography requires that you expend considerable time and effort, but then so does anything you want to do well.

Because of the ease with which most flowers can be photographed, the market is saturated. Photographs of flowers just do not sell well. When I was starting out in photography, Samuel Gottchos had the flower market sewed up. He was a very wealthy man because whatever flower photographs were purchased, were purchased from him. I was beaten out on a big sale to *Woman's Day* magazine by Gottchos. Afterward, I asked the art director how he thought my photos compared with those taken by Gottchos. His answer was, "Your photos are no better nor worse than his, but he is Gottchos." Today, no one has a corner on the flower market. Most pros don't bother photographing wildflowers. I do, even though I don't sell that many. Just to capture the beauty of the flowers on film is reason enough for me to continue to photograph them, and I always will. I always include a number of wildflower photographs in my general lectures. The general public loves wildflower photographs, and I do all I can to enhance that appreciation.

Responsibility

According to the latest statistics, over 20,000 plants are now on the worldwide endangered plant list. Too many people have picked too many flowers for too long. It has got to stop. Most flowers growing along the sides of roads or out in fields and meadows are exceptionally hardy and plentiful, although some, like the fringed gentian, a meadow plant, have become rare. Our greatest concern is for the delicate, beautiful woodland plants—the real "spring flowers" that bloom in the forests before the leaves appear on the trees. Their beauty has always been their undoing. Today, progress in the form of a bulldozer often destroys the plants and their habitat forever with building developments. Many people make it a point to get permission to go into an area to be developed and remove and transplant the wildflowers before the bulldozers go to work. This situation is about the only one in which we can condone the transplanting of wildflowers. Most people cannot or do not duplicate the conditions of acid soil, shale, and the

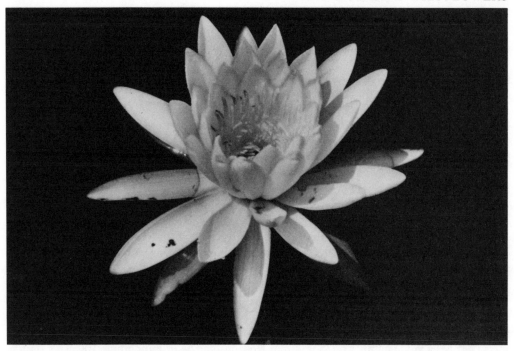

This sweet-scented white waterlily was photographed in the Okeefenokee Swamp in Georgia. The tannic acid in the water made the water very dark.

like, which most of these plants need to thrive. So when you are photographing wildflowers, look at them, photograph them, and appreciate them—but leave them.

Equipment Needed

When I first started in photography, there were no macro lenses or micro lenses. The average 35 mm camera focused down to 18 to 24 inches with the normal 50 mm lens. This was when I first began to use the 135 mm lens as my main lens. The 135 mm focused down to only 4 feet, but the magnification was more than 2½X. Then I went to portra, proxar, or close-up lenses, pieces of optical glass that went on over the regular lens like a filter. A set had three different elements, to be used according to the distance you wanted to be from your subject. They caused no loss of light for exposure, but they were not needle sharp on the outside edges. Portra lenses are still a good investment for those who cannot afford the macro lenses. Two of these lenses can also be used together for even greater magnification, but the photo quality suffers, and you may get vignetting.

I then went to extension tubes and a bellows. These devices allowed the photographer to get very close to the subject and rendered a high degree of magnification. You also had to be a mathematician because there was no through-the-lens metering system. Your exposure had to be taken with a hand-held meter and then you got out the charts and calculated the proper exposure according to the extension tube, or tubes, being used or the extension you had on your bellows. Both methods caused a considerable light loss. Both methods are still commonly used today and give excellent results. The calculations no longer have to be made because most 35 mm cameras now give meter readings through the lens.

The introduction of macro lenses and micro lenses made it even easier to do close-up work because the extension tubes are built right into the lens and allow focusing down to 5 to 7 inches. These lenses can also be used in conjunction with extension tubes for extreme close-ups. An extension tube usually is provided with the 55 mm micro lens, allowing a 1:1 ratio, giving an image on the film that is the same size as the subject being photographed. There is considerable light loss using these combinations. Many photographers overcome the light loss by using very small electronic flash units.

Another method of getting extreme close-ups is to get a special adapter ring and use it to reverse your regular lens. This cuts off all the automatic features of your lens for exposure. You have to manually open your lens to its widest aperture in order to get enough light to focus and then close it down manually to the proper f stop for exposure. When I started out, all lenses were manually set for exposure; many large-format camera lenses still are.

The use of a bellows also disengages the automatic lens coupling device for aperture control so that the lens must be closed down manually.

Using the reversal ring allows you to get greater magnification than with the extension tubes, but it also means that you have to be within 2 to 3 inches of your subject. A lot of your subjects are just not going to stand for such familiarity.

Ringlights are circular electronic flash tubes that fit around your lens like a lens hood. They give a soft, flat, shadowless light, although there is better separation between subject and background with color than there is with black and white. A ringlight is fine for photographing flowers, but it is objectionable for living creatures because, used at close distances, it makes a donut-shaped highlight in your subject's eye.

A better way is to use a small electronic flash that sells for $15 or $20 and has no adjustments but has a guide number of 35 or 40 for Kodachrome 64 or Fujichrome 100. This flash is then placed on a bracket that extends it to the front of, and slightly above, your taking lens. A series of test shots must be made at various apertures and notes taken recording the lens and extension tube being used (if any), the aperature stop, and the distance from the end of the lens to the subject. When your transparencies come back, view them on a light table and pick out the one that gives you the best color exposure.

You can duplicate the original results by using the same setup. The only variation that will affect the exposure is if you are going to be photographing either darker or lighter subjects than your test subject. If darker, open your lens one-half to one stop; if lighter, close down your lens one-half to one stop.

Some photographers prefer to use two flash heads when doing close-up work. You can mount both flash heads on brackets at the end of your lens. Or you can mount one flash on the bracket at the end of your lens and put the second flash on the hot shoe of the camera.

I prefer the latter because the first system, with both lights at an equal distance to the subject, gives the same shadowless flash as do ringlights. Where the one flash used on the bracket is used as the main light, the second flash on the hot shoe, being farther from the subject, will act as a fill light.

I have also used reflectors to bounce a little light on flowers that need it. A piece of aluminum foil crumpled up and then stretched flat on a piece of stiff cardboard makes a good reflector. Or, use a piece of a space blanket in the same way.

To get the depth of field you desire, you have to use either the electronic flash or a tripod. Whereas I usually prefer to photograph in good sunlight, many of the most beautiful, moody photographs of flowers are taken either in the shade or on overcast days. A skylight filter helps take out some of the blue caused by the shade.

The small tabletop tripods work well, and I have a half dozen different sizes and makes. When I use my large Gitzo tripod, I remove the center post and flatten out the legs. I then use the 6-inch center post. If this does not get my camera low enough, I reverse the main center post so that I can get the camera almost to ground level.

A problem may arise if your lens's aperture does not close down beyond $f/16$. Some lenses do not. Most lenses close to $f/22$ or, better yet, to $f/32$. If you find that your electronic flash is

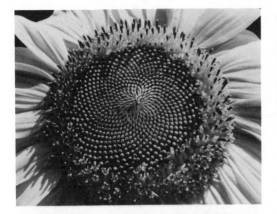

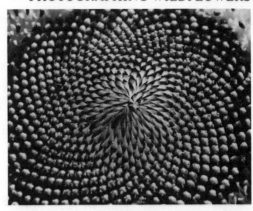

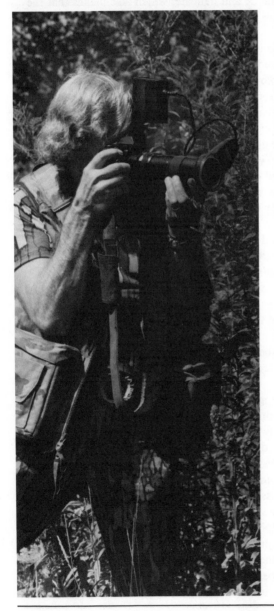

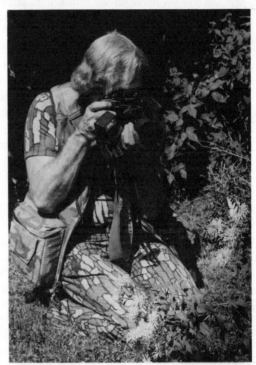

Top left I have always been fascinated by the designs in nature. This arrangement of the sunflower's seeds is called the Fibonacci Sequence.

Top right Using the macro lens fully extended allowed me to shoot just the seed head.

Bottom left A ringlight gives a soft light that works well for close-ups of flower photographs in color.

Bottom right A small electronic flash placed on a bracket off to one side of your lens, but equidistant to the subject, works well for flowers or insects.

still too powerful at close distances for the film you are using, you will have to move the light farther from the subject or diffuse either the light or the lens.

You can cut your light's output in half by shooting through one layer of an ordinary white handkerchief. Two layers will cut the light in half again. For close-up work, however, some photographers do not like the soft, diffused light produced by shooting through handkerchiefs.

Your only other recourse is to place neutral-density filters over the lens. These filters are made with various degrees of light-reduction abilities; the one most commonly used cuts the light in half. These filters are seldom needed with color film, but they are often used with black and white film.

Flower Photographing Techniques

As I mentioned, most spring wildflowers are fragile and delicate, which also means that they move about in the wind as if they had St. Vitus's dance. A number of tricks can be used to coax them to hold still.

I have a 12-foot-long roll of 18-inch-wide camouflage cloth that I use for a windshield. Using six to eight thin metal rods, which can be pushed into the dirt easily, I make a 3½-foot circle around the plant. This prevents the wind from blowing the flower about.

With any but the smallest flowers, a thin, strong florist's wire can be pushed in behind the plants and fastened to the stem with a plastic-bag tie wire. Just keep the tie wire out of the section being photographed. I have often just picked up a dead twig from the forest floor, split one end with my knife, pushed the twig into the dirt, and supported the flower in the split.

I photograph wildflowers with a natural background if it is pleasing. If the background is detracting or if I want the flower to really stand out, I prefer the background to be dark. If I cannot make use of a natural tree shadow to blacken the background, I have an assistant stand to one side and with the shadow of his body or by using a piece of cardboard, have him create a shadow that will fall behind the plant.

If the flower is a very common one, I cut it and take it home to photograph in a "black box." A black box is simply an oversized cardboard carton painted black inside. I set the flower in a holder in the box so that the flower is in sunshine but the back of the box is in the shadow created by the top of the box. This cuts wind movement and gives me a beautiful, jet black background.

I also use a portable flower clamp and bracket that I fasten on the camera body. The bracket holds the flower in the clamp out in front of the lens. This allows for extremely sharp focusing. I can use this in the black box or in front of any background that pleases me.

Make sure that you take a gray card reading for your exposure, or take a meter reading off a neutral background. Do not try to get a meter reading from a small flower against a black background. The black will influence your reading adversely.

"Gardening" is the term used to remove unwanted grass blades, leaves, and the like that are around the plant you want to photograph. Rarely can some of the surrounding foliage be used for framing. Most of the time it just proves distracting and is better removed. Selective focusing, by controlling the depth of field, can lessen the effects of a distracting background.

The angle or perspective at which you photograph a flower is often determined by the flower. Low-growing clump plants, such as moss pink, are best photographed straight down. Some lilies are best photographed up toward the sky so that their tubes are outlined against the sky. Some flowers, such as the jack-in-the-pulpit and the mayapple, are best photographed from ground level, looking up under the leaves in order to show the blossom. I like to photograph my two favorite flowers, the hepatica and the pink moccasin plant, at their blossom height, which is about 3 inches and 9 inches respectively.

Flowers are often enhanced if photographed in the early morning when the dew is still on

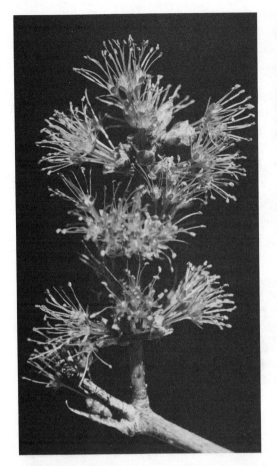

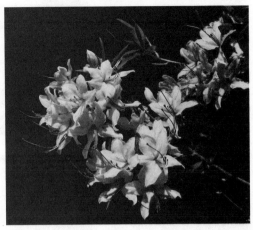

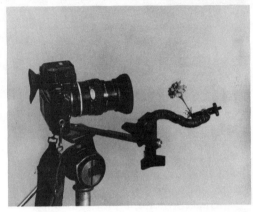

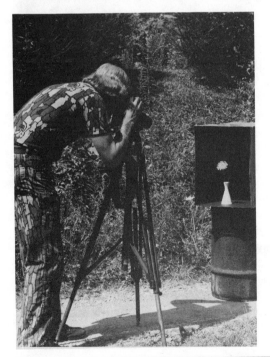

Top left These red maple flowers were photographed using a black box.
Top right The completely black background of a black box highlights the blossoms of the wild pink azalea.
Bottom left A black box in use.
Bottom right A flower clamp in use. Photo by Irene Vandermolen

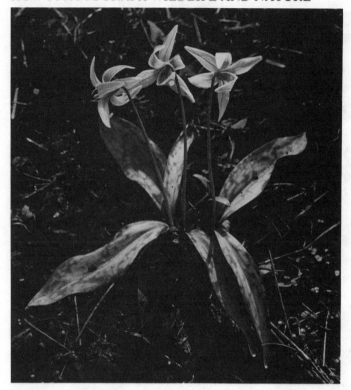

Left I removed some dead grass stalks and leaves from around these trout lilies.

Opposite page: Left Trees rimed with frost.
Right A person gives scale to this 400-year-old white oak tree.

the blossoms, or after a rain. If there is no dew or rain, make your own by misting the plant with a misting waterpot, or use an empty spray bottle that window cleaner comes in. Some photographers prefer to mist with glycerine, but I have found that regular water does just as good a job.

Be on the alert if you have a sudden late-spring snowstorm after some of the flowers have started to bloom. Flowers capped with snow make fabulous photographs. If the weather turns very cold before it snows, most of the flowers will freeze and wilt.

Don't put your camera away in the winter. Although the flowers will be gone, many plants, such as barberry, multiflora rose, and pokeweed, will retain their bright berries until the birds eat them. When the berries are encased with ice, they make very attractive photos.

Photographing Trees

Trees are photographic subjects in their own right and should not be thought of as simply material for framing scenics. Many trees have flowers as beautiful as the smaller plants and often have more of them. The buds of trees make fascinating close-ups.

I like to photograph bare trees in winter with backlight so that they stand stark as silhouettes. I like to backlight trees on misty mornings when the sun's rays produce cathedral effects. I have done a lot of close-up photography of various tree barks because most trees can be identified by their bark alone.

Trees weighted down with loads of soft, wet snow assume grotesque but beautiful forms. I like to take photographs with my camera held against the tree trunk, shooting straight up to show trees as most people don't see them. Photographing the same tree from the same spot at the four different seasons of the year is one of the finest ways to show the passage of time. It also creates the illusion that trees live forever, even though they don't.

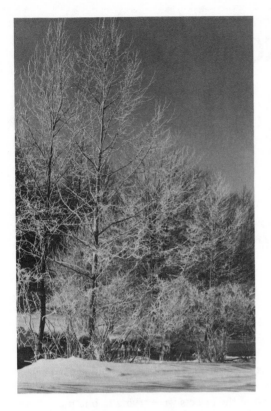
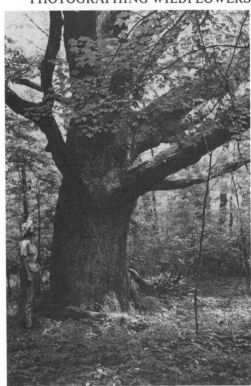

I have taken many photos of trees that have died and are being returned to the soil by various fungi. Trees are included in so many of my wildlife photographs because trees provide homes for so many species.

I like to photograph entire forests of trees, and I like to photograph the lone giant of a tree that stands by itself, defying the elements. I have photographed trees as trees, as tree products, as saw logs, as lumber, as boards, as firewood, and as pulpwood.

We cannot think of trees without thinking of their leaves, of the blazing glory of their foliage in autumn. Photos of fall foliage do not sell that well, but I go right on photographing fall scenics, individual colorful trees, branches of colorful leaves, colorful leaves against the blue sky, leaves with the sun shining from behind them, single leaves of great beauty, and leaves floating on water.

The list could go on and on. The subject matter is limited only by your photographic eye and your imagination. People often claim that I look at the world through rose-colored glasses. I do. I look for beauty wherever I go, and I find it. I hope you do too.

PHOTOGRAPHING INSECTS

I learn more every day so that I have more to teach tomorrow.

—L. L. Rue III

One thing about photographing insects: You will never run out of subjects. There are at least three times as many insects as there are all other living creatures in the world. And at times I have been sure that most of the insects were trying to bite me at the same time, even though biting insects make up only 1 percent of the total insect population.

As with anything that you attempt to do, you must have a good basic knowledge of your subject. Although insects are all around us, and even on us, the more knowledge you have about insects, their habitat and their habits, the more successful you will be.

Insect populations took a tremendous beating a few decades ago when the government was spraying DDT on everything. The purpose of the spraying was to control the gypsy moth caterpillar, which was devastating forests in the northeastern woodlands. The gypsy moth is still with us in force, but many of our common butterflies, moths, and dragonflies were all but annihilated. Since the ban on DDT was imposed, these insects have made a slow but steady comeback. If you want to see what we lost, just go to an area that has not been sprayed.

Here is a very small sampling of some of the basic knowledge needed:

Some insects are active all day long and hide at night. Some insects remain hidden all day and are active all night. Most night-flying insects can be attracted by using a light.

Dragonflies and damselflies have favorite perches that they return to time after time. Both insects are easier to approach when they are mating. Water striders and whirlygig beetles favor certain spots of still water in a pond or lake. Many different kinds of flies can be baited with a small piece of tainted meat.

Butterflies are best photographed in the early morning when they are more apt to spread their wings out to catch the warmth of the newly risen sun. A cool morning slows down almost all insect life.

Spiders, although not insects because they have eight legs, can be approached quite easily, particularly when they have a web. Orb spiderwebs in the fall, when they are bejeweled with dew, make beautiful subjects, with or without the spiders. Don't try to photograph the webs if there is even a slight breeze because they will move almost constantly. The webs can be misted with water from a spray bottle if there has been no dew. Spider webs are best shot with the light behind them.

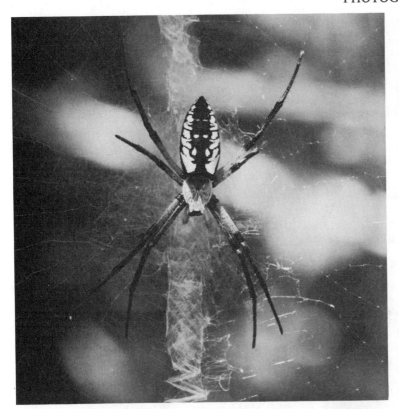

Top The large yellow and black garden spiders are easy to photograph as they will remain motionless on their webs. Photo by Len Rue, Jr.
Bottom An orb spider web bejeweled with dew.

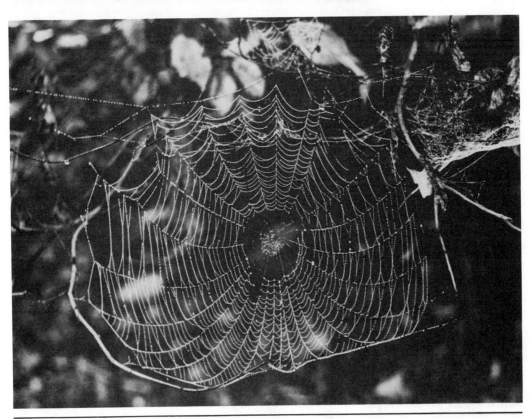

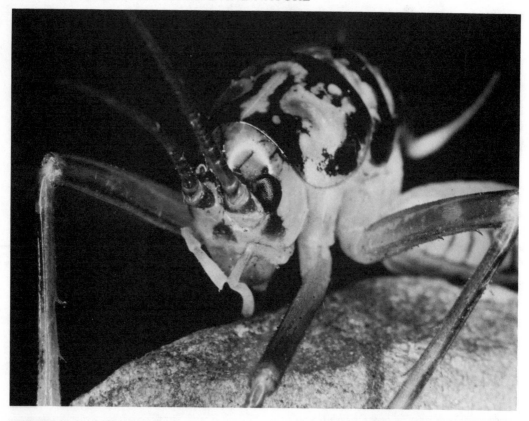

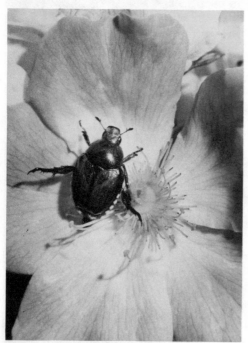

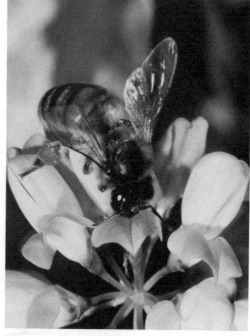

Top This cave cricket was photographed many times its natural size.
Bottom left This Japanese beetle was photographed larger than life size.
Bottom right A wild honeybee.

Crickets can easily be found in August and September. Just turn over dry cowflops, old boards, or flat surface stones.

Ants are common, and their hills can be located easily. They can be baited to almost any desirable spot by the use of cookie or cake crumbs. Just try keeping ants or yellow jackets away from a picnic.

The nests of wasps and hornets can be located under the eaves of porches or in the attic. Honeybees are easily located by watching whatever plants are flowering. The bees can be kept in one spot by placing a drop of sugar water or a drop of honey and water in the flower you want them to sit on. They can be called long distances by the odor of burning beeswax.

The carcass of any bird or animal will attract flies first, some butterflies, and carrion and scavenger beetles. There is a whole progression of various insects according to the state of decomposition. Some of our most beautiful butterflies flock to various kinds of animal excrement. They should not be photographed there, but they can be caught there and removed to a spot where you want to photograph them.

And on and on. A number of good books can tell you more about insect habits and habitats.

Equipment

The basic equipment we discussed for photographing wildflowers is needed to photograph insects: zoom lenses, macro lenses or micro lenses, extension tubes and/or bellows, and close-up strobes. According to the size of the insect—and some are mighty tiny—you may want to move even closer to the insect than you would to wildflowers. So you may use the reversed lens more frequently, or you may use the bellows. To get the needed light, though, you will have to use the ringlight or two small strobes mounted on either side of your taking lens.

Some Tricks That Help

You can bait most wild creatures and insects are no exception. The old adage "You can catch more flies with sugar than with vinegar" is true. Flies, of course, can be attracted by tainted meat faster than with sweets, but "sugaring" attracts a tremendous number of insects.

Plain sugar added to water will suffice in many cases. A small amount of honey added to sugar water will thicken it so that it is easier to apply and will stay in place without dripping. This liquid, deposited with a narrow eyedropper on flowers frequented by butterflies, will not only attract them but will get them to stay in one spot for a much longer time.

Some time-honored sugaring formulas for moths are as follows: Mix 4 pounds of granulated sugar with one can of beer and a little rum. Another formula calls for the use of fermented or rotten fruit, such as bananas or peaches, mixed with sugar. These concoctions are painted on trees at night, and the next morning you can photograph half-crocked moths that have been on a binge.

Another, less messy attractant is the use of a blacklight for moths. Take care not to look at the light yourself for any period of time because the light could damage your eyes.

In using either sugar or a blacklight, it is better to take the photos as soon as the insects come in or catch them and take them to a studio. Moths form a large part of the diet of screech owls, bats, and flying squirrels, and anything that attracts moths is going to attract the predators that feed on them. Some moths do not become active until after midnight when the predators are less hungry, having eaten other prey.

In order to focus on the moths attracted to your bait, you will need a strong light shining on your subject. You can wear a headlamp, but it is much easier if you have an assistant who can shine the light while you concentrate on focusing the camera.

Many people raise their own moths from egg masses or cocoons that they find or buy. At a number of moth farms, you can purchase either eggs or cocoons. Each moth species feeds on selected plants, and if these are available in your area, you should be able to feed the caterpillars with no problem. This is how most life-cycle photographs are taken.

Most of the larger silk moths do not feed after emerging from the cocoon. They eat voraciously as caterpillars but not as adults. The sole goal as an adult is to find another adult of the same species and breed before they die.

The antennae on male moths are much larger than those on females, which makes it easy to tell the sexes apart. If a female is confined to a small wire cage and hung out in your yard, she will attract every male within miles that are downwind. Her pheremones are a powerful attractant, and you will soon have dozens of males to photograph. Although you may want to photograph butterflies on their food plants, you do not need flowers in the photos of silk moths unless you want to show the foods they eat as caterpillars.

A friend of mine, who is an excellent butterfly photographer, catches his subjects with a net and pops them into a small, portable ice chest. The ice or coolant is covered with a towel so that the insects do not get wet. He collects very early in the morning when butterflies are sluggish.

When he has done enough collecting, he seeks out suitable wildflowers or plants on which to photograph his subjects. Cooled by the ice, they are easily handled. As they warm up and start to become active, he takes his photographs. If he has only one or two specimens of a particular kind, he returns them to the cooler before they fly away. If he has a goodly number of specimens, then he simply lets one fly off while he works on another one. He releases all his subjects before he returns to his home, preferring not to keep any in captivity.

Some photographers take specimens home to a studio where they use a simple set-up with plants and flowers that they have brought in from the field. The background may simply be black, or they may use a natural foliage. Blue paper can be used to represent the sky, or a painted background, which is kept out of focus, can be used as background. When using paper backgrounds, a strobe is usually set up to illuminate them and to get rid of any shadows cast from the electronic flash used to illuminate the insect.

When doing studio work, some photographers place the insect in the freezer and really chill it. Then they place it on the desired spot and speed up the thawing process by having an electric light shine on the insect to warm it. A butterfly will usually spread its wings to soak up the heat from the lamp. However, some butterflies, such as the skippers, sulphurs, and hairstreaks, almost always keep their wings upright.

Caterpillars can be worked in either the field or the studio. One of the easiest methods is to set your camera on its tripod, focused on an inclined twig with a suitable background. The caterpillar will climb up the twig and can be photographed when it reaches the focused-on spot. When the caterpillar reaches the end of the twig, it can be started up at the base of the twig. If the twig is held in a holder, simply turn the twig upside down and let the caterpillar climb up it again.

Some photographers prefer to stalk their subjects in the field, some prefer to set up cameras on tripods and let subjects come to them, and some prefer to take subjects home where they can be kept under strict control. Each method has its good and bad points. I use all three methods.

Some Precautions

In the past, photographers used different gases to overcome insects so that they could be managed. Some of these substances were also poisonous to humans. Today, every insect photographer I know chills the insects instead.

Many insects bite, sting, or suck blood. Usually the photographer is kept busy trying to keep

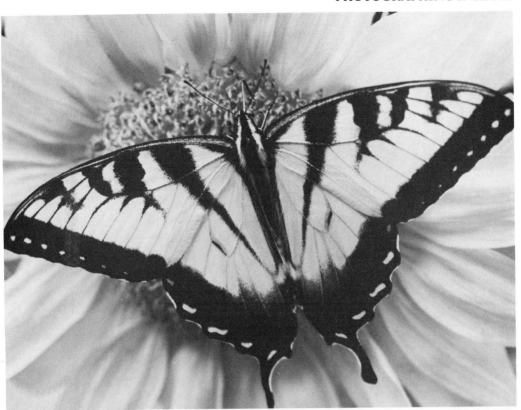

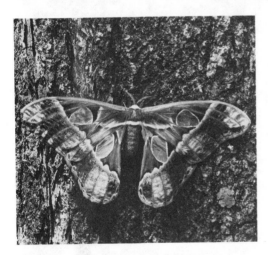

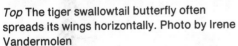

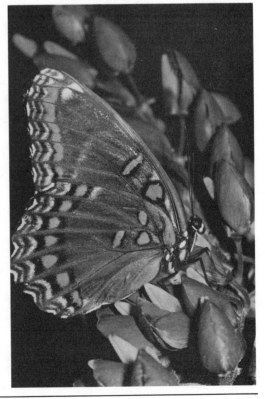

Top The tiger swallowtail butterfly often spreads its wings horizontally. Photo by Irene Vandermolen

Bottom left The huge, beautiful Rothschild moth was attracted to a blacklight in Barro Colorado, Panama. Photo by Irene Vandermolen

Bottom right This red-spotted purple butterfly was photographed in a studio with flash. Photo by Len Rue, Jr.

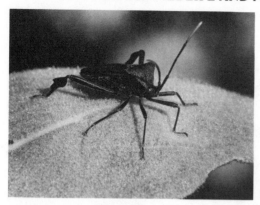

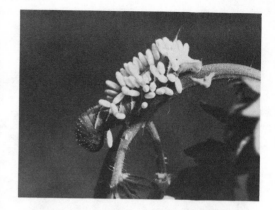

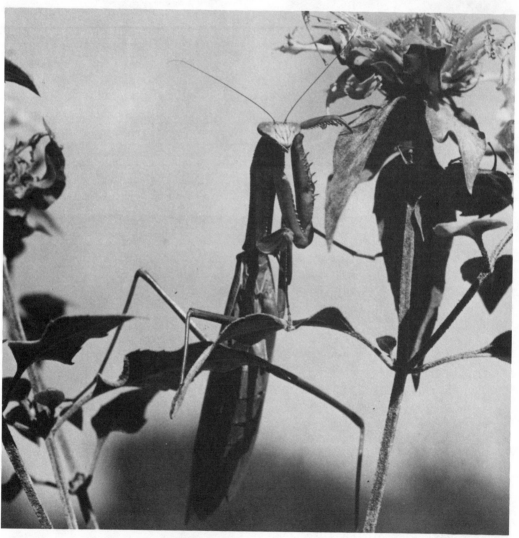

Top left This leaf-footed bug was photographed outdoors with natural lighting.
Top right This parasitized tobacco hornworm was photographed outdoors with natural lighting.
Photo by Irene Vandermolen
Bottom I photographed this praying mantis, just as I found it, with a 55 mm macro lens.

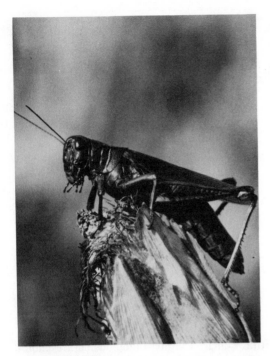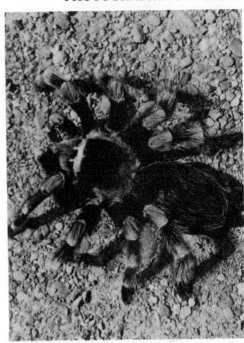

Left Careful stalking got me within range of this grasshopper.
Right Tarantulas can give a painful bite but are not generally considered poisonous.

these insects away while more desirable insects are photographed. I personally use Cutter insect repellent because it gives hours of protection. It can even be put around your eyes, and it does not harm clothing materials.

If you are in an area that has chiggers or ticks, and the latter do carry Rocky Mountain spotted fever, put the insect repellent liberally on your ankles, socks, and lower pants. Powdered sulfur also works well, especially for chiggers.

The venom of yellow jackets, wasps, hornets, and bees is painful to everyone and could be fatal to anyone who has an allergic reaction. People with such allergies can go into an anaphylactic shock in seconds. The symptoms are an immediate breaking out in welts or hives and difficulty in breathing. In extreme cases, breathing stops. Most people know if they have such an allergy, and if they do, they should always carry an Anakit, available by prescription, which has adrenaline-based medications. Those who do not have an allergy can get relief from the pain of the stinging by using Cortaid, which contains hydrocortisone.

Although spiders are not insects, people who photograph insects usually photograph spiders as well. Most spiders do not bite, but some do. Two spiders are definitely poisonous enough to kill children, or even adults who are not in the best of health. Ice cubes, where available, help in all cases. Cortaid helps relieve the pain of nonlethal spider bites, as do percogesic tablets. The bites of black widow and brown recluse spiders call for immediate professional medical treatment.

PHOTOGRAPHING REPTILES AND AMPHIBIANS

I never say that I am lucky; I always say that
I have been truly blessed by God.
                    —L. L. Rue III

I recently had a telephone conversation with a woman who takes fabulous nature photographs. She confessed that she is terrified every time she works in our southern swamplands because she is deathly afraid of snakes.

Most people do not like snakes, although a few people really like them. Some people are terrified by them, but nearly everyone is fascinated by them. Most of this dislike of snakes is a fostered fear that goes all the way back to the first book in the Bible: Genesis 3:15. Babies do not have an innate fear of snakes; their reaction to snakes is in imitation of the fuss made by older children and adults.

I have stated repeatedly that knowledge dispels fear. The more you know about anything, the less reason you have to fear it. Nevertheless, a knowledge of wildlife should teach you to respect wild creatures for their speed, strength, and, occasionally, their danger.

There are only two poisonous lizards in the world: the gila monster and the beaded lizard. Both are found in parts of New Mexico, Arizona, and Old Mexico. These lizards are about 18 to 24 inches in total length; they are sluggish in action and rare enough to be on endangered animal lists. Their cryptic coloration makes them readily identifiable so that there should be no problem of misidentification. The largest lizards in the world are the komodo dragons of Malaysia. These giants range up to 8 to 10 feet in length. They are not aggressive to humans.

The crocodiles of the world are a different story. Both the Nile and saltwater crocs may be up to 18 feet in length and can be extremely dangerous to humans. On land, for a short distance, they can outrun a man. I was not allowed to set up a blind on a riverbank in South Africa to photograph the crocs because they were too aggressive. Below Murchison's Falls in Uganda, the crocs were stacked up like cordwood. It was only safe to photograph them from a motor launch.

For a long time, here in the United States, there were only two authenticated deaths by alligators. Then, in the 1960s and 1970s the number of alligators was reduced to where they were considered endangered, and they were given complete protection. Today, alligators have made such a population comeback that in some areas they are considered nuisance creatures. Now there are many, many cases of unprovoked attacks.

The most venomous snakes in the world are the sea snakes of the South Seas. On land, the king cobra is probably the largest deadly snake, but mambas are the fastest. The krait, tiger

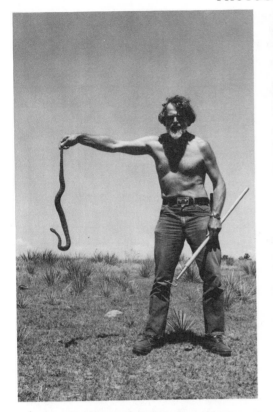

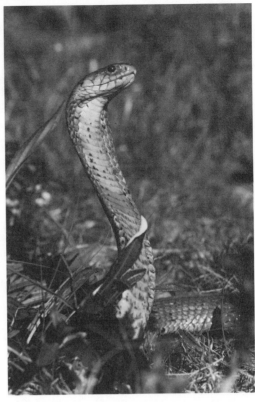

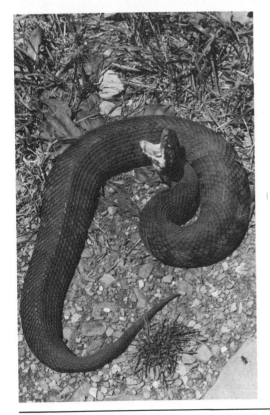

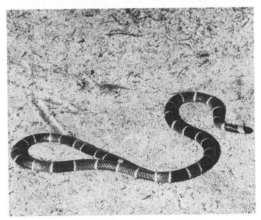

Top left Knowledge of what a snake can do allows me to pick up this prairie rattlesnake by the tail. Don't try it! Photo by Len Rue, Jr.
Top right The forest cobra of Africa is an extremely deadly snake.
Bottom left The cottontail moccasin is primarily a southern snake and is found only around water.
Bottom right The coral snake carries the same poison as does the cobra.

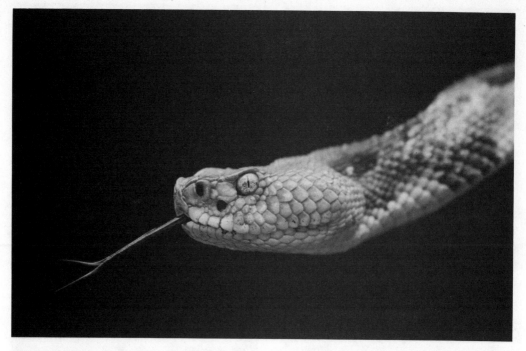

This photograph of a timber rattlesnake shows its elliptical eye, nostril, heat-sensing pit, and forked tongue.

snake, gaboon viper, and many others are extremely dangerous. Borneo, Australia, Southeast Asia, and parts of Africa have a large number of these and other very deadly snakes.

Most of these snakes rear up and strike out and down. The large ones can rear up to 6 or 7 feet above the ground; the only real protection is to avoid them whenever possible. Most photographers working in areas with dangerous snakes hire guides; the safety of the photographer is in the guide's hands. Ringhals or spitting cobras can squirt their poison for a distance of 8 to 10 feet into a person's eyes.

In North America we have four species of snakes that are poisonous to humans, although some additional small species of rear-fanged snakes also have poison. The copperhead, the cottonmouth moccasin, and the various rattlesnakes are all pit vipers; they have a hemorrhagic venom that affects the red blood cells and capillaries. The coral snake, our only elapid, has a neurotoxic poison that causes paralysis and respiratory failure.

Although the venom of the coral snake is the more deadly, the snake is usually inoffensive and remains hidden in the underbrush. It delivers its poison by chewing. As the snake is small, it has to chew on a finger or toe to inflict damage. Its bright coloration makes it easy to confuse this beautiful little snake with a humber of harmless species. An old Boy Scout rhyme will help you to identify it: "Red and yellow, kill a fellow; red and black, a friend of Jack." In the extreme southern states, any little snake with the red pattern touching the yellow band is a coral snake.

Pit vipers are all poisonous, but their individual deadliness is determined by their size, fang length, and many other factors. These snakes strike up and out of a coil or from an S curve in the body or by swinging sideways. None of them can strike more than two-thirds of their body length unless they are striking downward from an elevated perch. Lying as straight as a pointer, they cannot bite an object 3 inches in front of their mouths. Knowing this allows me to photograph a 6-foot snake at a distance of 4 feet. Don't take chances, however. Use a telephoto lens and photograph them at a safe distance.

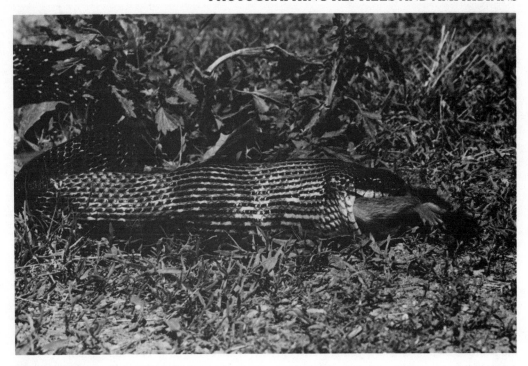

A black rat snake swallowing a chipmunk. Photo by Irene Vandermolen

Several kinds of good snakeproof boots are available; mine are made by Gokey. There are also several kinds of metal-encased leggings and metal mesh leggings. Bob Allen just came out with cordura nylon leggings that are snakeproof. If I am working in known snake country, I wear boots or leggings, carry a Cutter compact snake kit, watch where I put my hands and feet, and forget about snakes. I have never been threatened by a poisonous snake in the wild.

When collecting snakes for photographs, I use either a homemade snake hook or a pair of commercial snake tongs. I use good heavy-duty fine-mesh seed bags to carry the snakes, and I put those bags inside a wooden pack basket. People have been bitten by carrying snakes in a bag and letting the bag brush against their legs.

Photographing Snakes

Snakes, like most creatures, are found near their food sources. That means near rocky talus slopes because wood and pack rats live there. Or near woodland stone rows because chipmunks inhabit such areas. They are found near farm feedlots to prey on mice, or in your garden because of insects. Water snakes festoon the trees along pond, lake, and river banks, from which they can drop into the water after frogs or fish or to escape from their enemies. Poisonous snakes are more active after dark because they are night feeders. A drought will concentrate the snakes near available water.

Warm roads on cool nights are good places to find snakes as they seek the comforting warmth. Rock ledges on warm mornings after cool nights are good spots for the same reason. Each spring and fall, the snakes will be found at their traditional, ancestral denning grounds. Most poisonous snakes go back to their dens in mid-August, just prior to giving birth to their young. This ensures that the young know where the den is when it is needed that fall. In my area the poisonous snakes are usually out of their dens by the time the dogwood trees bloom, and the snakes leave the den to scatter for the summer when the blossoms drop off. The temperature variations that cause the dogwood to bloom early or late are the same conditions that control the movement of the snakes. Nonpoisonous snakes are active earlier and later than poisonous ones.

I would say that 95 percent of all snake photos are taken under controlled conditions. Usually the snakes are collected and then released in the appropriate setting. Most zoo shots are studio setups, but the average nature photographer usually finds the snake and then releases it where it can be controlled.

An assistant is usually needed to keep the snake from crawling away or to keep a poisonous snake from getting too close to the photographer. Your perspective changes when you look through a viewfinder. You might be closer to the snake than you intended to be.

All reptiles and amphibians are cold-blooded, poikilothermic; their body temperature is the same as their environment. This basic fact must be kept in mind while doing photography.

You cannot photograph a snake in the hot sun because it will die. You can photograph it in the warm sun on a cool day. The warmer the day, the more active the snake, and so the best times for snake photos are early spring and early fall. Conversely, snakes cannot be photographed in winter in most areas of the continent because they are in hibernation.

In order to slow a snake down so that it can be photographed, I have often put it in a bag and popped it into a refrigerator for a short while. I did that with a western garter snake in California and found seven snakes in the bag when I got ready to take the picture. The female must have been on the verge of giving birth when I caught her. I did not realize she was pregnant because she was not that large. The episode was a real bonus for me, and at the end of the photo session mother and young were released where I caught her, all doing fine.

Don't put snakes in the freezer to cool them down; the tremendous drop in temperature will kill them. A refrigerator is usually about 40 to 45 degrees F., and snakes hibernate at 56 degrees F.

It is always best to photograph a snake in the exact habitat it frequents. I like to photograph pine snakes in pine trees, water snakes draped on logs in the water, and western rattlesnakes backed up against a cactus or a similar natural prop. It is usually easier to get a poisonous snake to pose for its picture because, being poisonous, it is not as apt to seek protective shelter as nonpoisonous varieties are. Still, when a poisonous snake decides to go somewhere else, it is almost impossible to get it to hold still.

One trick I have found to work well in getting a snake to hold still is to take it out on a cool morning and cover it with a plastic cake cover. If the sun is bright, have an assistant keep the snake cool by throwing his shadow over the snake. The snake usually settles down in a short time within the confines of the cake cover. The cover, being clear plastic, allows you to see what the snake is doing and to focus. When the snake strikes a good pose, whisk off the cover and take the photo.

To restrain a snake, to move it into better position, or just to lift its head up in a more alert pose, I prefer to use a snake hook rather than tongs because the hook will not injure the snake. The snake hook is always used to turn over rocks or reach into crevasses; this should never be done with your hands.

My snake hook and capture bag are standard gear in my truck or car wherever I travel. I release all snake specimens after photographing them. Various states are now enacting laws for the protection of rarer snakes, and you should be aware of these restrictions so that you do not violate them.

How to Photograph Lizards

Lizards, more than most reptiles, have a defined home area. I have found this to be true with most specimens, up to and including alligators. When you discover a lizard, it then becomes a

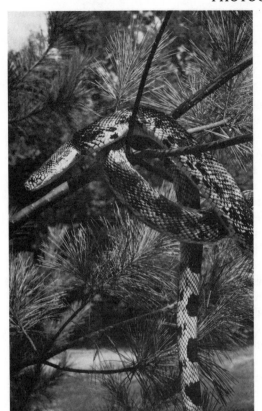

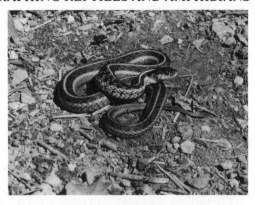

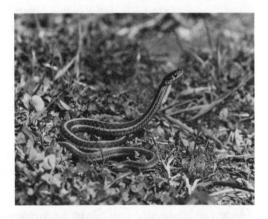

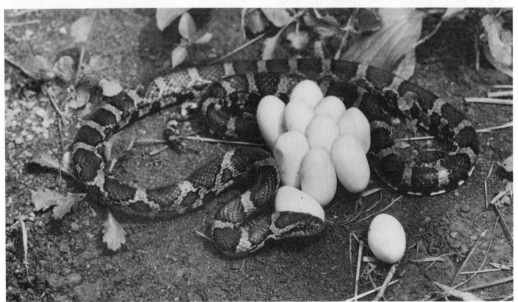

Top left A pine snake climbing in a pine tree.
Top right This is a typical pose of the common garter snake.
Middle right This is a better photograph of a common garter snake because the head has been raised with a snake hook.
Bottom Milk snakes lay eggs.

rather simple chore to sit and observe the creature, waiting for a pattern of its actions to emerge. This is the crux of most wildlife photography: Watch and study the creature until its activity pattern becomes apparent, and from those observations you will know when, where, and what has to be done to secure the photo you want. Although lizards are also governed by the temperature, many desert species can withstand heat that would cook a snake. Consequently, many lizards can be photographed when it is too hot to photograph anything else. I have also discovered that lizards pay absolutely no attention to you if you just hold still. Their eyes are geared to detect motion, and as long as you don't move, you become a part of the landscape.

As lizards dash about seeking food, they have favorite pathways and favorite observation spots. Focus on these spots and just wait for the return of the lizard. Even the largest American lizard, the alligator, has preferred spots that it will use for sunning. These spots can easily be detected by the pathways through the mud leading to the spot and by the crushed vegetation. If the days are fairly uniform in temperature, the alligator will be almost punctual. It will appear at the same time in the cool of the morning, haul out to sun itself in its preferred spot, and retire back into the water to cool off when it gets too hot. In swimming to and from its preferred spot, the gator offers excellent photo opportunities.

As mentioned, lizards are most commonly found among dry rock heaps, such as talus slides. They also can be found among piles of logs. I have had good luck in finding them around the piles of slash and sawdust at old sawmill sites. These spots are particularly favored by fence swifts.

The chameleons of the Southeast are likely to be found clambering about on all kinds of vegetation, but because of the excellent cover and their adaptive coloration, they are sometimes difficult to locate even where they are common. Many lizards, such as the yucca night lizard, come out of hiding only at night and must be hunted with a flashlight.

How to Photograph Salamanders

Salamanders in general are the antithesis of lizards. Salamanders like it where it is cool, dark, and damp. Whereas most lizards are fast moving, salamanders are slow. They are usually found under logs, rocks, or other debris on the forest floor. A word of caution: If you are turning over logs and rocks to look for salamanders, make sure you replace the logs and rocks exactly as they were. If you do not, you are destroying the salamander's habitat; it takes years for the rocks and logs to settle into the ground sufficiently to provide the protection salamanders must have to survive.

During rainstorms, salamanders by the hundreds can be found crossing the back roads in the northeastern states in late March and early April. They are leaving their woodland hibernation areas to seek out lowland pools and ponds in which to breed. Some of the aquatic newts and mudpuppies can be captured by seining the ponds and rivers with fine nets. Under stones along old woodland stone rows are excellent spots to look for salamanders.

Salamanders are best photographed on a beautiful piece of green moss or an appropriate rock or log. A different kind of patience is needed to photograph salamanders than to photograph lizards. With lizards, you have to wait until they reappear in the desired spots. With salamanders, you have to keep putting them back in the desired spots. Although they move slowly, they move deliberately; and when they decide to move, they walk right out of the picture.

Except for efts, which have a dry skin, skins of salamanders cannot be allowed to dry out as this may cause their death. And moisten your hands before you pick them up to put them back into place. The moisture on the salamander's skin is actually a protective mucous coating that reduces friction as the salamander squeezes about beneath the rocks and logs. As this mucous dries, it turns into a mucilage, and the salamander will actually adhere to your fingers unless they are moistened.

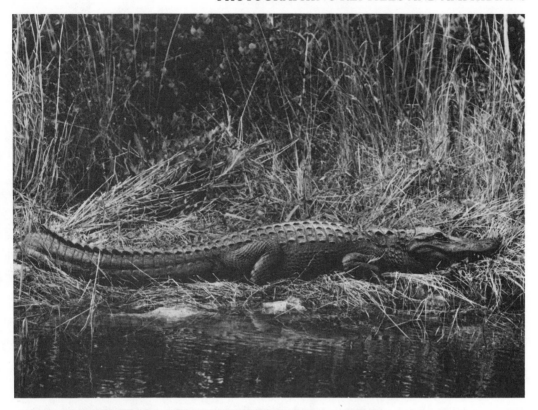

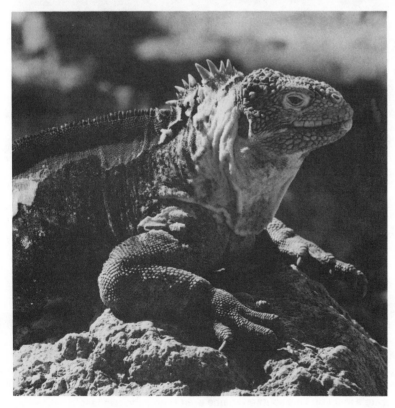

Top An alligator at its favorite "sunning" spot. *Bottom* A land iguana photgraphed in the Galapagos. Photo by Irene Vandermolen

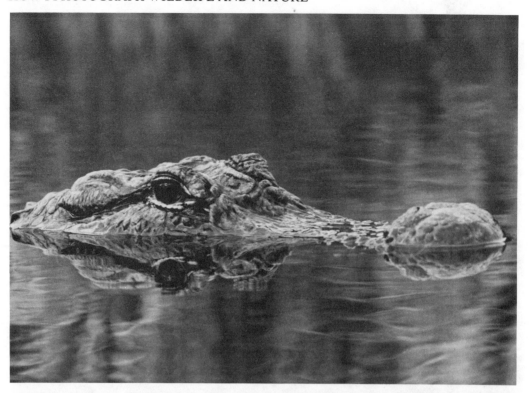

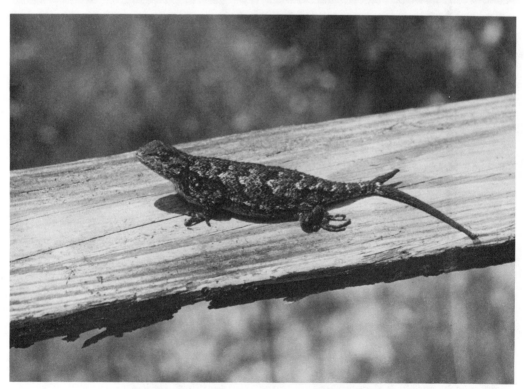

Top An "eyeball to eyeball" photograph of an alligator.
Bottom Lizards can regenerate a lost tail. This southern fence swift is growing two tails.

Photographing Frogs and Toads

Water is the key to photographing frogs and toads because most of them concentrate in and around water to mate, lay their eggs, and allow for the transformation of the tadpole into the adult. One toad does lay its eggs on land, and the young of some toads hatch out looking like adults, bypassing the transformation stage. The mating season of amphibians is not a well-kept secret; males advertise their presence to females, and the entire world, by loud vocalizations. The thrilling trilling of spring peepers announces to us that spring has finally sprung, but its real purpose is to signal to other peepers that the mating season has arrived.

Each species of frog and toad has its own time for the laying of eggs. For example, in northwestern New Jersey, where I live, peepers start the season off in early April, the American toad in early May, the green frog in early June, and the bullfrog in mid-June to early July.

Only the males sing, and they have inflatable throat membranes. During the mating season, toads and frogs may sing at any time during a 24-hour period, but the singing is almost continuous after dark. Males can also be encouraged to sing by playing a tape of their recorded voices. This stimulates most males into singing and thereby betraying their presence.

The use of hip boots, preferably waders, will facilitate your wandering about in the pond, locating your subjects without stepping on submerged sticks with the risk of getting cut. For working after dark, I use one of the Burnham Brothers' headlamps because it leaves both hands free to operate the camera. Although I use a red filter on the light when working with mammals at night, I have found that the white light does not bother frogs and toads. In fact the bright, white beam seems to pin the subjects in place. In warm weather, insects will be attracted by the headlight. A cottonball soaked in insect repellent and taped to the light will help.

If the frogs have not been molested, they will sometimes allow your approach in broad daylight if you move exceedingly slow and cautiously. Any sudden movement and all you will see and hear is the plop of their departure. If the frogs are leery and cannot be approached, I capture them with a net.

I then take them to a spot in the pond where the water is shallow enough so that if they jump away from where I place them, I can capture them again. If you want action shots of the frog jumping, get your strobes and camera set up and prefocused on the spot where the action should take place, before you put the frog down. An electric eye helps in a situation like this, but it is extremely difficult to get set up under natural conditions. It is much easier to use the electric eye in a studio setup.

Photographing Turtles

Turtles move slowly on land because of their stumpy legs and the weight of their shells. When they decide to move, however, it is done with deliberation and strength. A wood turtle that wants to keep moving is just going to keep moving.

A box turtle may withdraw into its shell and be very deliberate about coming back out. Each movement is a study in slow motion until just one foot touches the ground and then off it scoots. You can make it go through the same routine a dozen times or a hundred times, but you cannot get it to hold still when it wants to move. You might get the turtle to stop once, the first time you try it, by stamping on the ground about a foot or so in front of it, but this seems to work just once.

Most water turtles, such as the painted, the red-eared slider, and the yellow-spotted pond, like to bask in the sun on days when the water is cool and the sun is warm, especially in early spring. I have seen them lined up on the floating logs in my pond while the bulk of the pond was still covered with ice. When the weather turns hot, turtles sun only in the very early morning; they escape the heat of the day by going in the water.

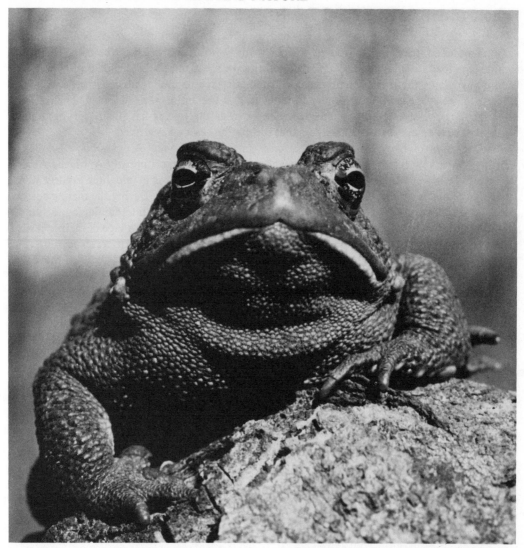

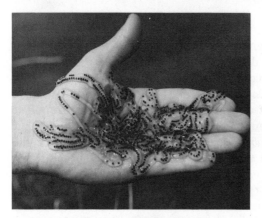
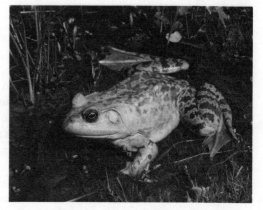

Top A portrait of an American toad.
Bottom left American toad eggs are laid in long strings, as many as 5000 at a time.
Bottom right This female bullfrog was placed in shallow water to be photographed.

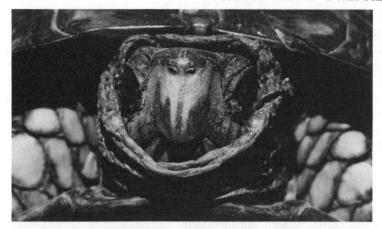

Top A box turtle s-l-o-w-l-y emerging from its shell.
Middle The ground-level angle has made this photo of a box turtle very appealing and a best-seller.
Bottom The largest land turtle in the world, the giant Galapagos tortoise. Photo by Irene Vandermolen

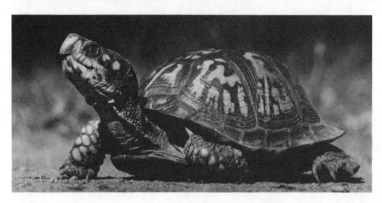

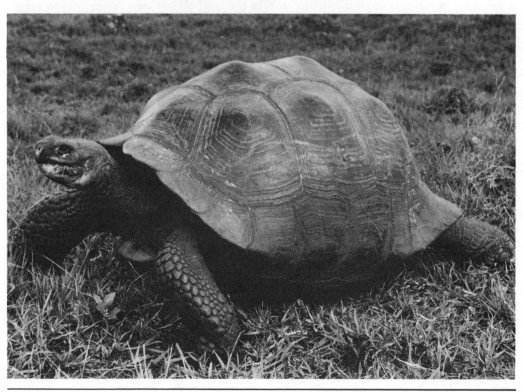

Turtles are usually very easy to locate by carefully searching every log, rock, or piece of debris along the edges of ponds and lakes. However, anyone working on turtles will immediately discover that turtles have fantastic eyesight. Long before you can get close enough to photograph them, they have you spotted; they dive into the water and head for the depths.

I usually photograph turtles in one of two ways. As the same turtles almost always climb out on the same log in the same spot, it is simple to set up your camera and trip it by remote, or you can use a blind. The simplest way is to catch the turtles with a net and take them to a suitable spot and then put them on the log or rock where you want them to be. It helps to have an assistant to keep catching the turtle and putting it back in the desired spot.

As I write this on a warm June afternoon, there is a large painted turtle laying her eggs in a hole on my back lawn. Never disturb the turtles at this time, or they will abandon the nest without laying all the eggs or covering them properly. Predation on turtle eggs is exceptionally heavy by skunks, raccoons, and opossums; don't add your name to the list.

A word of caution: Snapping turtles seldom sun themselves and are seldom seen except during this time of year when they too come to lay their eggs. Snappers can be picked up by their tails, but make sure that no part of your body gets within range of those snapping jaws. The snapper has an exceptionally long neck and will actually lunge forward as well. For a creature that walks slowly, the snapper's head can strike out with lightning speed—fast enough to catch fish.

Angles, Perspectives and Techniques

As stated earlier, I like to photograph wildlife at eye level or below eye level, and that goes for photographing reptiles and amphibians as well. Because these critters are usually small or close to the ground, eye-level photography sometimes takes a lot of doing.

In order to get my camera close to the ground without having to dig a hole for my chin, I use either a 90-degree right-angle viewfinder or take the head off my camera's prism and use a straight prism. Using either device, I can actually rest my camera on the ground. If I want the camera to be 6 inches or so off the ground, I use one of my very small tabletop tripods. These little tripods also work well if I am photographing in shallow water.

Particularly with turtles—but I also do it with frogs, toads, and water snakes—I like to get in the water and photograph the subject against the land. I like this perspective because others photograph these subjects from the land.

To make it easier on the body when doing this "low-down" work, I often use athletic knee and elbow pads. Without protection, every pebble becomes a boulder; it's a real obstacle to getting good photos. Rubberized knee protectors, such as those worn by stone masons and available in hardware stores, are the best to use in the water.

Some frog and toad shots are better taken slightly above the creature because such shots may provide better identification or show the colors and patterns of different species. If it is early in spring, hip boots or waders will be needed as protection against the cold water.

I find macro lenses are best for this type of work, and I have them in the 55 mm, 105 mm, and 200 mm lengths. If I want to get closer to my subject or make my subject larger than the lenses would normally record, I use the PK11, 12, or 13 extension tubes, or a bellows. With the PK13 and the 200 mm lens, I can get approximately the same image size on the film with the lens 16 inches from the subject as I can with the 55 mm lens at 3 inches. And it is easier to get 16 inches from your subject than it is to get 3 inches. Yes, there is a progressive light loss with each larger extension tube, but everything in this life is a tradeoff.

Portrait lenses give a larger image size without as great a light loss as extension tubes, but the quality of the pictures is definitely inferior. Because of the extension tubes, the light loss is a handicap when shooting with sunlight; it is minimized by the use of a small electronic flash.

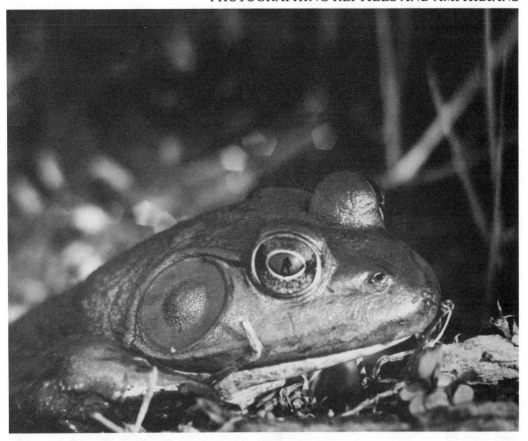

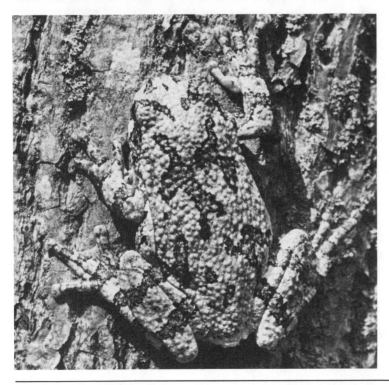

Above I took my own portrait, which can be seen in the eye, when I photographed this male bullfrog.
Left The camouflage pattern of this tree toad is best seen from above.

PHOTOGRAPHING BIRDS

The Rue Formula for Success:
Hours expended = results achieved.

More people photograph birds than any other form of wildlife. About 650 species of birds breed in North America north of the Mexican border. At the end of summer, after the nesting season, it is estimated that the bird population of the continent is about 20 billion. Some areas have few birds, others have huge concentrations. Compared to the acreage covered, it comes to about three birds per acre.

Birds are among the best-known and best-loved forms of wildlife, and the most commonly seen. Most birds are diurnal and carry on their activities during daylight hours when they can be seen. Birds are appreciated not only for their beauty but for the beneficial role that many fulfill by consuming vast tonnages of harmful insects and weed seeds. The activities of birds are therapeutic; they bring joy and a sense of peace to all, particularly shut-ins. In each one of us is an atavistic attachment to wildlife and nature, and for many in city or urban environments, birds provide the only connecting link.

We photograph birds because of their beauty, because they are often seen, because they are easily baited, and because at some times of the year all birds are anchored to a definite breeding and nesting area. Because of the great interest in birds, there are more bird clubs in need of programs about birds than any other kind of nature club. More magazines are devoted to birds, and more books are published about birds, than about any other form of wildlife. This points up a most important fact to the wildlife photographer: Bird photographs are highly salable.

How to Locate Birds

There are many excellent books on finding birds in every area of North America; I list some of them in the bibliography. Pettingill's books tell you where to go, what you will find, and when to be there to find it. These books are invaluable and get you into the immediate area where you can begin to search for a particular bird.

The easiest way to locate birds is to ask someone who knows about birds and is familiar with the area. Local Audubon bird groups are in the field all year, and they are usually more than willing to share their knowledge, providing you can assure them that you will do everything possible to protect the birds.

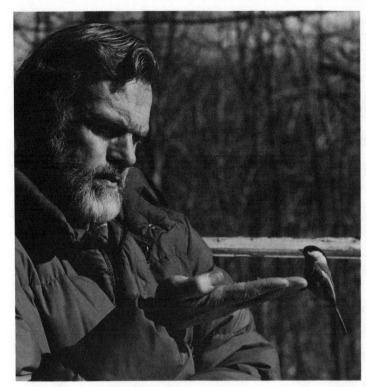

I like to study birds at close range. I have tamed many black-capped chickadees to eat from my hands or take seeds from my lips.

If you are going to photograph in a park or refuge, always go to the headquarters or nature center and speak to the people in charge. Explain to them what you hope to do. There is a good chance that they may even have the subject you need under observation.

If no one can help you, then you must rely on your own knowledge to locate the birds you want to photograph. A basic rule of bird behavior is that almost all land birds feed heavily in early to mid-morning, are quiescent until mid-afternoon, and resume heavy feeding from then until dark. This pattern changes if the birds are feeding young, for the demands of the young keep the adults gathering food most of the day. In any event, if there is a slack time, even when birds are feeding young, it will be around noon. An incoming winter storm can be foretold by a tremendous increase in feeding activity throughout the day. At such times the birds are much more tolerant of one another. There is less fighting because each bird is interested only in securing food.

Shorebirds also have two peak periods of feeding each day, but their activities are geared to the two daily tides. These birds feed heavily when the tide is flowing out, exposing the mud flats of tidal basins or wide stretches of sea beaches. Unless you are particularly interested in photographing feeding activities, this is not the time to photograph shorebirds. As their food sources are uncovered, the birds scatter over huge areas. Many times, you cannot follow the birds because of the depth of the mud. Also, these vast areas are wide open; nothing offers concealment. The time to photograph shorebirds is when the incoming tide pushes them off the tidal flats and concentrates them along the ever diminishing shoreline. The birds retreat in front of incoming waves, feeding as they do so, then gather to preen and sleep. It is exceedingly difficult to photograph smaller shorebirds, such as sanderlings, while they feed because they are a study in perpetual motion as they dash up and down the beach in front of each advancing and retreating wave. But even the most active birds slow down at high tide when their appetites have been sated.

Wading birds, such as egrets and herons, may feed over a wide area, but they have preferred

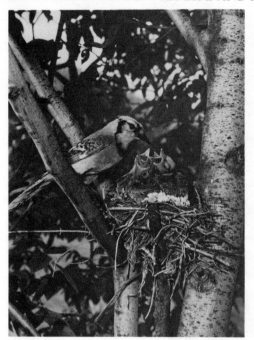 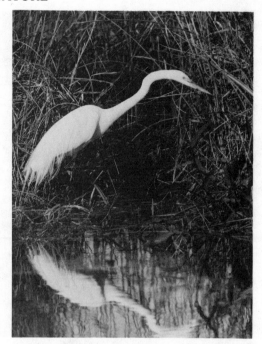

Left Birds with young to feed, such as this blue jay, are busy all day long.
Right Wading birds, such as this great egret, have favorite fishing spots that they return to every day. Photo by Irene Vandermolen

fishing spots that they return to day after day. Experience has taught them that they can catch the fish they need in certain spots with the methods they use, and all birds have different ways of obtaining food. Every human fisherman has preferred "hot spots," and so do birds. Learn these spots, and with patience, success will be assured.

Two conditions exist over which we have no control but of which, as photographers, we should be aware in order to take advantage of these occurrences. First, a prolonged drought in any area will dry up many shallow ponds and waterholes, concentrating fish and birds as they gather to feed on a bonanza. Even birds that don't feed on fish will be concentrated at the available waterhole to drink.

Second, the climate of our continent has changed drastically since the early 1960s with the jet stream often pouring oceans of frigid air over southern states that never experienced such weather before. Two years ago I was able to take advantage of such a happening. As I passed through Jacksonville, Florida, the temperature was 14 degrees F. at dawn. All of Florida was locked up in winter's icy grip, and no wildlife moved for five days. On the sixth day, as I entered the Everglades, the sun burst through, the temperatures soared, the fish became active, and the wading birds went into a "feeding frenzy." Because of their hunger, the birds threw caution to the wind; they paid no attention to anyone, they were too busy gorging themselves. For several days, I shot between 3000 and 4000 photos a day. I was able to do some of the best bird photography I have ever done. Only twice in my life have I been in the right place at the right time to such a great advantage. Now that I have made you aware of it, perhaps you can take advantage of it the next time it happens.

Many game birds can be located by their calls in the spring. Male ruffed grouse, using a favorite log or stump, make a drumming sound with their wings. The grouse use this log consistently throughout the breeding season. Turkeys gobble as males attempt to lure females to a favored area. The bobwhite and other quail call from favored fence posts and rocks. Sharp-tail grouse, prairie chickens, and sage grouse boom, call, and dance on traditional breeding

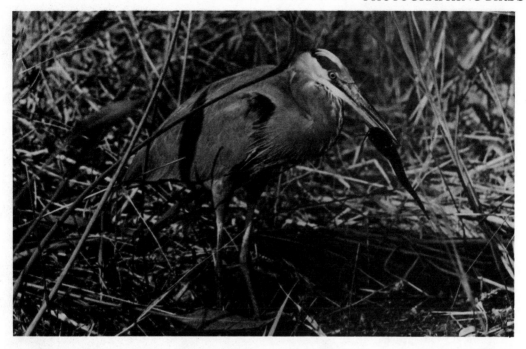

A great blue heron breaks the spines off a catfish before attempting to swallow the fish. Photo by Irene Vandermolen

areas called *leks*. Most of these spots have been used annually by these birds and their ancestors since before the coming of man. Leks have been recorded by the various state game agencies, and their biologists are always willing to share their knowledge of a lek's location with dedicated nature photographers.

Owls can be located by going out at night and playing recorded tapes of their calls. After learning their whereabouts, their daytime roosting spots can be located by carefully searching any stands of conifers, or other dense cover, in the area and looking for owl pellets. Owls swallow small prey whole. The owls' body acids digest the meat, and the undigestible bones, feathers, and fur are regurgitated in a mass known as an owl pellet. Owls are creatures of habit, and finding the pellets means finding the owl.

Wild creatures are no different from us. They, too, look for the easy way.

Fish-cleaning facilities at marinas always have a large entourage of gulls; and in the South, pelicans wait for a free hand-out. Garbage dumps are excellent places for gulls, crows, blackbirds, and so on.

Ponds in city parks have resident flocks of geese, many varieties of ducks, and in New Jersey, my home state, mute swans. Kids love to feed birds, and the birds love to eat what the kids feed them. Unfortunately, what is fed the birds is usually white bread; a better food, for both kids and waterfowl, would be natural grains.

The most difficult birds to locate and photograph are small warblers and other perching birds. These birds usually frequent the tops of the tallest trees, and most of them will not respond to bait or water. They do like quiet forested areas near small streams.

Many of these birds can be lured within camera range by making a high-pitched shishing sound with your mouth, repeating the sound over and over again. The higher you are able to make the pitch of the sound, the more effective it will be. The birds can hear a much higher sound frequency than humans can. Some people make a kissing sound, while others actually kiss the backs of their hands or make a squeaking, sucking noise on the back of their hand. For

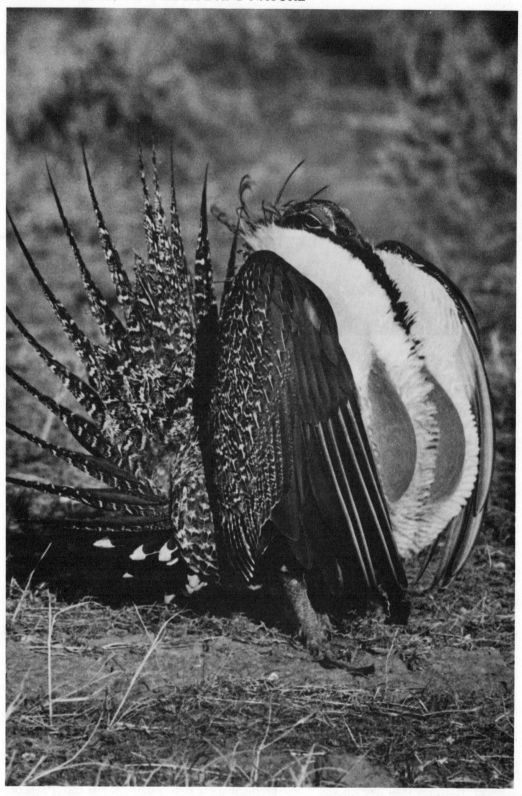

A sage grouse cock "booming" on a traditional territory called a *lek*.

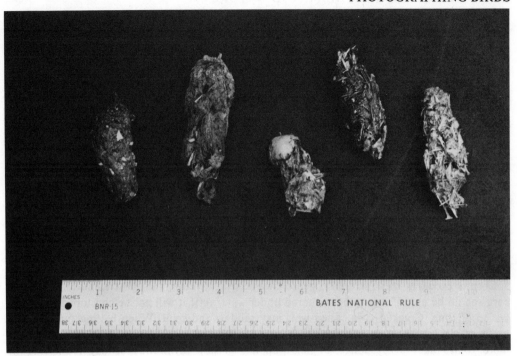

Regurgitated owl pellets show not only where the owls can be found but also what they have been eating.

those who have difficulty making any of these sounds, the little Audubon bird call works very well. A wide variety of high-pitched squeaks, clucks, and trills can be made when the little pewter handle is turned, with varying degrees of force, against the wood.

Small birds also respond well to a whistled imitation of the call of the little screech owl. Don't make the call of any of the larger owls because this will cause the birds to leave the area to seek protective shelter.

Woodpeckers, especially the pileated, often respond to the sound made by rapping on the trunk of a dead tree with a piece of wood.

Clicking fist-size stones together in a marsh often draws a vocal response from the various rails. If the birds are seen but slink off, they can sometimes be called back into the open by this method.

If you are in a marsh, in a canoe or boat, in the early morning, you can often startle rails and gallinules to betray their location by making a sharp, loud noise. You can pound on the side of the canoe or boat, or slap your paddle against the water. The birds won't come to these sounds, but by their cries you will know where to look for them.

Feeding and Baiting Birds

The area around my home is a jumbled, jungle of vegetation, and it was planned and planted that way. I love being surrounded by wildlife. And I am. I take thousands of photographs a year from my house or in the immediate vicinity. As I write this, a mockingbird is feeding on the multiflora rose hips in my yard.

Birds must have food, water, and shelter—and perhaps shelter is the most important. If you can provide all three, you will have birds. I have about 20 different species of birds visiting my feeders every day, with as many as 150 birds at a time in the vicinity.

HOW I PHOTOGRAPH WILDLIFE AND NATURE

I have planted thousands upon thousands of food-producing shrubs such as autumn olive, tartarian honeysuckle, multiflora rose, and barberry on my property. Wild dogwood shrubs abound in the woods. These plants produce untold thousands of berries, which are relished by many different species of birds. The rose hips and barberries remain on the plants all winter. The dense brushiness of all these plants provides fantastic shelter in which the birds can build nests; they also use the brush as a haven from their enemies.

A bird will not cross wide-open spaces no matter how much feed you put out. It will seek food that is near shelter. I have bushy lilac and spirea bushes planted at all the corners of my house and a brush fence row within 8 feet of the corner of my porch. The birds feel safe because they are safe.

The birds that come to my feeders have different feeding preferences both for food and in the placement of food. A knowledge of both makes it easier to photograph them.

Peanut hearts and sunflower seeds have to be at the top of any seed-eating bird's food list, and both are highly nutritious for the birds. Peanut butter and suet enable insect-eating birds as well as seed-feeders to produce body heat. Millet, cracked corn, cracked wheat, and milo are also good foods. Niger seed is a favorite of finches.

Corn is excellent bait for ducks, geese, swans, wild turkeys, and most game birds. Whole corn should be used if it is to be scattered under water or if it will not be consumed in a short period of time. Cracked corn, when wet, may mildew and spoil. When baiting for turkey, I prefer to use cracked corn because it is harder for the deer to pick up, and so the turkeys get more. It also takes turkeys longer to pick it up, and so they stay in the area longer, allowing the possibility of more photos.

Halved oranges and sliced apples are attractive to many birds, particularly where water may be scarce. The birds come to the fruit as much for the moisture as for the food content.

Water is an attractant, particularly if it is falling with a splash. Birds need water to drink, and they love to bathe. A tin can with a very small hole punched in the bottom can be filled with water and suspended above any shallow water pan. The resultant drip will draw birds like a magnet. I have three free-flowing springs near my home, so I don't have to provide water, but I have built a rock-garden waterfall and pool that I operate in the summer. Electrical heating elements are available that will keep your outdoor water ice-free for the birds. Desert waterholes are a mecca for the birds.

Hummingbirds, orioles, and jays can be lured with feeders containing a solution of one part sugar or honey to two parts water. This mixture approximates the sweetness of a flower's nectar, which is the main source of high energy needed by the hummers. A harmless red vegetable dye is usually added to the solution to make it even more appealing to the color-conscious birds.

A slick trick used to hold sanderlings and sandpipers in a desired area is to cut dried spaghetti into 1-inch pieces, soak them, and spread the pieces along the beach in the desired spot. The spaghetti looks like worms to the birds and is avidly eaten.

There is no place for squeamishness in wildlife photography. If you want to photograph vultures, eagles, and some hawks, there is no better way to do it than by baiting the birds with carrion. Road-killed wildlife such as rabbits, woodchucks, and squirrels abound, unfortunately, and if picked up early in the morning, they will not have had time to decompose and become odoriferous. Dead skunks can be shoveled into a box fastened to the bumper of your car, and they do make good bait. Dead fish are great for vultures and eagles. Deer frequently perish by falling on the ice of rivers and lakes and will be visited by any eagle in the area.

Cardinals, white-throated sparrows, juncos, and the like prefer to feed on the ground or on open feeding platforms. They will go to hanging feeders but not by preference. Titmice, chickadees, nuthatches, finches, and the like prefer hanging feeders.

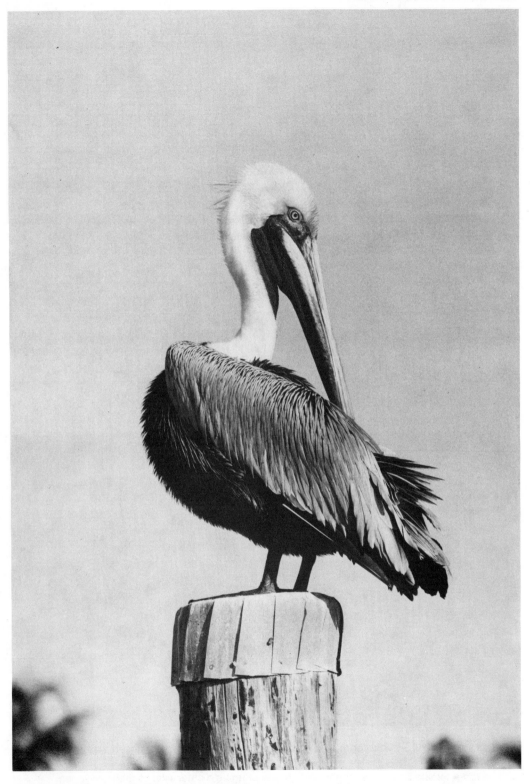

The brown pelican population is increasing. Pelicans are commonly seen sitting on pilings near fish-cleaning operations. Photo by Irene Vandermolen

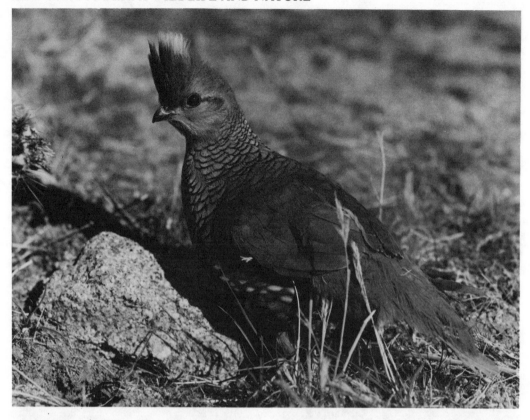

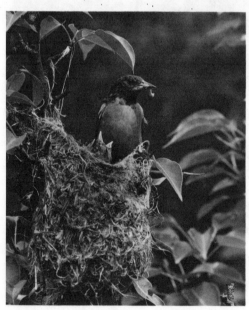

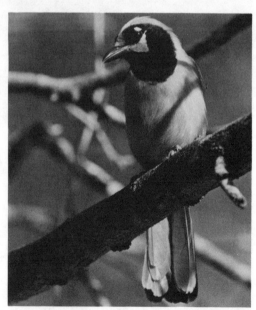

Top This scaled quail was photographed as it was coming in to drink at a desert waterhole. Photo by Len Rue, Jr.

Bottom left A female Baltimore, or northern, oriole bringing a caterpillar to feed her young.

Bottom right Green jays are found only along the Mexican-Texas border. Photo by Irene Vandermolen

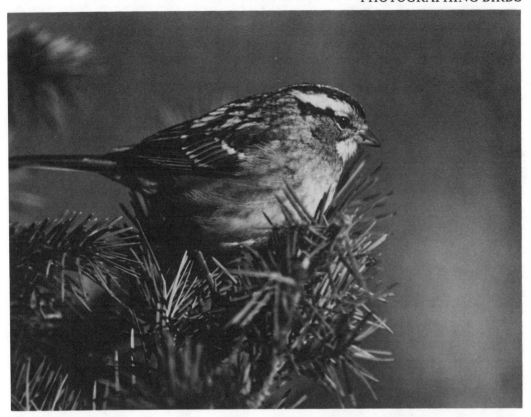

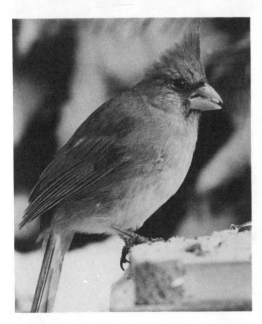 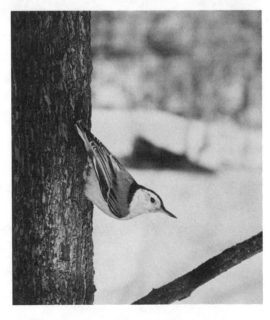

Top This white-throated sparrow is perched on an old Christmas tree that I stuck in the snow outside my window.

Bottom left Cardinals prefer to feed up on flat, open feeding shelves or on the ground.

Bottom right This nuthatch came to get the sunflower seeds I had hidden in the tree hole by its tail.

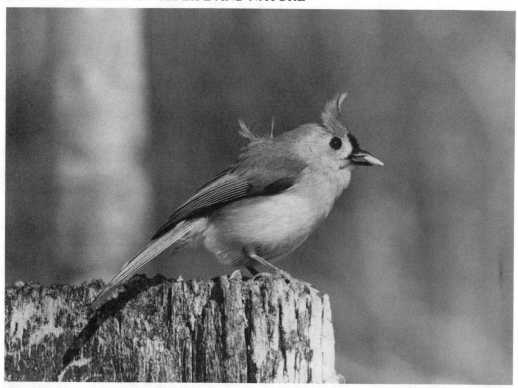

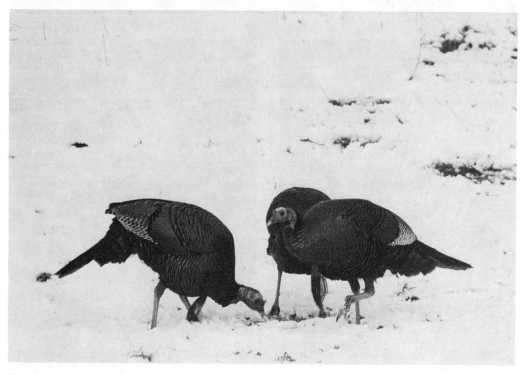

Top If you do not want it to be known that the bird was photographed at a feeder, don't take photos of it with a seed in its bill. This seed-eater is a tufted titmouse.
Bottom I baited these wild turkeys with corn hidden in hollows in the snow.

How to Photograph Birds Using Baits

Unless you want to feature birds at feeding stations, you must hide, disguise, or eliminate the feeder from the area to be photographed. Here is how it is done.

There are always many more birds waiting to get to the feeder than can feed at one time. The birds usually sit all over the nearby trees and bushes. Photograph them sitting on their natural perches. If there are no trees where you want them, plant some. Or have a live tree in a tub and move it where you want it. Or better yet, use cut perch trees and branches that can be stuck in the ground or nailed to a block of a stump to hold them erect. Your old Christmas tree can be used here.

If a cut perch tree is placed 6 to 8 feet from your feeder, bird after bird will perch on it just before flying in to feed. Naturally you don't want all your birds sitting on the same tree in the same spot. You can turn the tree around so that the birds use different branches, or you can put a change of background foliage behind the perch, or you can keep substituting different trees. If you are using a cut tree or branch, you can eliminate all the extra branches from the tree so that the birds are forced to land precisely where you want them. Just keep any signs of "gardening" out of the area being photographed. Although I often photograph wildlife by baiting or under controlled conditions, I don't want any evidence of it to show.

If I want birds to sit on a certain limb, I pin a paper cup full of food to the tree trunk, out of sight, near the desired spot. An oak tree near my home has a horizontal dead limb. I have hollowed out the top of the limb with a knife and often put seeds in the hollow and have the birds sitting on a natural limb. Prop up a piece of a dead tree trunk vertically so that it looks like a regular tree. Drill a large hole horizontally into the trunk and fill it with suet or peanut butter. Turn the trunk so that the hole is not visible from the camera angle. Now you can put the trunk where you want it and get great photos of woodpeckers, nuthatches, and so forth climbing up the tree trunk.

I gather every tree stump that contains an old woodpecker's hole after it has fallen to the ground. I prop it up where I want it and throw sunflower seeds inside. Within a day or so I have the cavity-nesting chickadees, titmice, and nuthatches—and often squirrels—popping in and out of the hole.

Shelf feeders can be hidden behind pieces of dead wood or can be made out of rough sections of hollow logs. Remember, though, if you are hiding the feeder, to take the photograph of the bird as soon as it lands. There is no point in hiding the feeder if you then take photographs of the bird with a seed in its beak.

When I bait game birds, I put the corn behind a piece of fallen wood, behind leaves, or in a hollow on the ground. I don't want the yellow corn to show. I have had some great turkey photos spoiled because the turkeys scratched and uncovered the corn so that it could be seen. Wheat often works better because it is smaller and blends into any brown background. With game birds that scratch for food, you have to keep changing the area you use because they soon have it scratched bare. You can extend the life of such an area by bringing in baskets of dead leaves and scattering them about.

When baiting ducks and geese, don't use the game bird food because it floats and will show up in the photograph. Corn sinks to the bottom and is good if you use a low camera angle so that the corn cannot be seen under water. The waterfowl, tipping up or diving beneath the surface of the water to feed, will give you wonderful action photos. Pictures of waterfowl are always enhanced when the birds are covered with droplets of water.

Photographs of hummingbirds at feeders are fine, but photographs of hummers at flowers are even better. Because the hummers dart constantly from one flower to another, it is next to impossible to prefocus on the flower that they will use. The simplest method is to get them to use a feeder that has an extended glass tube. Then take the blossom of whatever large-blossomed flower the hummers are visiting, such as the hollyhock, trumpet vine, or coral bells,

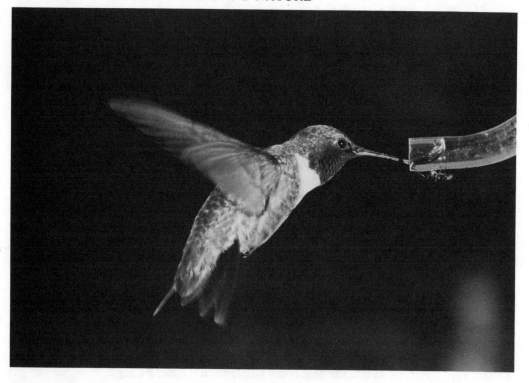

A male ruby-throated hummingbird and an ant, both feeding at a sugar-water feeder.

and fasten the flower over the end of the glass tube with an elastic band or a paper-covered tie wire. By being careful with your framing, you can eliminate the tube and elastic band and get just the hummer visiting the flower.

How to Locate Bird Nests

The simplest way to find bird nests is to go out in any area frequented by birds and sit down. If you remain motionless for a while, wildlife will soon resume its normal activities. If you dress in camouflage, as I do much of the time, it will be easier for you to blend in with your surroundings.

The peak of the nesting season for small birds is from mid-April to the end of June. Some species nest much earlier, and many birds raise two and sometimes three broods, and so the season may extend into August.

If you start early in the season when the birds first come back from the South, you can locate their general nesting areas by locating the males on their singing territories. With many species, the males arrive first and select the nest territory and defend it against other males of the same species by singing and, if need be, fighting.

As nest building gets under way, you can observe the birds gathering material and watch where they go with it. Any bird flying with material in its mouth is carrying it to build a nest somewhere. Robins and swallows carrying mud, hawks and herons carrying large sticks, orioles carrying string, and flycatchers carrying cast snakeskins are a few examples. Woodpeckers can be heard as they excavate nest holes. Or their holes may be discovered by the wood chips lying on top of the leaves at the base of the tree. After you locate a woodpecker's nest, a dentist's or mechanic's mirror will allow you to see if there are eggs in the cavity.

Most hawk, owl, and eagle nests, although large and bulky, are usually difficult to locate in

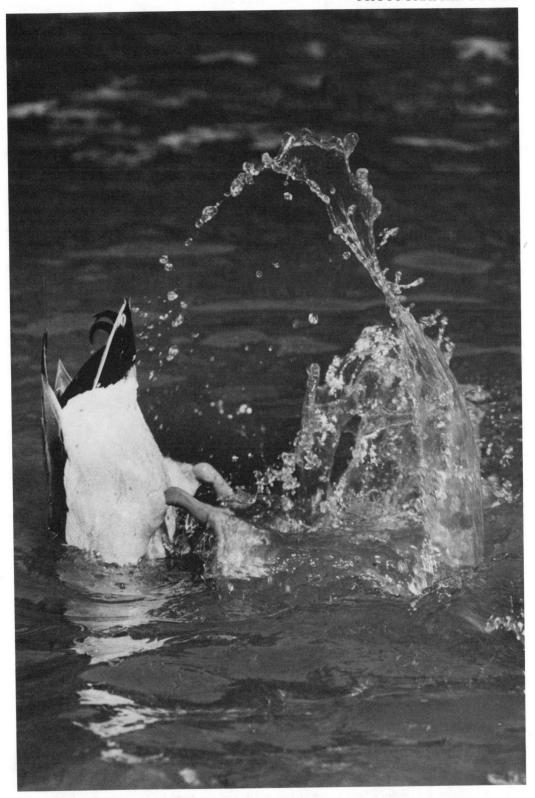

Corn scattered in shallow water will get "puddle" ducks like this mallard to tip-up to feed.

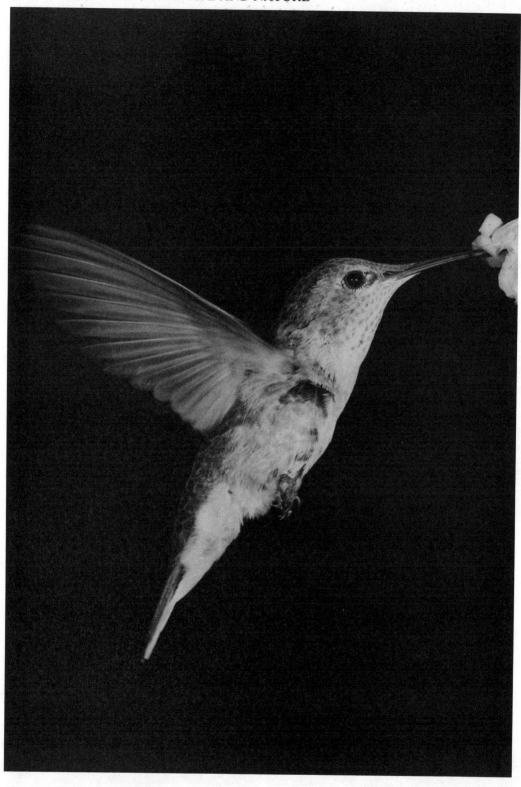

You can disguise the feeder's tube with a flower, as my son did when he photographed this female broad-tailed hummingbird. Photo by Len Rue, Jr.

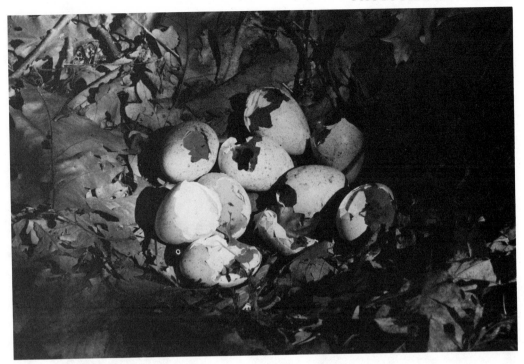

Crows destroy a tremendous number of birds' nests by eating the eggs, such as these wild turkey eggs.

the eastern half of the continent because of the millions of trees the birds have to choose from and that hide them. Finding raptor nests is much easier in western states because there are more hawks there and because of the scarcity of trees. Both the birds and their nests are more easily seen. All you have to do is scan the few trees growing along the creek bottoms, and the bulky nests stand out like sore thumbs.

If you find a bulky nest but do not see the hawk or owl near it or using it, check the nest carefully with your binoculars. Raptors usually lay claim to a nest and show their intention of using it by putting a twig of evergreen branch in the nest. If evergreens are not available, they will put a branch with green leaves in the nest and replace the branch with a new one when the leaves turn brown.

Check any steep-sided sand bank or gravel pit for the nests of swallows and kingfishers. Such areas are used annually if the banks are not disturbed. Check under the rafters of buildings for the nests of swallows, phoebes, robins, and so on.

Many species, such as the bluebird, tree swallow, chickadee, titmouse, and house wren, will readily utilize the birdhouses you erect for them. You can photograph birds at the house, or you can erect a perch nearby that they can land on before flying to the house. All of these birds are so closely associated with humans that pictures of the birds and their man-made environment are not only acceptable but often desired.

When birds begin to lay eggs, incubate eggs, or feed young, they often become very secretive. Many birds, particularly those of the grasslands such as meadowlarks, bobolinks, and prairie horned larks, do not fly directly to or away from their nests. They land at a considerable distance from the nest and then sneak through the vegetation to the nest. They leave by the same procedure. After such a bird has been seen landing in the grass, two people can approach the spot from different angles. If both mark the spot where the bird is flushed, the nest is somewhere nearby. The bird can also be flushed from its nest by two people walking 100 feet

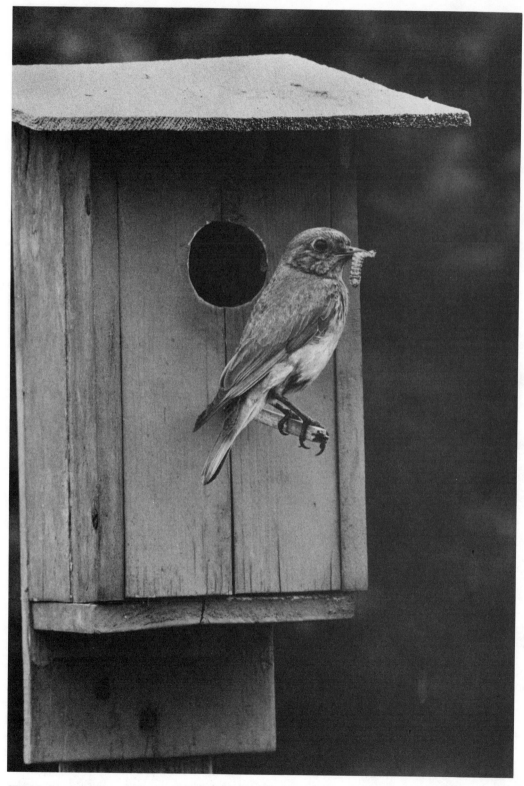

Bluebirds need man-made houses because there are not enough natural tree cavities in which they can nest.

apart and dragging a rope over the grass tops between them. Extreme care must be taken when searching for hidden nests so that they are not stepped on.

If you are searching for bird nests in a dense bush or a brushy fence row, do it from the shade side and look toward the light. This causes the bulky nest to be silhouetted against the sky. If you search for the nest with the light behind you, the nest often blends into the vegetation and remains undetected.

Any time you find a songbird flying with a white object in its mouth, you are seeing a bird that has just come from its nest carrying the waste material of the young in a fecal sac. If you noted where the bird came from, you can locate the nest. Birds may go to their nests in a circuitous fashion but often leave in a direct flight.

Killdeer, stilts, avocets, and the like all put on a distraction display, feigning injury to get your attention when you get near their nests. Do not follow the bird, which is what the bird wants you to do. Look in the opposite direction, and the nest can be located.

Some bird nests have to be approached with extreme caution because the birds often actively protect their nests. Terns, in particular, will flock in a screaming mass as you approach their rookery. Many individuals will dive down and strike you on the head. I have had jaegers fly off with my hat and have had jays bloody my scalp. Always watch your eyes because birds instinctively go for the eyes; they know that this is a very vulnerable spot. Hawks and owls have attacked many people, blinding some and knocking others out of trees. It is wise to wear a construction worker's "hard hat" with a wire-mesh face protector when photographing raptors.

The most dangerous time of life, for most birds, is when the young are just about large enough to leave the nest but do not really have the strength to fly. If you approach the nest at such a time, the young may abandon it prematurely, flapping and fluttering about among the underbrush, screaming for help at the top of their lungs. As you catch the young and attempt to put them back in the nest—they seldom stay—the parents may attack your eyes. And you may be attacked by any other birds in the area because they instinctively know there is strength in numbers and usually respond to the distress calls of another bird. Unfortunately, such distress calls attract many predators, looking for an easy meal of young birds. For the birds' protection and your own, do not attempt close-up photography of young birds that are large enough to leave the nest.

Most birds do everything possible to conceal their nests from predators, which is why nests are so hard to locate. I often wonder how any form of wildlife is able to reproduce itself because of predation and other factors, although in most instances, with most species of both birds and animals, predation plays a negligible factor in the species' population.

Almost 60 percent of all birds' eggs and young are destroyed before the young are large enough to leave the nest. This does not represent a total loss because most of these birds will nest again at once. In some instances, the second nesting may be more successful because the later hatching date coincides with a heavier vegetation cover for shelter and more food is usually available.

Because birds' nests are hidden, they are hard to photograph. Do not cut away the intervening foliage. That foliage is needed to protect the birds from predation. In some cases the vegetation is also important as shade to protect the bird, its eggs, and its young from the heat.

I always carry light nylon cord with me and use this cord to tie back interfering pieces of foliage. When I leave, I simply untie the vegetation, and it springs back in place again, concealing the nest.

Do not approach a nest any more than you absolutely have to, to minimize the disturbance of the parent birds. Their anxiety and distress calls will be heeded by all predators, who will be attracted to the area. Although birds have a very poor sense of smell, that of mammals is particularly keen. Many animals will follow a man's tracks or will be attracted by any disturbance in the out-of-doors done by man. If predators follow your tracks to a bird's nest, they will surely decimate it.

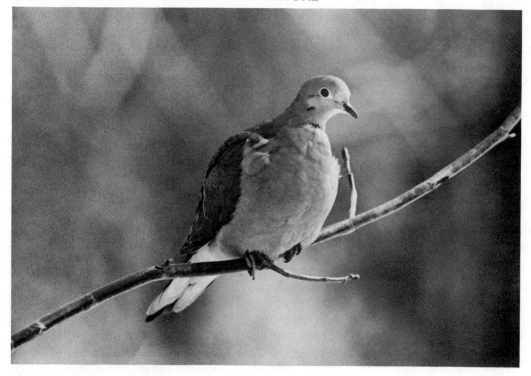

This mourning dove is sitting in a tree just outside my home.

Blinds and How to Use Them

Blinds, or hides, as they are called in Europe, are any device in which, or behind which, a photographer can secret himself and remain undetected from the subject being photographed.

I use my entire home as a blind, although I do most of my photography from just two windows that are in the same room. From time to time I see articles that claim that you can take photographs through the windows in your home without opening them. This should be done only as a last resort. Most houses have storm windows or double-layered thermo-paned insulating glass. That makes two layers of glass and four surfaces of glass that can reflect and refract light. Window glass is not made to optical standards, and photos taken through such glass suffer in quality. If pictures must be taken through the glass, the room should be darkened, if at all possible, to cut down on reflections. Or a large black cloth can be hung up with just a hole for the camera lens. Shooting at an angle to the glass also reduces reflections.

I prefer to raise the window. I have a special drape with a V-shaped hole cut in it through which I can stick the lens. The drape also masks any movement I make. Some photographers use a piece of wood or cardboard that is the same length as the window's width and about 8 to 10 inches in height. They raise the window just high enough to put the board under it. The camera lens is then stuck through a hole cut in the middle for that purpose. I don't like the restrictions imposed by the inflexibility of wood or cardboard. My cloth drape allows me to move the lens to a more oblique angle, if that should be required, and it also masks my activities, which the low board does not do.

My pickup truck has a camper on the back, and it is backed right now to the edge of my lawn. I have been baiting both deer and turkeys to a spot in the woods about 75 feet from the truck. I haven't moved the truck lately, and so the wildlife accept it as readily as they do any of the buildings on my property. When I want to take photos, I get out before the wildlife comes in, prop the camper door open, drop a drape across the door, and sit inside and shoot out. I

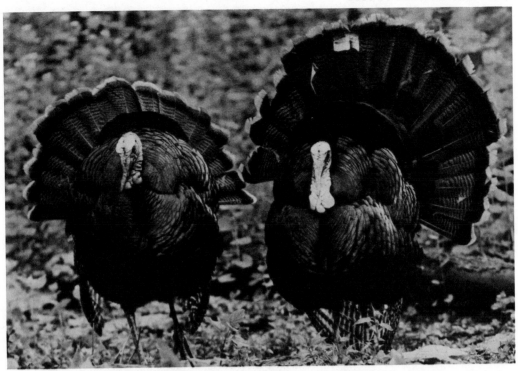

I photographed these wild turkeys in my yard by using my truck as a blind.

have taken many rolls of excellent photos so far, and I am anxiously awaiting the turkeys to start displaying for the spring breeding season in another three or four weeks.

Every wildlife photographer should always carry his camera and telephoto lens already coupled to a window bracket wherever he travels. Wild creatures in most areas will pay no attention to a vehicle, and there are many opportunities where photos can be taken through the open car window. Your movements inside the vehicle have to be done slowly, but there is little need to hide. Do not attempt to get out to use a tripod or get additional equipment. This usually causes the wildlife to fly or run off. Be sure to get in the best position possible and then make sure to turn off the engine. The slightest vibration of the engine can affect the sharpness of your photo. Starting the engine again may startle your subject, and so it is very important to get in the best position possible before shutting off the engine.

Blinds can often be made out of natural materials that grow in the area in which you are working. However, do not attempt to do this in any park or refuge. It is illegal to cut the vegetation, and stiff fines accompany the ordinances. On private land, make sure you secure permission before you do any cutting.

A framework of poles driven into the ground and tied together, or nailed, is usually all that is needed. Then such vegetation as cattails, phragmites, small scrub cedar trees, cornstalks, or tree branches can be tied in place to offer concealment. The material used in the blind must match the surroundings.

I once made a good blind at the edge of a cornfield for deer by making a tripod of long poles and fastening long cornstalks to the framework. The blind looked exactly like a shock of stalked corn, and it worked very well. A friend of mine once made a blind out of bales of hay at the edge of a hayfield.

Usually it is much simpler to use a regular blind, be it a commercial blind or homemade. My Ultimate Blind, which is the result of years of building blinds, is quick to put up, weatherproof, large enough to be comfortable, light enough to carry, and reversible to match either a green or brown background. A white covering is also available for use with a snow background. A waterproof groundcloth can also be snapped in if the area is wet and muddy.

I am adding here, in photos, diagrams of how to build a portable blind. It is easier to show you the details than to take pages to tell you how to do it. One thing that I find highly desirable and important in building blinds is that the top be waterproof and that the material be dense enough so that your outline is not silhouetted by the sun shining behind it. Most people never take these two factors into consideration.

Many people say that they do not intend to use the blind during the rain anyway. I don't either. Many times, however, I've had a sudden squall or thunderstorm come up and spoil a beautiful day, while I sat out the storm snug and dry in the blind. If the top of the blind is not waterproof, it will leak drops of moisture long after the storm has passed. It is next to impossible to get snow or ice off the top of a burlap blind, whereas it will shake off easily from a canvas top.

The material for the back of the blind must be doubled in thickness or be of opaque material to be an effective screen. A single piece of burlap in the rear of the blind will allow the sun to shine through, and the wildlife will be able to see any motions you make inside. You will appear only as a shadowy figure, but a movable shadowy figure, and that may scare them off.

The pup tent makes a fine blind, and many other tents can also be modified and used as blinds. Do not buy tents made of the bright blue or blaze orange material that so many tentmakers favor today. Many green, brown, and tan tents are available. Early Winters is the only company I know of that is making tents in camouflage colors. For use on the western plains, where the constant wind can be brutal, some photographers make low plywood blinds, which do not move or make noise, as canvas blinds may do. The advantage of using tents for blinds is that you can sleep in them if you are going to be working on sage grouse, prairie chickens, sharptail grouse, and the like. These birds usually arrive on their leks about one and a half hours before sunrise and leave perhaps half an hour to an hour after the sun is up. If you want to photograph these birds, you have to be up and into your blind before 4:30 A.M. or you risk scaring off the early-arriving birds. It is better to sleep in the blind; then you are ready to start taking photographs when there is sufficient light. If the day turns out stormy, just go back to sleep.

There are two major reasons to hide your blind with camouflage. The more important is that the more the blind blends in with the surroundings, the more acceptable it will be to wildlife. The second, perhaps of equal importance, is to prevent people from seeing it. Common courtesy demands that you do not approach a blind. I have had many subjects scared off because someone wondered what the blind was, or what I was doing, and so on. I have also had a number of blinds stolen when people discovered them and I was not in them. Unfortunately, theft is common everywhere in the country today.

Curious cattle can also wreck your blind, if you set it up in a pasture or on rangeland. The cattle may simply want to rub against it to relieve an itch, but blinds aren't built to withstand such a rubbing. Under such situations the best protection for the blind is to use the smallest model electric fence charger you can get. Then, with some very lightweight insulated poles and some very thin light wire, you can put up an electric fence around your blind. If you are photographing a small bird's nest, enclose the nest in the protected fenced-in area so that it does not get trampled. This is impractical when photographing a large area such as a lek.

For most subjects, particularly those on a nest, it is very important that the blind be introduced to the area gradually. I usually take three days to set the blind in place before I use it on the fourth day.

The first day, I may set the blind up about 100 feet from the nest I wish to photograph. The blind must be fastened securely so that it does not blow or flap about. If the blind does not move, the birds accept it quite readily. On the second day, I move the blind in to about 50

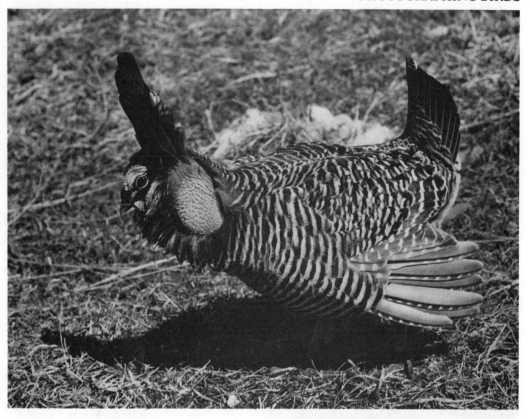

PATTERN FOR A BLIND

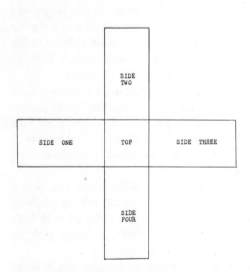

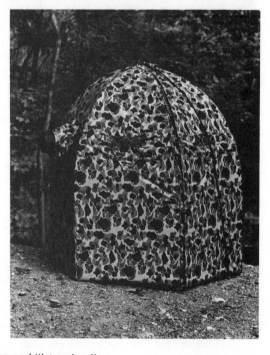

Stitch side one to side two, side two to side three, side three
to side four. Leave side one which is adjacent to side four open
for entering and exiting blind. Strips of velcro, ties or pins
may be used as closures for this side.

Top A male greater prairie chicken male displaying and "booming."
Bottom left A pattern for making a simple blind out of any material.
Bottom right My Ultimate Blind can be put up in 30 seconds.

feet. The third day, I move it to whatever distance I intend to shoot from. If the blind has not been flapping or moving in the breeze, the birds will have accepted it by this time. On the fourth day, I can start working.

Whenever possible, move the blind and get into and out of it when the birds are not on their nest. Use binoculars to check this. No matter what wild creatures I am photographing, I always try to prevent their associating me with the blind. If at all possible, have someone accompany you to the blind. Then, if you are observed at the blind, the birds will feel safe when your companion leaves the area. I have also found it of great help, particularly with crows and larger birds, if when your companion leaves the area, he or she carries an overcoat on a hanger extended at arm's length. This creates the illusion of two people walking away. If you think this is a lot of nonsense, try it. Crows can count to three or more. If they see two people walk toward the blind, and only one leaves, they will not approach it. They can be fooled by the use of the overcoat.

I have always wished that I had one of those "cherrypicker" hydraulic baskets that utility and tree-trimming companies use so effectively for high work. I don't, and unless you are really well-to-do, you won't be able to afford one either. To photograph high nests takes some doing, and it is not a task for anyone who is not in good physical condition. Every time I get 40 or 50 feet above the ground in the treetops, I ask myself, "What am I doing up here?"

There are a number of ways to get up in high trees. You can use a 40-foot aluminum extension ladder, painted dead-grass color. This is one of the safest ways, but it is awkward to carry the ladder any distance, and it does require help to put it up. Once erected, the ladder can be tied in place, which makes it very easy to use.

I frequently use climbing spurs such as those used by timber toppers. Although spurs take some getting used to, they make an easy way to climb. Because spurs do scar trees, however, they cannot be used in many areas. When you use spurs, or do any tree work, always wear a safety belt and have two ropes that go around the tree. Naturally you only use one rope at a time, but when you come to a large limb, you need two. Then you fasten one rope above the limb before you unfasten the one below it, and you are safe. I learned this the hard way. I was working on a red-tailed hawk's nest that was 70 feet above the ground, with the first major tree limb 40 feet up. I didn't have too much trouble going up because I could hold on to the big limb, climb above it, and tie on again. Coming down was another story. I could hold on to the big limb with one arm, but I had to throw the rope around the big tree and catch it with the other hand. It took me a long time; I still wonder how I ever got down without falling.

I do not like to screw metal steps into a tree, nor do I like to nail on wooden cleats. Nowadays I use metal steps, made by the Martin Manufacturing Company, that fasten around the tree with a chain and are very easy and safe to use. You can put them on the tree and take them off as you come down so that they are not stolen. Or you can leave the higher ones in place and just remove the bottom three or four. They can be purchased with chains long enough to go around the largest trees.

Using a bow, or better yet, a crossbow, you can shoot an arrow, pulling a light line over a tree limb. Then, with the light line, you can pull up a climbing rope. You can use the climbing rope to pull up a wire scaling ladder. In climbing an aerial ladder, don't climb up with both feet on the same side or the bottom will tilt sharply upward, and you may slip. Climb with the ladder between your legs, and put each foot in from the opposite direction.

All these methods are satisfactory to get you up in the treetop if the nest you want to photograph is in the same tree or very close by. You will still need a platform to work from. Some good 2″ X 4″ boards will make a sufficient base if the span between the limbs and the trunk is not too great. If the trunks are over 6 feet apart, I use 2″ X 6″ boards for the base. A piece of ⅝″ or ¾″ plywood makes a good deck. You can then erect your blind on the platform.

This is too much trouble to go to if you plan to use the platform just once or twice. When that is the case, I use a portable tree stand such as is used for hunting. I use a Baker tree stand

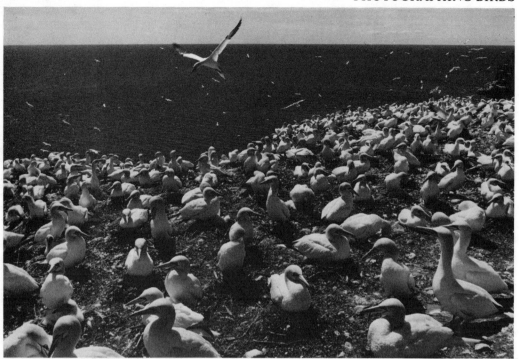

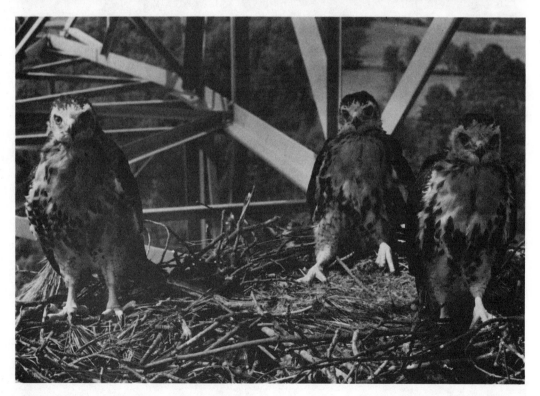

Top Seabird colonies, like these gannets on Bonaventure Island in Quebec, can be photographed without using a blind.
Bottom I photographed these young red-tailed hawks on the top of an electric transmission tower. It was the first time that this hawk was known to have used a man-made structure.

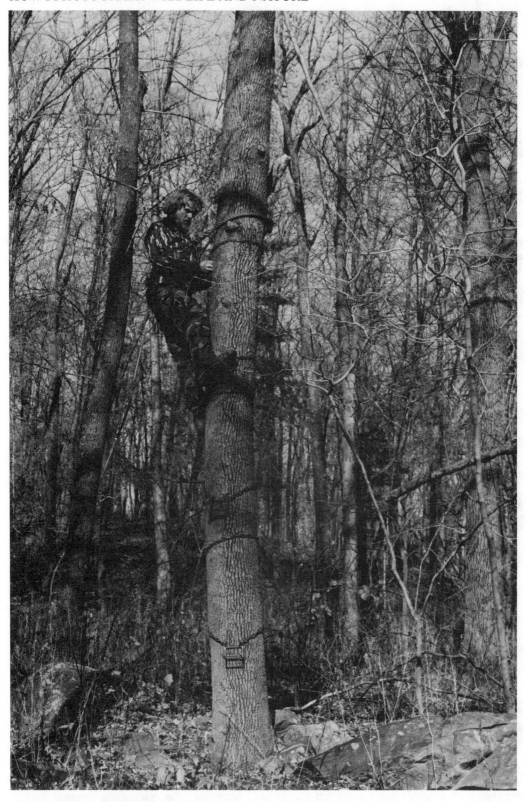

Martin tree steps can be used to get up to high nests without damage to the tree.

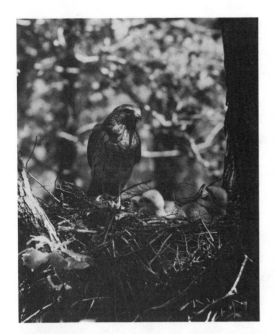 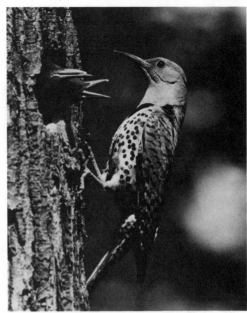

Left This adult red-shouldered hawk, nest, and young were photographed from a blind I had built in an adjoining tree.
Right I photographed this female yellow-shafted flicker from the raised bucket of a front-end loader.

and have modified it so that I can use it for photography. You can actually climb with the stand itself or climb up by another method and fasten the stand where you want it. The photo on page 46 shows the modifications.

For long-term, treetop projects where there are no nearby trees, a pylon must be erected. Pylons mean a tremendous amount of work and must be securely fastened with guy wires to prevent them from collapsing. The base legs must be buried in the earth to give the desired rigidity. Help will be needed to erect such a tower, as well as a supply of straight, strong trees of 4 to 5 inches in diameter that can be cut. The advantage to building a tower is that it can be built back in the woods where you cannot drive a vehicle.

If I can drive a pickup truck or a four-wheel vehicle near the site, then I prefer to use regular construction scaffolding. These sections are usually 4 feet wide by 4 feet high by 6 feet long, and they are heavy but go together easily. If you use them, be sure to have wide planks under the base legs so that they do not sink into the earth and cause the tower to tilt. Again, they must be securely guyed with wire to be safe. This scaffolding is too expensive to buy if it is to be used only once or twice. For such usage it is cheaper to rent scaffolding from a construction company.

Whether you build a wooden tower or put up tubular scaffolding, you must do it in sections to give the birds a chance to become accustomed to it. You should not work more than an hour, and preferably a half hour, at any one time. Such towers cannot be moved and must be placed at the exact distance from the nest that you want to work from. Once the towers are erected and the blind is in place, you can work in comfort and safety and photograph entire nesting sequences. Unless you plan to use flash, place the tower on the south side of the nest, if possible, so that you can get the maximum benefit from the sunlight. If you plan to use electronic flash, and this is almost a must for owls, get some lightweight metal channels on which you can mount your flashheads to get them closer to the subject for greater light intensity and higher *f* stops.

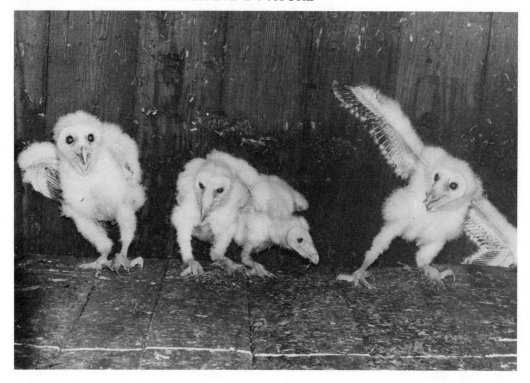

These baby barn owls were photographed in a silo with the flash held just above the camera.

For water or marsh birds, a John boat, skiff, or duck-hunting sneak boat or other flat-bottomed boat can be covered with camouflaged or natural materials and used as a floating blind. One photographer used a kayak camouflaged as a floating log and propelled it with a silent electric motor. He was able to move right in among flocks of ducks and up to water birds' nests. Because a breeze usually blows around water, such boats must be anchored securely with poles thrust down into the mud and held securely to the gunwale of the boat to prevent it from drifting about and stabilize it sufficiently so that long lenses can be used.

Fishermen have long used tire tubes from trucks as a means to getting to some good fishing spots when it was not possible to use a boat. Today, photographers are doing the same thing. What is needed is the largest truck tube and a canvas harness to go over it. Several companies sell such covers; they can be found advertised in any sporting magazine. I got mine from Cabela's.

The canvas covers go over the tube and have crosspieces on the inside that form a seat that keeps you from slipping through the center of the tube. The photographer wears chest-high waders and a pair of footfins with which he propels the tube. These fins fold back when the foot is brought forward and fold sideways to resist the water when the foot is brought back. So, with a walking motion, you can "walk" through the water.

A piece of 1½-inch poly pipe is made into a circle by joining with a wooden plug that fits into both ends of the pipe. The hoop is made slightly smaller than the circumference of the tube. It is then placed over the tube and tied underneath with rope. Four holes are drilled, one in each quarter of the hoop, and two fiberglass rods, from bicycle safety flags, are inserted to form two arches. Over this goes some camouflaged netting, and your floating blind is complete. With this device you can float-walk around marshes and ponds for all kinds of water bird photography. I use an old tripod that I cram down into the mud when I want to get in position to take photos. This blind, if moved very slowly, is readily accepted by wildlife. Do not

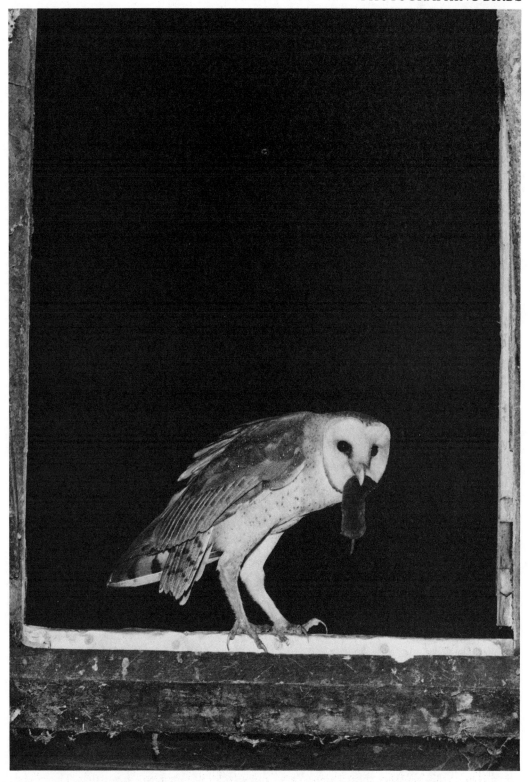

This adult barn owl, with a meadow mouse, was photgraphed in the doorway at the top of a 40-foot silo. The flash was fastened to a metal bracket and the camera tripped by remote control.

use this device in areas that are inhabited by alligators. Alligators usually do not attack humans, but your moving legs may provoke an attack.

Some photographers dig pit blinds, which have the advantage of getting the photographer at the wildlife's eye level. Pit blinds are also easily concealed because of their low contour. The disadvantages are that they are often next to impossible to dig because of rocky soil. In clay soil they fill up with water, which they hold because the water cannot drain away. In sandy soil you have to put in a wooden form to keep the walls from collapsing. Where it is possible to use them, however, pit blinds are good.

One word of caution in the use of blinds: They also offer shelter to different forms of wildlife. Always check the blind before you get into it to make sure that a snake has not crawled inside. In desert country, watch for scorpions. Spiders may take up residence in a blind. Paper wasps and mud dauber wasps will build egg nests in any blind that is left up for an extended period. These wasps can be dispatched with any wasp-killer spray. Gypsy moth caterpillars will festoon the blind with shed instar cases.

Many people make their blinds too small. I fully realize that the smaller the blind, the lighter it will be in weight when it has to be carried. Also, a smaller blind is easier to conceal. But, a small blind is an abomination because such a blind will not allow you to be comfortable, and if you are not comfortable, you will not put in the hours of waiting that you must put in if you are to be successful.

A blind should never be less than 3 feet square; 40 inches is better. You have to have room to set up your tripod. I always place mine with two legs against the front of the blind and the third leg protruding back into the blind. I may place the two legs on the inside of the blind's frame or outside the frame, depending on the length of the lens I am using. And I often have the third leg longer than the front two legs so that the camera and lens are pushed forward which facilitates getting the lens farther out the front of the blind.

By all means, have a comfortable stool to sit on. There are good ones available that even have comfortable backs on them. For me, the backs are a must; I can sit forever, but I have to have a back support. The back cover of the stool is usually just pushed on over the frame, and so I drill through the cover and the frame and lace the cover on so that it cannot be lost.

Most stools have the four legs ending up as points that sink into the earth as you sit on the stool. The better stools are tubular, and each set of legs is bent out of the same pipe so that there is a piece of horizontal pipe between the legs, which prevents the stool from sinking. I would not use any other kind of stool. My stool also has a zippered bag suspended between the legs. This is handy for holding all types of gear needed in the blind, such as insect repellent and a notebook and pen. A shoulder carrying strap facilitates carrying the stool. I got my stool from Cabela's, whose address is listed in the appendix.

Some people read while waiting in the blind. I cannot, and I don't think you should either. It is all right to take down notes of activities you are observing because that keeps you alert to all that is going on around you. But if you read, you may become engrossed in your reading, which may cause you to miss action and perhaps photos. You are in the blind to record activities on paper and film. Do it.

Occasionally I doze off in the blind. This cannot be helped, particularly if you are putting in long hours and the action is slow. Perhaps my years of being with wildlife has made me more like them in the fact that I do not fall into a deep sleep but just doze for the shortest of cat-naps.

In cold weather, always dress warmer for sitting in the blind than you would normally do if you were to be active. I use an Orvis down coat and insulated overpants. Carry your extra clothing to the blind; do not wear it. If it's worn, the activity of walking may cause you to perspire, and this moisture means you will be quickly chilled when you are sitting. The hours of inactivity will allow the cold to seep in, although the confines of the blind will keep it slightly warmer inside than the ambient temperature outside. In cold weather, I either use a

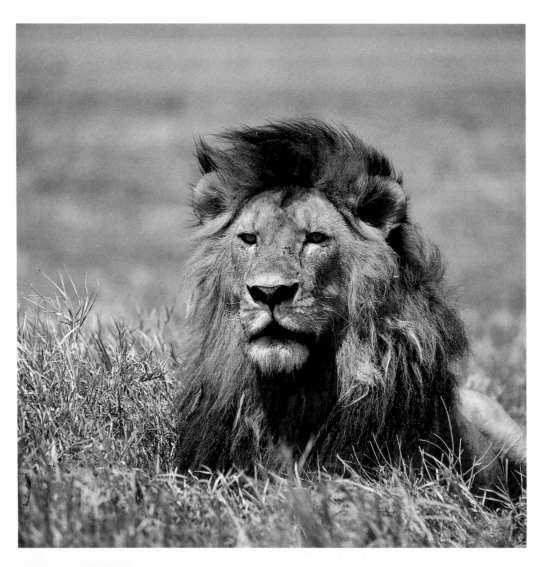

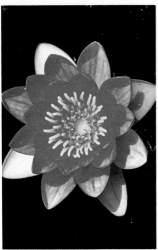

Above This, the finest male African lion I have ever seen, was photographed in Ngorongoro Crater in Tanzania from a Land Rover.

Left Most people start their nature photography right in their backyards—as I did when I photographed this water lily.

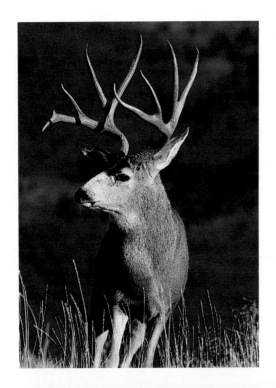
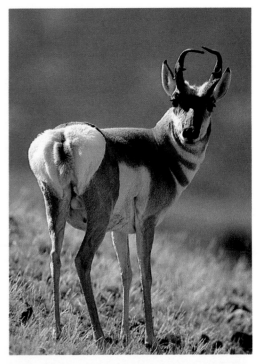
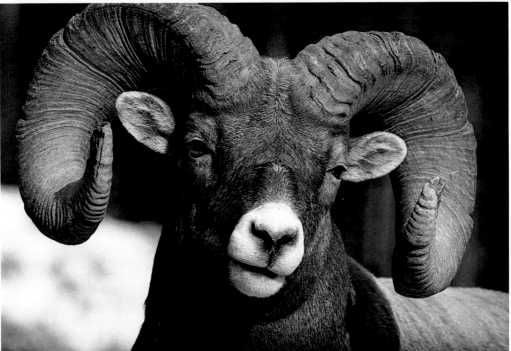

Top left This photo of a superb mule deer buck is made more dramatic because I photographed him against the black background.

Top right This pose of the pronghorn buck is one of my favorites. I like the animal to walk away, then stop and turn to look back.

Bottom I think this is the finest portrait I have ever done of a Bighorn sheep ram.

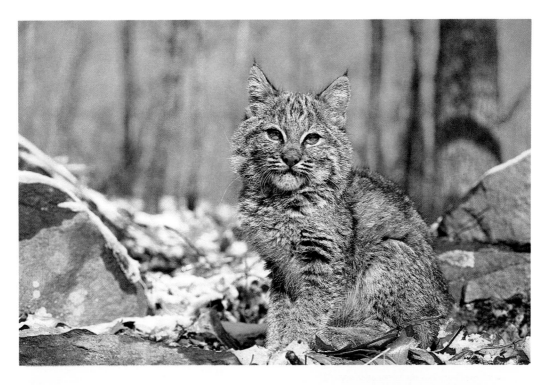

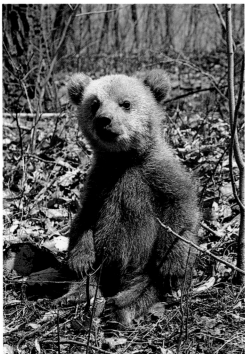

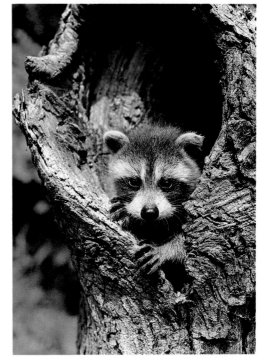

Top Portraits of wildlife, such as this young bobcat, should be taken at eye level or lower.
Bottom left Everyone who sees this baby grizzly bear falls in love with it. It makes them remember the cuddly toy bears most people had when they were little.
Bottom right That this baby raccoon was photographed in a hollow tree establishes the fact that raccoons seek such trees as dens.

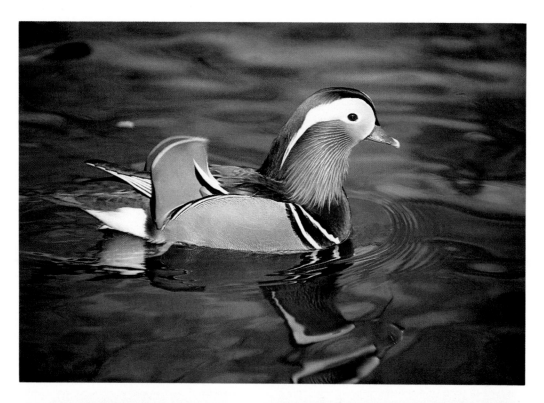

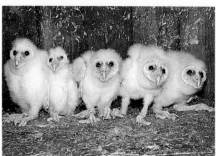

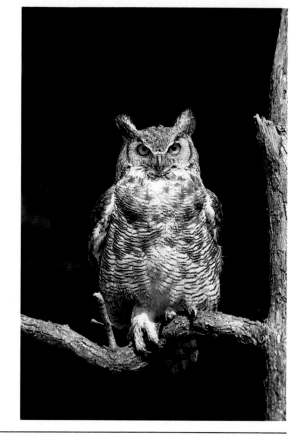

Top The Mandarin duck is probably the most colorful duck in the world and is common in many parks and collections.
Above left The first wildlife photos I ever took were of baby barn owls. These, taken thirty years later, are much better.
Right Now protected by law, the increasing population of great horned owls should be easier to photograph.
Opposite The use of DDT pushed the bald eagle to the brink of extinction. Since the poison was banned, the eagles are slowly regaining their numbers.

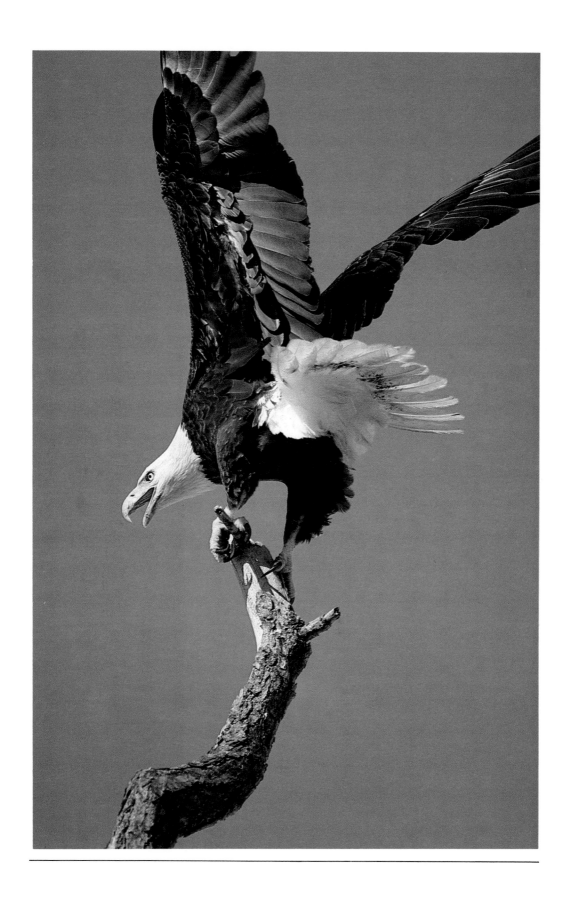

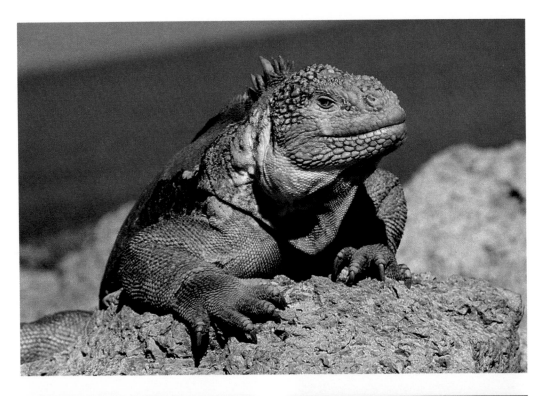

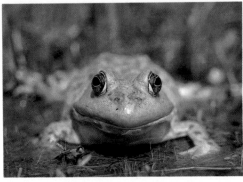

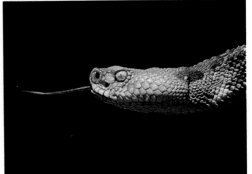

Top All of the creatures in the Galapagos Islands, such as this land iguana, allow photographers to approach closely.

Above left This low angle view of a bullfrog shows that I was in deeper water than the frog was.

Middle right Extreme caution should always be used when photographing poisonous specimens such as this timber rattlesnake.

Bottom right Dragonflies will return again and again to the same perch, which makes them easy to photograph.

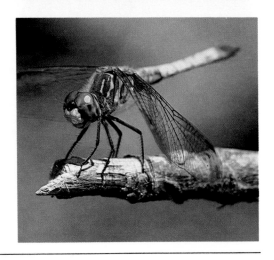

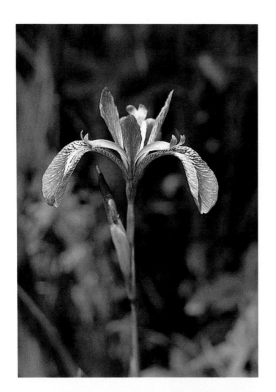

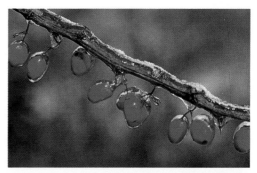

Left Although wildflower shots do not sell well, I continue to record the flowers' beauty, as I have done with this wild blue flag.
Below right Don't put your camera away in the winter. Photos such as these ice-encased barberries await those who brave the cold.
Bottom I deliberately cast a black shadow over the background in order to make this teasel blossom stand out.

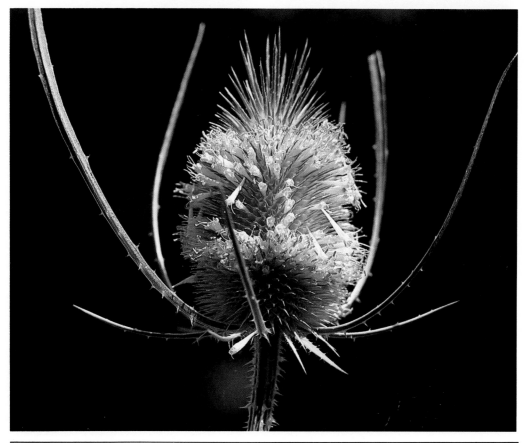

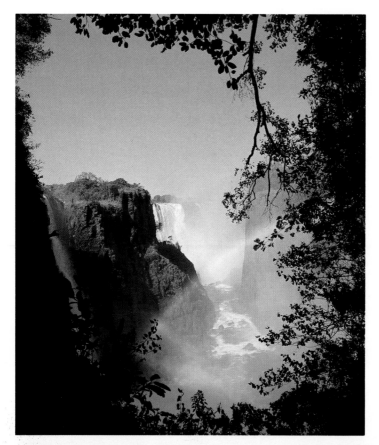

Top Victoria Falls on the Zambesi River, taken from the Zimbabwe side, is a scenic photographer's delight.
Bottom My camera lens was opened wide and the shutter was held open allowing the lightning of this desert storm to etch itself upon the film.

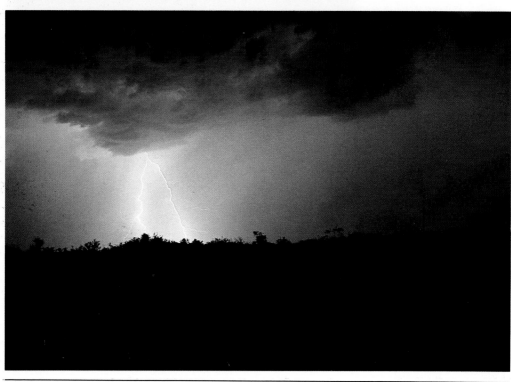

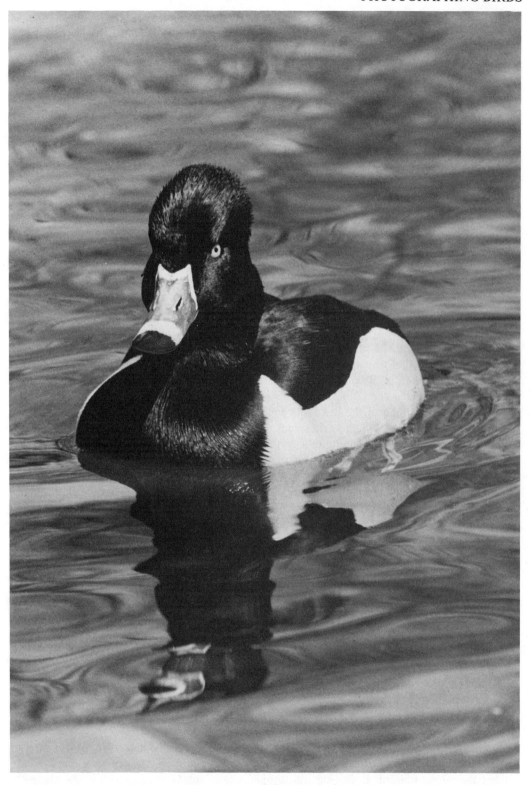

The lower you can get your camera, the better eyeball-to-eyeball perspective you can get on your subject. This is a male ringed-neck duck. Photo by Irene Vandermolen

bottom in the blind or bring something, such as a burlap bag or a piece of old rug, to put under my feet. Flex your toes and fingers as much as possible to increase their circulation. In bitterly cold weather, use some sort of a heater, if only a candle lantern.

I find it better to snack lightly while in a blind rather than eat a large lunch. Snacking gives you something to do when the action is slow, whereas a large lunch may make you sleepy.

Be sure that you have gone to the bathroom before you go to your blind, and urinate at the last possible moment as you leave your car to start for the blind. I carry a wide-mouth, one-quart plastic bottle with a tight-fitting lid to hold urine while in the blind.

Bird Photography by Remote Control

It is often much simpler to take bird photographs by remote control, camouflaging the camera, instead of building a blind. In instances such as photographing raptor nests on cliffs, it is the only way.

I always prefer working from a blind where possible because then you can swing and refocus the camera as the subject moves or comes in from an unexpected angle. With remote control, you have the camera set up and focused on a fixed spot and can work only when the subject enters that spot. If birds are coming to a nest or den hole, the area covered is usually sufficient to take in the action. Also, when using a remote release, a shorter telephoto helps ensure greater area coverage, a greater depth of field, and a greater possibility of getting your subject in the frame.

In order not to scare the birds off their nests, the camera should also be brought into the area in stages. Instead of leaving the actual camera out, I make a dummy camera out of a block of wood with a tin can in place of the lens. A tripod of three sticks can be used to hold this apparatus. My cameras are all black, and so I paint the dummy camera and tin can black, except for the "lens" end of the can. This end I leave bright so that the birds can be accustomed to the bright "eye" of the actual lens when it is in place. When the birds are accustomed to the dummy camera, simply substitute the real camera, and you are ready to shoot.

The camera can be tripped by the use of an air hose, an electronic tripping device, or a radio control unit.

The most sophisticated tripping device is the electric eye. We have all experienced having a door in a shopping mall or supermarket open as we approached it. Somewhere, as we approached, we broke a beam of electricity, which activated the door-opening device.

To use the electric eye, you must know the path that the wildlife will take to go to feed or to its nest or den. Only experimentation can tell you how far beyond the broken beam the wildlife will travel before the camera and flash go off. When this is ascertained, the electric beam and its receiver are set up opposite one another and out of the area seen by the camera lens. As the wildlife passes through the beam, the electricity is interrupted, and the impulse is carried by wire to the motorized camera, which is then activated and a picture is taken. A more complicated but more foolproof system employs the use of a laser light and reflecting mirrors, which bounce the beam of light back and forth, making a grid instead of a single beam for the wildlife to pass through. After setting up an electric eye, a motorized camera, and electronic flash, you can take an entire roll of film without being there. All you have to do is to come back now and then to change the film.

To get the ultimate sharpness to your photos when using any lens, but particularly when using long telephoto lenses, whether tripping the camera by a remote electronic release or by a cable release, fasten the mirror on the camera in the *up* position. The movement of the mirror with the taking of each picture is just one more cause for vibration that can be eliminated by locking the mirror upward. If you can also support the telephoto lens, as well as the camera, that will reduce vibration. Hanging a weight from your tripod's center column will greatly reduce the possibility of vibration. Placing a sandbag on the top of the lens, over the tripod

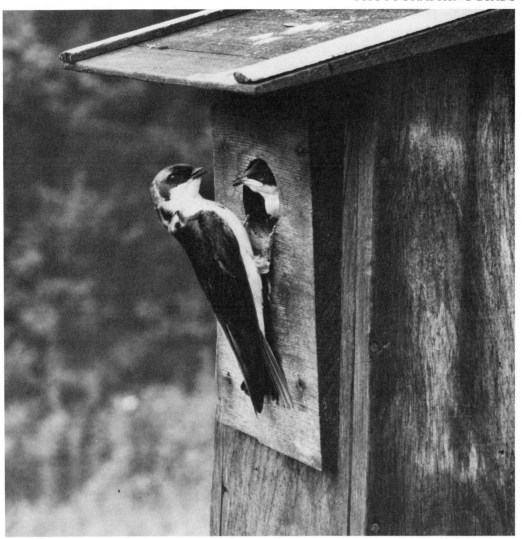

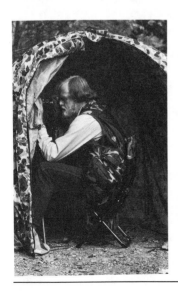

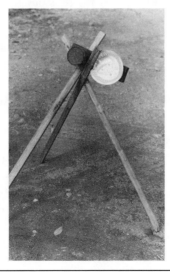

Top This photograph of a male tree swallow feeding its young was taken by a remote release. The focus was set for 1 inch outside the hole. *Bottom left* A photo stool must have a back for support and tubular sections across the legs to prevent the stool from sinking in soft soil. *Bottom right* A dummy tripod, camera, and flashgun to be put near a bird's nest before putting up the real equipment. Photo by Irene Vandermolen

center, will reduce vibration. Anything that reduces vibration increases the sharpness of the picture.

When you are using your camera by remote you should also close the viewing eyepiece, if your camera has this feature, because it may affect the light metering system. When you are taking the photograph with your eye at the viewfinder, your face and the eyecup block out most of the extraneous light. When your face is not blocking the light, the light can enter the eyepiece and be bounced into the camera's interior by the mirror. It may give a false exposure reading.

Lighting for Bird Photography

I have repeatedly stated that I do not like to use flash for any subjects, but at times it is a necessity. I dislike using flash because it usually makes it appear as if the photos were taken at night. Synchro-sunlight lessens this problem. Multiple flash puts too many highlights in the subject's eyes, instantly identifying it as a flash setup and most often a studio setup. Most wild creatures accept flash without being unduly alarmed because they have become conditioned to natural lightning flashes. If a wild creature seems to panic when a photograph is being lit by flash, it most likely has been frightened by the sound of the shutter and film advancing mechanisms rather than by the light of the flash.

Electronic flash photography with most focal plane shutter cameras is difficult because the flash can be synchronized only at 1/60 or 1/80 of a second. The new Nikon FM2 will sync at 1/125 of a second. With regular focal plane shutter cameras there is no problem if the picture is taken at night or in dark situations. When a flash picture is taken in good light at these sync speeds, a "ghost image" occurs, recording as a blur the movement of the subject that was not stopped by the peak of the electronic flash discharge.

To avoid this problem, many photographers use cameras, such as the Hasselblad, that have a leaf shutter in the camera's lens or body. These leaf shutters synchronize with electronic flash at any shutter-speed setting.

When using just one flash, the flash should always be off to one side of the camera and raised slightly so that the lighting will not be flat and shadowless. This will also prevent the "red-eye" reflection of your subject. Most flash units are capable of being used either in the manual or fully automatic mode, and there are advantages to both.

When the flash is set on automatic an electric sensor reads the amount of light that has reached the subject and is being bounced back. When sufficient light has reached the subject to allow the photo to be properly exposed at the set's designated f stop, the unit is shut off before all the stored electricity has been discharged from the capacitor. Most people use their electronic flash at automatic because it is easier and usually results in comparatively foolproof photos. Most strobes have a ready light that glows to let you know the unit is charged. I suggest that to get a full charge, you wait about 5 seconds after the light begins to glow before you shoot.

I would like to interject one note here: You should test your lens, flash, and film combination on simulated subjects under field conditions before you do any serious shooting. Most manufacturers' guide numbers and recommendations are made for indoor shooting by the average photographer. When shooting indoors, depending on the colors involved, most surfaces of walls and ceilings will bounce back most of the light flashed on them, and there is usually additional ambient light. When you shoot outdoors, most surfaces will absorb the light without reflectancy, and there may be no ambient light at all. The differences in the actual guide numbers or f-stop settings that you have to use may vary as much as three complete stops (maybe even more) from the manufacturers' recommendations. The only way that you can tell what your unit will do and what it will enable you to do is by extensive testing.

Another advantage of using the flash on automatic is that the duration of the flash becomes

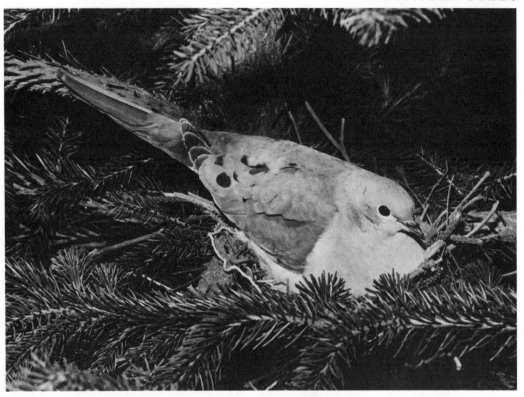

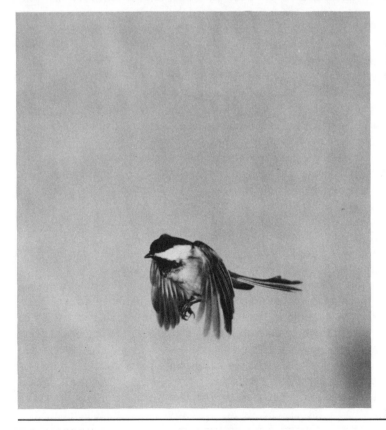

Top This mourning dove was photographed with a single flash to the right and above the camera. *Bottom* This black-capped chickadee took its own photograph by flying through the beam of an electric eye.

shorter (i.e., faster) the closer the light is moved to the subject. With many of the small commercial lights, speeds of 1/50,000 of a second are possible at distances of 12 to 18 inches. Also, by using the flash automatically, conserving part of the power in each shot, the batteries used for recharging will last longer, and more shots can be taken.

The advantage of using the flash manually is that the unit discharges completely with each flash, giving far more power, and so a higher guide number can be used. This allows the lens to be closed down for additional depth of field. Conversely, the complete discharge of the unit drains the batteries quicker, lessening the number of flashes possible with the unit.

A disadvantage of using any flash by remote is that the unit must be turned on before you leave the area. Most units cannot stand the drain of being left on for 6 to 8 hours at a time, not counting the flash discharge of power. I know of no commercial flash unit that can be turned on and off from a distance, although units can be customized by electronic experts. If the unit could be turned on and off from a distance, it could be left off till the subject came into the area and then switched on. When the subject left the area, the set could be switched off. That would save a lot of battery power, pictures, and photographers' frustration.

When possible, two strobes should be used, one main light situated above and slightly off to one side of the camera. The second light should be on the opposite side of, and away from, the camera about 3 feet and farther back or set at one-half power to be used as a fill-in flash.

The ideal situation is when a third light can be used behind and above the subject to act as a backlight. This will cause rimlighting and allow the subject to stand out in contrast to the background. The backlight must be high enough so that its light does not shine into the camera lens and cause halation. It must also be back farther from the subject than the main light so as not to throw a shadow in front of the subject. I don't like a backlight because it does not give the subject a natural appearance. Both fill-in and backlights can be connected by cords to, and fired by, a main battery pack, or they can have their own batteries and be fired by slave units.

The new Nikon F3, the Olympus, and some other cameras have a specialized electronic flash, known as dedicated flash, which is metered right from the film plane. Using these lights, the exposure for regular flash is supposed to be perfect every time. It is, for most normal situations. I have found that I cannot use my unit in deep shade to photograph nests. The sensor does not know what object is to be read, what it should concentrate on. The blinking diode inside the viewfinder keeps calling for more light even when there is sufficient light to expose the photograph properly. So, from personal experience, I have found that the dedicated flash units just do not work for nature photographers.

There are hundreds of different flash units on the market, running in cost from $10 to thousands of dollars. The flash units come with many different modes. Some units can only be used manually, some can be used manually or automatically. On some units the amount of power discharged can be controlled manually or automatically. Some units do the same thing by allowing you to set the power by dialing the f stop you desire to shoot. Some units are battery powered, some are AC powered, and many can be used either way.

With the flash unit you purchase will be a sheet of instructions that gives the recommended guide number or the light output of the flash in Beam Candle Power Seconds (BCPS).

If you are using your flash unit manually, use the guide number as a starting point to make the tests I've suggested. Set your camera on the 1/60, 1/80, or 1/125 shutter-speed sync line, if using a focal plane shutter, or on any desired shutter speed if using a leaf shutter. Measure the distance from the flash, not from the camera, to the subject. Divide the number of feet from flash to the subject into the guide number to find your f stop number. If the guide number is 80 for a film speed of ASA-ISO/64, and the distance is 10 feet, your f stop is f/8. But test this under actual field conditions, and bracket two or three stops on each side of the designated number. Then, when your film comes back check to see which f stop was perfectly exposed and multiply that f stop by the distance to get your own tested guide number.

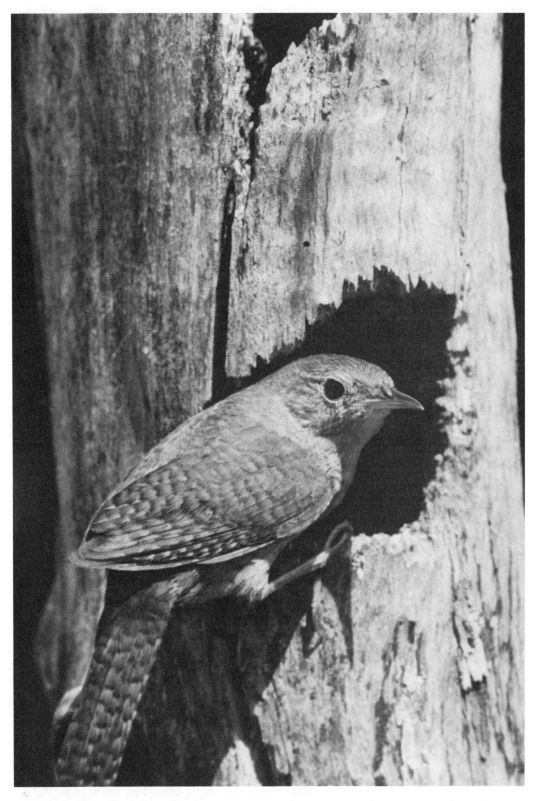

This house wren's photo was taken using the new Nikon MLI red-light transmitter and receiver.

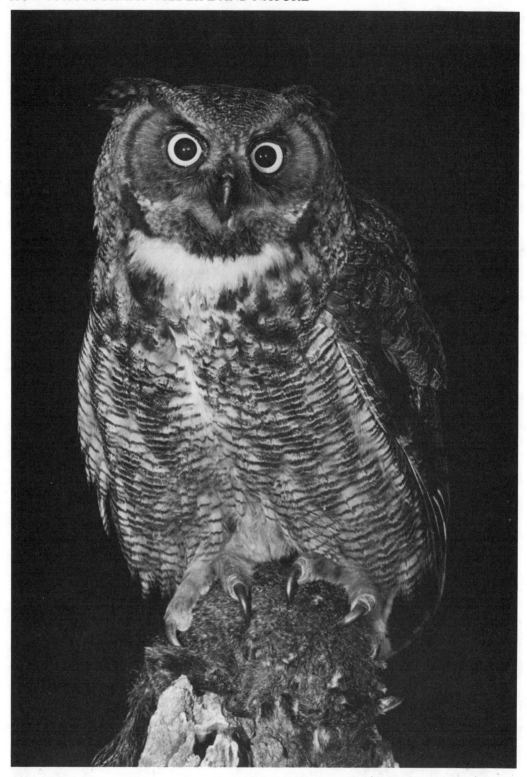

This great horned owl was attracted by the bait of a road-killed squirrel. The photo was taken with two flash units.

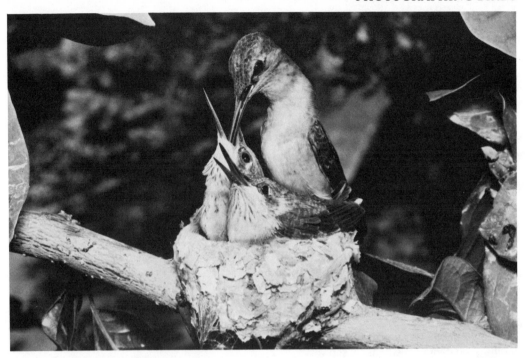

Two lights were used to take this photo of a broad-tailed hummingbird. The left-hand flash was about 3 feet from the camera; it does not show in the birds' eyes because of the angle of their heads.

Flash units that supply the BCPS number usually supply a nomograph or chart with the unit. To find the guide number, you line up the BCPS number and the ASA-ISO rating, and that gives you the guide number. Then you must run the tests described above. A flash meter may also be used to determine proper exposure.

Many photographers take all their wildlife photographs with flash, even when the subject is in the sunlight. They do this because the speed of the flash stops all action, and they can still shoot even if a cloud temporarily covers the sun.

I will state again: I do not like to do this. I prefer natural light, even though I miss pictures because of some blurring or because of some cloud. If you are going to use a strobe, it is important that the speed of the light discharge be as fast as possible. Most strobes flash at between 1/1000 to 1/2000 of a second. That is much faster than you can ever shoot color film without flash. However, those speeds will not stop all motion in wildlife. A flash at 1/5000 will stop most action; 1/10,000 is better yet. The wings of hummingbirds usually make 75 to 200 complete strokes every second, and insects' wings beat even faster. The fantastic insect flight photos by Stephen Dalton were taken at 1/25,000 of a second. His customized, specialized equipment allows us to see sights never before seen.

If you want to shoot wildlife photographs with flash so that pictures do not appear to be taken at night, you must understand how to synchronize sunlight with your flash. This cannot be done with all cameras or with all flashes, as I have already explained. The key to the entire setup is this: Sync the camera's shutter speed to the available daylight, and sync the lens f stop to match the electronic flash output.

Here is how it is done. It does not matter whether the bird and its nest are in sunlight or in deep shade. Even if the nest is in the shade, you can usually see daylight through the bushes beyond the shaded nest. Meter the daylight, which in the eastern half of the United States is

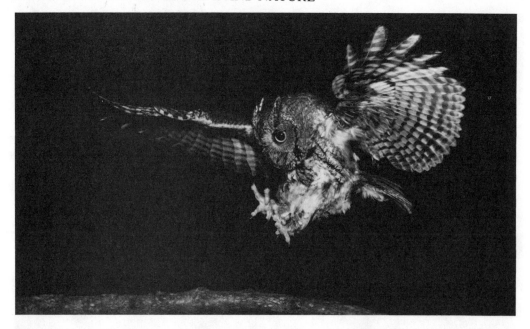

This photograph of a screech owl was taken with my custom-made electronic flash set on manual for the good depth of field that is shown.

about 1/125 at $f/9$ on a bright, sunny day. Using my Nikon FM2 or my Hasselblad, I set the flash sync at a shutter speed of 1/125 of a second. I set my lens opening at $f/9$ and my Metz strobe on automatic at $f/9$ and shoot. I use my Sunpak strobe manually, and if I am 6 feet from the nest, I set the strobe dial at $f/9$, which cuts the unit down to 1/6 power and shoot. Both the nest and the background are now perfectly balanced, eliminating the nighttime appearance.

Basically this is how it is done with the equipment I use. Using this information as a guide, you will have to test whatever film, camera, lens, and strobe that you use.

Birds in Flight

Stopping birds in flight with an electronic flash and an electric eye is comparatively easy if you have the proper equipment. Stopping birds in flight in a natural environment is much more difficult, and your success depends almost entirely on your abilities. Nevertheless, some specialized equipment can help you do the job better and easier.

The fastest focusing lens I know of is the Novoflex system. This system consists of a basic pistol-grip focusing device with interchangeable lenses, a shoulder pod, build in extension tubes, and an adapter to fit almost any camera made. By squeezing the focusing device, the lens slides forward or backward, and that's fast focusing. My Nikon 3 is aperture preferred, so by presetting the f stop, I use the camera and lens like a rifle. As I follow my subject, the camera adjusts the shutter speed, and my exposure is correct throughout the different sky shades.

The gradation of light on a bright, sunny sky can vary as much as four full camera stops, being brightest nearest the sun and darkest on the horizon away from the sun. To do flight shots, I usually meter the sky, not my subject, which may be much lighter or darker than the sky. By metering the sky and having the blue correctly exposed, any bird in the sky will fall within the proper range and be exposed correctly. But be sure that you meter the portion of the sky that the subject is in. Watch those different bands of light. The metering I have just

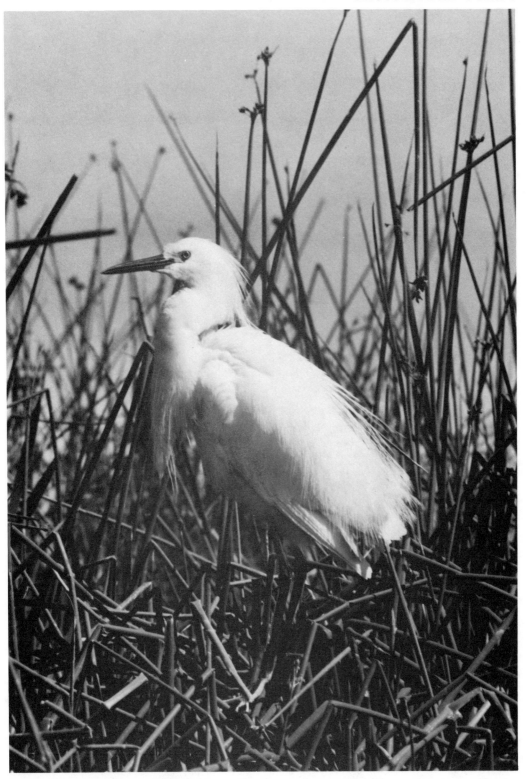

I took this photograph of a snowy egret with normal daylight lighting. The sun was high, as you can see by the bird's belly being in shadow.

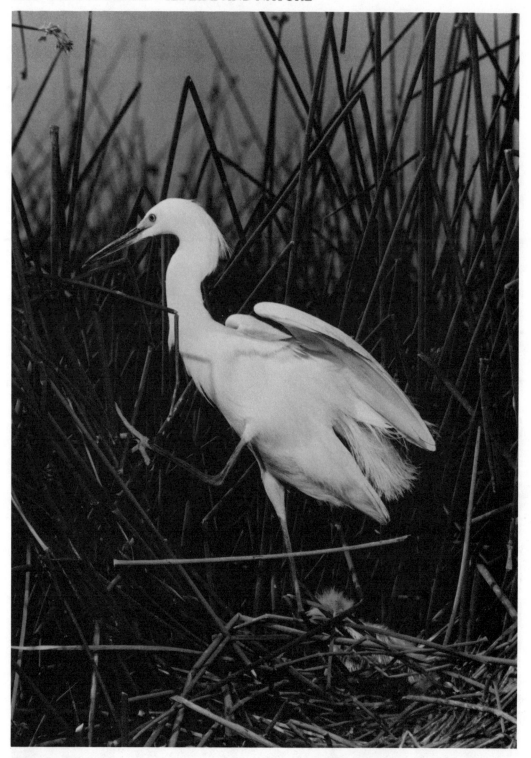

This snowy egret was photographed in daylight using the sunlight synchronized with two flash units. The sky is just one stop darker, and the photo does not have the appearance of being taken at night. However, I do not like the unnatural flat appearance caused by a lack of the sun's shadow.

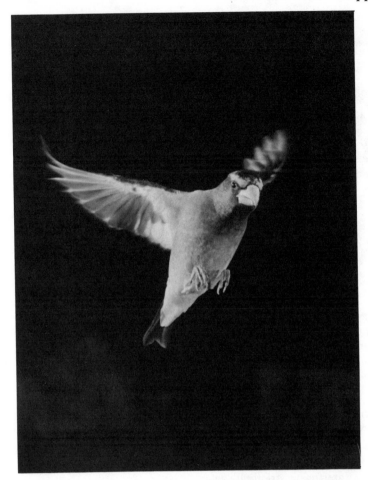

Most commercial electronic flash units will not stop the wing action of birds unless they are 12 to 18 inches from the subject. Most birds will not approach lights set that close.

given is for either a light or a dark subject photographed against a blue sky. If the sky is filled with puffy, white clouds and if the subject is either a white gull or a black vulture, meter the clouds and open the lens two stops and shoot.

Naturally, the larger the bird, the easier it is to photograph. And the slower the bird flies, the easier it is to photograph, which is why soaring birds are easier to photograph than flapping-flight birds. Ducks are among the fastest fliers, exceeded only by some swifts, hawks, and falcons. By knowing that most larger birds have to take off into the wind, you can gauge in which direction they are going to fly. Birds taking off or flying into a headwind are flying much slower than if they have the wind behind them. When a very strong wind is blowing, some birds flying into it are almost stopped in midair. Good flight photos can be taken from ships or from the tops of cliffs, for many soaring birds remain almost motionless in such air currents . Large birds also land into the wind.

Although many photographers want to hand-hold all their flight shots with a shoulder pod, I prefer using my tripod. I use either a Gitzo ball head or a Miller fluid pan head on my tripod, and I shoot the camera and lens as I would an antiaircraft gun. Both heads allow me to pan smoothly and prevent the camera from moving up and down as I move sideways.

When I cannot use a tripod, for example on a bouncing boat deck or in a plane, I use a gyroscope stabilizer. With a battery-powered gyro spinning at high speeds, the camera and lens almost take on a life of their own. Despite the ups and downs I make, the gyro keeps the camera level and allows smooth panning horizontally. The gyroscope can be a real boon to the bird photographer doing flight shots.

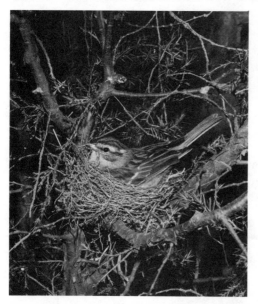

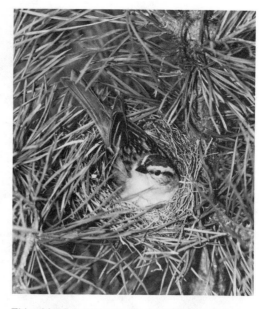

I shot this chipping sparrow with a single flash unit, and although the light illuminated both the bird and the nest, the photograph appears to have been taken at night.

This chipping sparrow photograph was taken using synchro-sunlight. The bird and the nest are illuminated beautifully, yet the background is still lighted by sunlight.

Decoys for Birds

I mentioned some of the various calls that can be used for birds, but some calls work even better if used with decoys. A stool of decoys is very important for luring ducks and geese within gun range and can also be used effectively for flight photos of these birds. If you cannot use a duck call convincingly, you can use an electronic call, but only for photographs. The use of an electronic call for hunting waterfowl is strictly illegal.

Decoys are also being used more frequently in hunting wild turkeys. The decoy and a good turkey call can be irresistible to an old gobbler. I have found that a decoy works better if you can move it ever so slightly now and then by pulling on it with a black thread looped around two different trees so that the decoy can be pivoted.

Another trick that works well with a turkey decoy is to fasten a couple of small turkey feathers by a thread hanging below the decoy's head. The feathers will stir in the breeze and will create the illusion of movement needed for success.

I don't know of anyone else doing it, but I have found that the use of a shorebird decoy or two helps attract, and hold, shorebirds of all kinds. I also use a "fear allaying" decoy in the form of a great blue heron decoy. These herons are among the wariest of birds, and all other birds seem to recognize this fact. So, if I'm trying for photographs of ducks, geese, herons, or shorebirds, I stick my heron decoy somewhere near my blind. When the other birds see that the heron is there, they know the area is safe for them. Cabela's Outfitters has just put out the first commercially available heron decoy. My secret is out; now others will be able to do as I have done. I use crow and dove decoys as well, when I'm working with these birds.

I live only a few miles from the Appalachian ridge that is followed by most of the hawks, in the eastern states, in migration each fall. An owl decoy, even one made of papier-mache, stuck up on a high pole, will have the hawks barreling in to attack it. It takes fast camera handling to follow the dive of some falcon at speeds of up to, and over, 100 miles per hour. Although good photos of these birds in flight are hard to come by, they are readily salable because most photographers don't try for them.

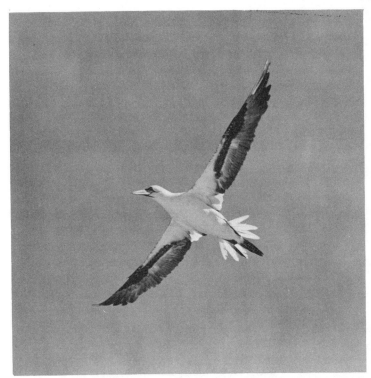

Top The easiest flight shots are of birds like this gannet that soar by on the air currents. *Bottom* The Novoflex lens is the fastest-focusing lens system in the world. The lens is focused by squeezing the pistol grip.

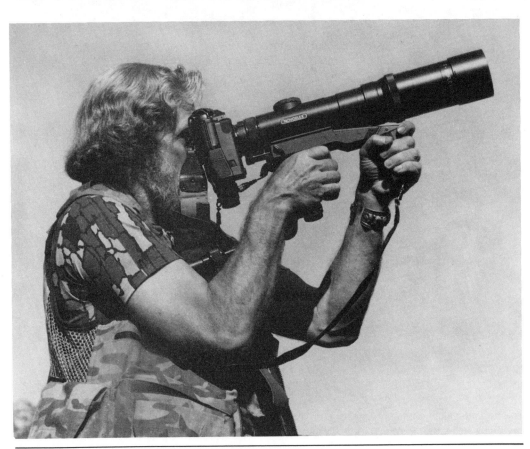

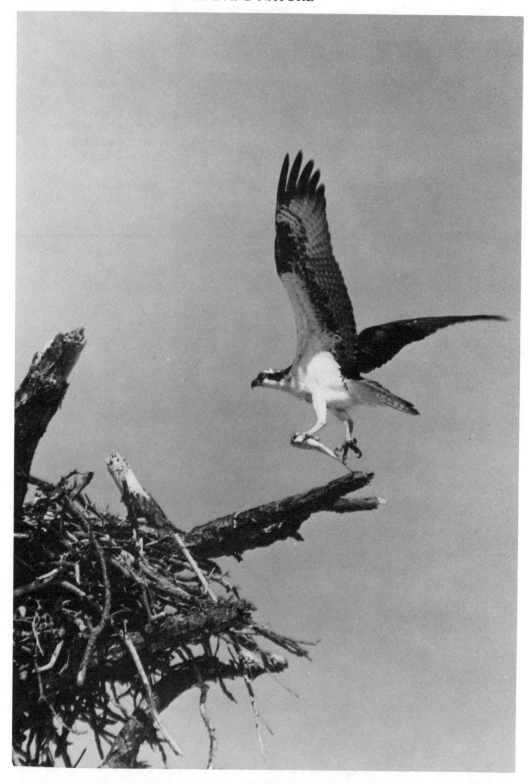

This beautiful flight shot of an osprey carrying a fish was possible because of the bird's comparatively slow wingbeat. Photo by Irene Vandermolen

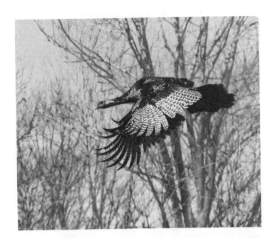

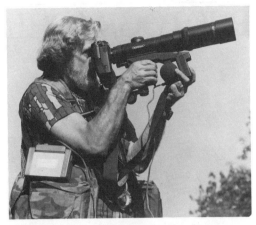

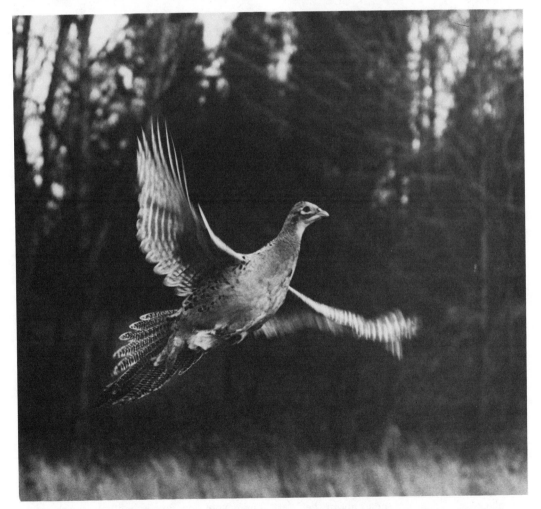

Top left The high speed of the black and white film allowed this fast-flying turkey to be frozen in midair. Note the pinions bent under the force of the wing stroke. Photo by Irene Vandermolen

Top right A gyroscope stabilizer is great for flight photography because it allows you to hand-hold a large lens without using a tripod.

Bottom I was almost able to stop this hen pheasant in flight, except for its rapidly beating wings.

PHOTOGRAPHING ANIMALS

I pray as if everything depended on God and
work as if everything depended on me.
                                    —Anonymous

Although I photograph everything in the great out-of-doors, I am happiest photographing animals. I love all of God's creatures, but I love animals most of all. Perhaps they shaped my life more than any other form of wildlife. I am a naturalist first and foremost; my first interest has always been, and always will be, studying the life history of wildlife. I am a naturalist today because I was a trapper as a kid. That's how I got my basic knowledge about wildlife, particularly animals. I am a photographer because I am a frustrated artist. I always wanted to draw and paint wildlife, and I cannot. I capture it on film instead of canvas. I lecture and write because I want to show the beauty of God's creatures to others and share my knowledge of these creatures with others. Photography and lecturing and writing about wildlife allow me to make a living so that I can spend time studying wild creatures, particularly animals.

How to Locate Animals

Many good books, including mine, can tell you where to look for wildlife generally. I have included a list of these books in the bibliography. Long before you go out to photograph animals, you should either be in the field learning about them or at home reading all you can about them—preferably both. I read every wildlife book I can get my hands on because we all have so much to learn. The more you know about animals, the more successful you will be in photographing them.

Each animal is adapted to live in a specific habitat. The muskrats, beaver, nutria, and river otter are found only around water. The sea otter can be found only along the Pacific coast from California to Alaska. Wild sheep and goats live only in our western mountains. Pronghorn antelopes are dwellers of the plains. White-tailed deer are found almost everywhere; mule deer and black-tailed deer are seen only in the West. The coyote now dwells in all the continental states, while the wolf has been extirpated from most of the lower 48 states. Woodchucks are found in the Northeast and across the continent to Alaska. Their cousins, the marmots, live only in the West. There is only one chipmunk east of the Mississippi River—and 14 species west of it. The cougar, which is thought of as a western cat, is now reappearing in mountainous

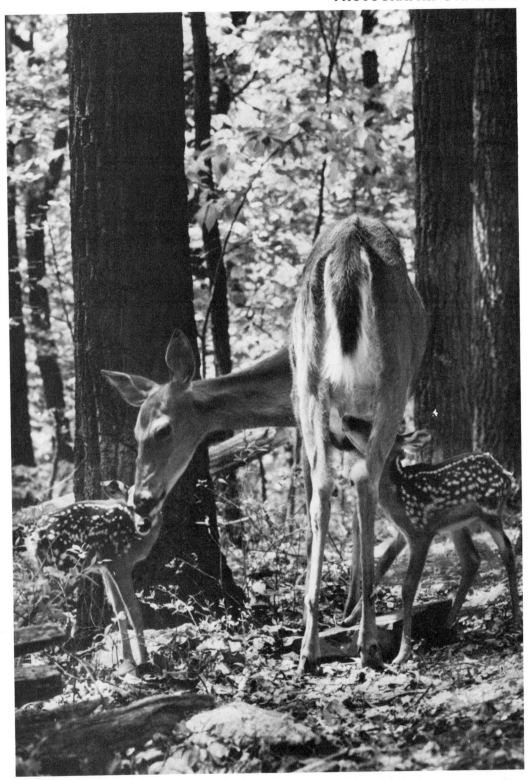

This photograph of a white-tailed doe and her fawns is one of my favorites, not only because it is aesthetically pleasing, but because it has been published at least 100 times.

areas of our eastern states. There are over 100 species of mice, some of which are found in every conceivable habitat in North America. Some mice have a widespread range, some are restricted to a very small area. Bats are our second most numerous animal form and are found across the continent, but they are not well known and are seldom seen because of their nocturnal habits. With the exception of the bison herd near Delta, Alaska, there are no "wild," free-roaming bison in the United States. There are bison living wild in our national refuges and parks, and a large number live on private land.

All of the above is just general knowledge, but it is the kind of basic knowledge you need. One thing you must keep in mind is that when you are out-of-doors, for every creature you see, probably a hundred have already seen you and have either run or flown off or have hidden. You just do not see that much wildlife most of the time. I don't have to. I can read sign, tell what animals are in the area by their tracks, droppings, dens, bits of hair or fur, cuttings, prey remnants, and so on. The better you can read sign, the better equipped you are to take advantage of what the out-of-doors has to offer.

If you are going to work in a national park or refuge, reading sign is of less importance because the animals are protected and usually do not fear humans. The best way to locate wildlife in the parks is, first, to speak to the park naturalists and rangers. Take a topographic map with you and have these experienced people mark the actual area in which they have seen the various species you are interested in.

The best way to locate wildlife in the parks is to drive along slowly in a car. Wild creatures are not afraid of a car as they are of a person on foot, and so they are not as apt to hide or run away. With a car you can cover a hundred times more territory than you can on foot. I'm not trying to encourage laziness; a car is the only practical way of covering large areas. It takes a high degree of skill to spot wildlife from a moving car, but it is a learned skill. I have seen many people who had no previous experience develop into exceptional game spotters. And you don't always look for the obvious animals; you look for the odd shape, the bump, the twitch of an ear or tail, the flash of an antler. You look for what is "out of place." Once you become familiar with an area, with its trees, stumps, logs, and rocks, you will quickly note the additional "blob" that may be an animal.

In national parks you will find a lot of animals by finding other photographers who found the animals first. Although the park animals belong to all of us, common courtesy demands that you respect the rights of other photographers. If a group of photographers is working on an animal, it is permissible to join in. But, use your long lenses; don't push in front of others. Most wildlife photographers use long lenses so that they don't "push" the animal they are working on. Many tourists shoot with instamatic cameras with short lenses. The tourist is much more likely to run up to get close to the animal, either forcing the animal to flee or endangering himself and others.

If a single photographer has found an animal and is working on it, ask permission to join him before you move up. I have never been refused such a request, nor have I ever denied it to others. Be courteous and be safe.

The sign of some animals are so conspicuous that they cannot be missed. Beavers cannot hide their whereabouts. Their white stump cuttings can be seen at a long distance. Beavers can alter their environment more than any other animal, and their dams create ponds and lakes. Dead trees standing in flooded areas are a sure sign of beavers even when you cannot see the dam. Beavers also build large bowl-shaped lodges, dig canals, and make well-worn trails.

Muskrat houses are conspicuous in swamplands. Their feces on rocks and stumps advertise their presence even when they live in holes in the bank.

Squirrel den holes in live trees usually exhibit white edges where the squirrels cut back the bark to keep the hole from growing closed. Their leaf nests in treetops are basket-size and cannot be missed. Hawk and crow nests are near the trunks of trees, squirrel nests are in the uppermost branches. Cut-open nut shells identify the squirrel's work.

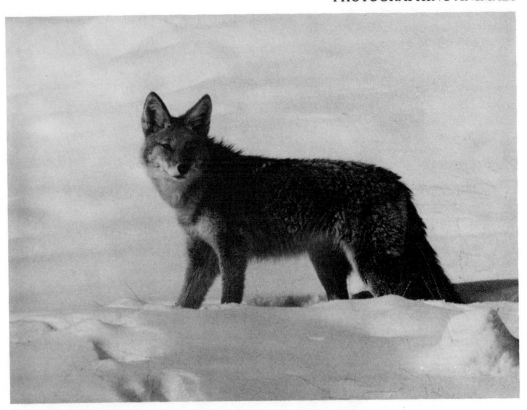

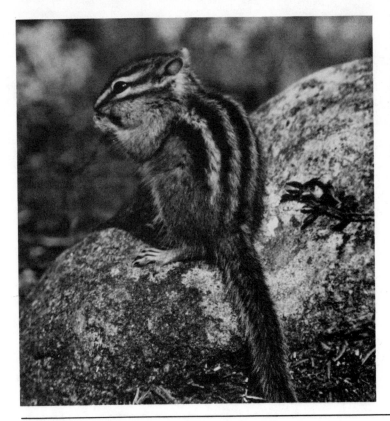

Top The coyote is undoubtedly the most intelligent wild mammal in North America. Photo by Len Rue, Jr. *Bottom* The least chipmunk is just one of dozens of ground squirrels found west of the Mississippi River.

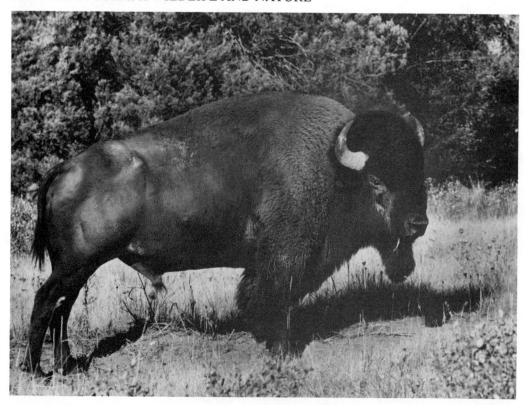

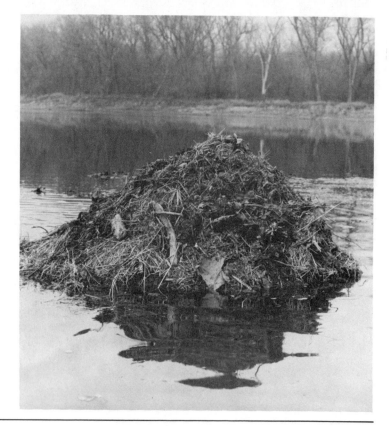

Top In the early days the bison was found in the eastern half of the United States as well as on the western plains.

Bottom Muskrat houses are large mounds of vegetation that can easily be seen.

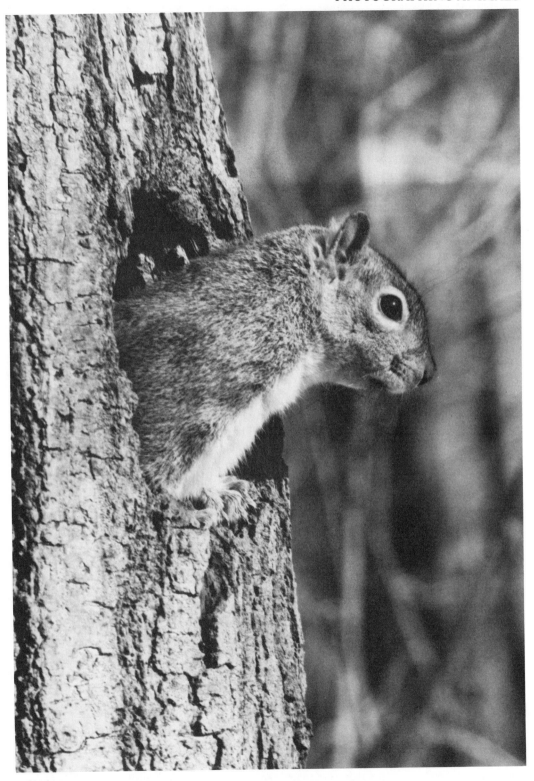

Gray squirrels live in natural tree cavities or abandoned woodpecker nest holes. Photo by Irene Vandermolen

The excavated dirt from the burrows of woodchucks is easily and commonly seen. Their cousins, the marmots, make similar mounds. The miniature volcano-shaped mounds of the blacktailed prairie dogs' burrows cannot be confused with that of any of the other ground squirrels. Most other ground squirrels excavate dirt, but in much smaller quantities. Because the squirrels are smaller, so is the diameter of their burrows. Eastern chipmunks have only a single entrance hole with no excavated dirt visible.

A red fox will frequently take over the burrow of a woodchuck after eating the original owner. The fox, being long legged, will remodel the burrow with the resultant shape of the opening a vertical oval. Because of the extra excavation, a lot more dirt is scattered in front of the fox burrow. As red foxes use a burrow only to raise their young, there will be remnants of prey animals scattered about that were brought in by the parents to feed the young. All of these facts about red foxes are true, but on a larger scale, for coyotes and wolves. Red fox burrows are most frequently found in open areas; coyote and wolf dens are more apt to be found along the banks of arroyos, gullies, and rivers.

The trunk of every hollow tree should be checked carefully for claw marks and hair pulled from the belly of raccoons. Raccoons also frequently defecate on the limbs and exposed roots of their den trees.

Dens of the big cats are hard to find unless snow is on the ground and then they may be tracked. You can often smell cats' dens as they frequently urinate on the rocks or stumps to proclaim ownership. You will seldom find their feces because most cats cover them with dirt, leaves, or snow. However, the raked-up covering will identify the cats' work.

Bears are constantly hungry. Find a food source in the wilderness, and you will find bears. The McNeil River in Alaska has the world's largest concentrations of Alaskan brown bears during the summer salmon run. Most grizzly bear photos taken today are taken at Sable Pass in McKinley National Park, Alaska. Most polar bear pictures are taken at Churchill, Manitoba, Canada. Any town dump or lumber-camp dump in a wild area will have bears feeding there on a regular schedule. Bear signs are easy to spot. Their huge, conspicuous tracks, claw marks on trees, and berry-filled feces proclaim bear. Most Dall sheep photos are taken in McKinley National Park, whereas most bighorn sheep photos are taken in Alberta in Jasper Provincial Park, Canada, or in Yellowstone. Photographers go to Glacier National Park in Montana for mountain goats. Alaskan moose are photographed in McKinley National Park and the Shiras moose in Yellowstone National Park. Pronghorn are also plentiful in Yellowstone. With all of these animals, most photographers look for the animals instead of their signs because these are the traditional spots that have been visited for years by the pros.

Deer trails, tracks, rubbed trees, bedding spots, and pellets are all common deer signs that can be located and read by even the novice. All deer east of the Mississippi River are whitetails. Most of the deer in the Rocky Mountains are mule deer. The deer found along Pacific coastal areas are usually black tails. Again, most photographers look for the deer, but reading sign simplifies the process. This is not a book on how to read tracks and tracking. However, I have gone on at some length here to help you locate animals and to impress upon you the importance of knowing about wildlife intimately. The photographer who can read animal signs will find more wildlife and will get more photographs than one who cannot.

Animal Behavior

As important as finding animals to photograph is the knowledge of what the animals you are attempting to photograph are likely to do when you attempt to photograph them.

All wildlife has a "flight or fight" distance. Most wildlife will allow you to approach to within a certain distance, for that particular species, before it will run off or hide. When you are beyond the flight distance, the wildlife will be aware of you in most instances but will not be too concerned because the distance increases its feeling of safety.

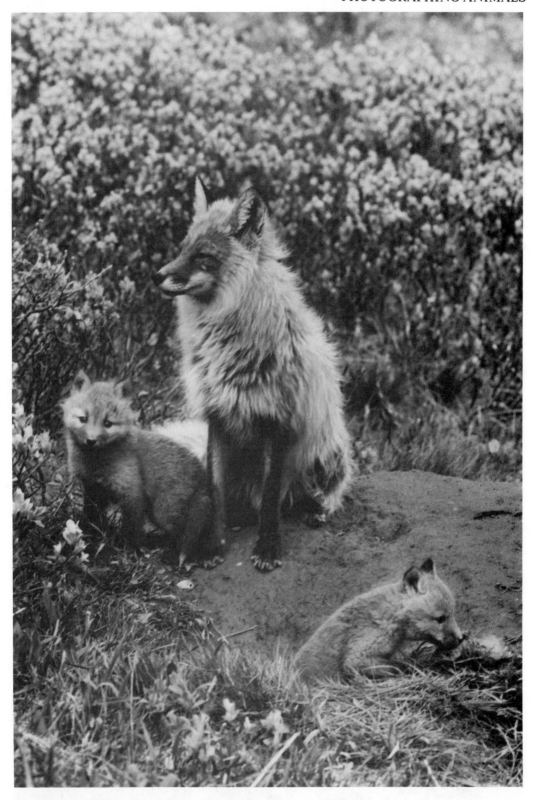

The red fox can dig its own den, but it usually takes over and enlarges that of a woodchuck.

Top This coyote pup is emerging from its den. *Bottom* Bobcats are seldom seen, but they can be tracked after a snowfall.

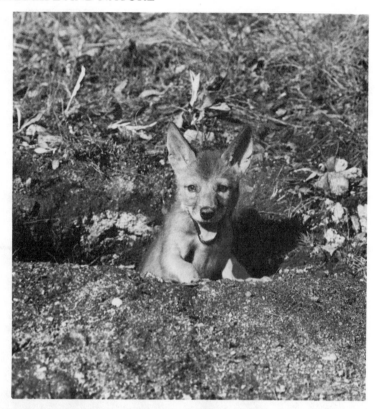

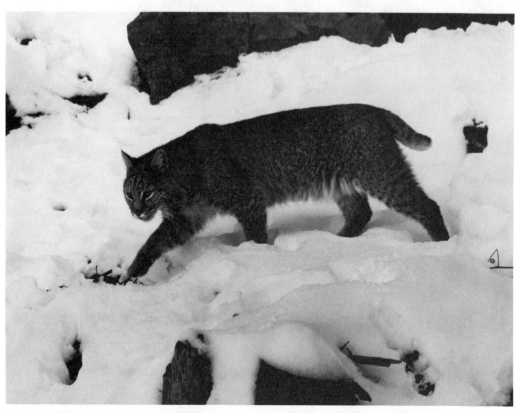

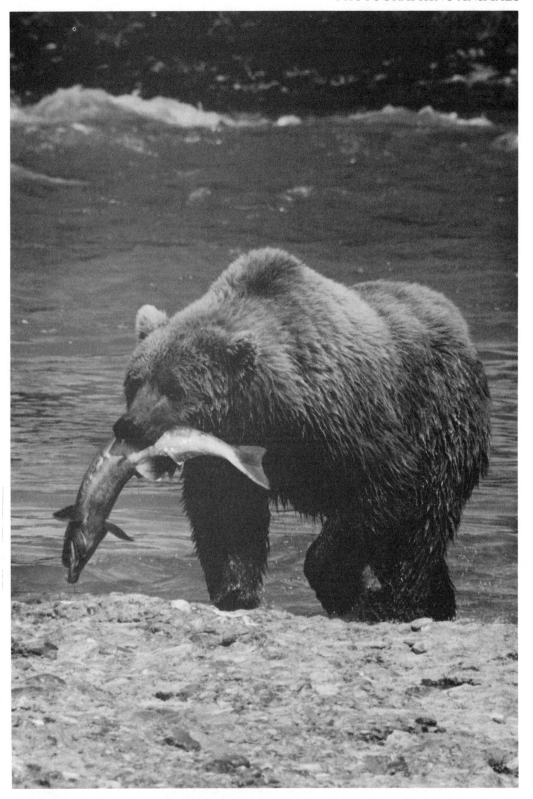

This Alaskan brown bear has caught a 28-inch salmon, one of a dozen it will eat each day.

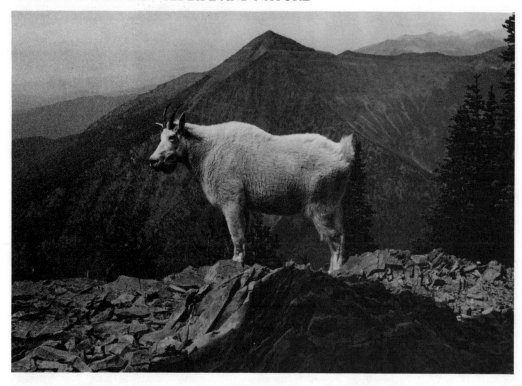

Mountain goat photographed on Brown's Peak in Glacier National Park, Montana.

As you come closer, the wildlife will become concerned because you are entering its flight distance. This distance is usually determined by the animals' size, strength, speed, and the amount of pressure a particular animal has been subjected to.

Most wild animals photographed today live in national parks and refuges. They have become accustomed to humans and do not flee at the sight of a man, as their heavily hunted counterparts do outside protected areas. Where animals are protected, the flight distance is greatly reduced or even eliminated. What remains is the "fight" distance.

Fight distance varies with the species, the sex of the animal, the time of year, and the individual animal. By fight distance is meant the area that when invaded, causes the animal to feel that its life, or the life of its young, is threatened. It feels cornered and attacks to protect itself.

An animal's concept of being cornered and our concept of its being cornered are usually two entirely different things. To us to be cornered is to be "boxed in." An animal may feel cornered in the wide-open spaces if you come upon it suddenly and surprise it.

The general behavior and response of wildlife to certain situations can be learned. I can inform you of some animal reactions. Knowledge of these facets of behavior could save your life. It must also be remembered that while the species as a whole usually does a certain thing, an individual creature may not. Wild creatures are individuals just as humans are. While most animals, most of the time, respond in a normal fashion, some individuals do not. So, always approach all wildlife subjects with the caution and respect they so rightly deserve.

I am constantly appalled by the ignorance exhibited by so many people when they attempt to photograph the wildlife that abounds in our national parks. I learned about wildlife by spending most of my life out-of-doors, living with and studying the wildlife I photograph. Most urban residents know only about the wildlife they see on television. There are good documentary shows about wildlife. Far too many of the shows, however, particularly the big-name shows

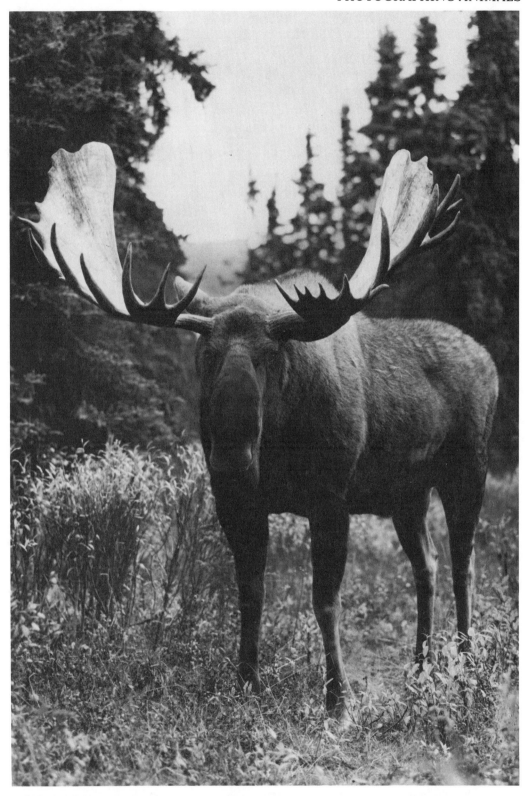

The Alaskan moose is the largest antlered animal in the world. Photo by Len Rue, Jr.

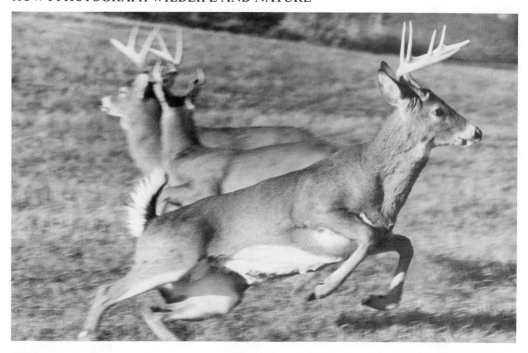

The flight distance of these white-tailed bucks has been violated; they feel threatened and are dashing to safety. Photo by Irene Vandermolen

or serials, humanize or anthropomorphize the wildlife and depict wild creatures as either "cute" and "cuddly" or "vicious" and "ravening." The tamed animals on the shows may be cute and cuddly, but wild animals are just that—wild animals. They are not vicious, although they can be dangerous.

I respect all wild creatures, both large and small, for their unbelievable strength and speed. I use a telephoto lens so that I don't have to approach an animal too closely and cause it to flee or feel it has to attack. If you keep your distance, the wildlife is more likely to carry on its activities in a normal fashion.

Most of the western national parks have rules and regulations against feeding bears. Bears are seldom encountered in the parks today because too many tourists fed too many bears in the past. When the bears lost their fear of humans, many unfortunate incidents occurred. Most of the bears have had to be removed to protect the tourists from their own stupidity.

When in bear country, always remember that you are a trespasser in the bear's domain. The most dangerous bear is the one that is not seen. Make every attempt not to surprise a bear. In bear country, talk as you walk the trails, and wear bells on your packs. Keep a clean campsite and suspend your food supplies high between trees and away from your camp.

Female bears with cubs are probably the greatest animal danger you can encounter in the wild. The smaller the cubs, the more protective the mother will be. Any time you get within 150 feet of any bear, you are in potential danger, but females with cubs can be a threat at even greater distances.

A bear that is curious stands up on its hind legs in order to see better. When angry, the bear erects the hair on its body and extends its head out as far as possible. It may huff a warning, growl, or pop its teeth. It may drool strings of slobber. The bear may circle to get your scent better.

Adult grizzly bears don't climb limbless trees, although they can climb a branched evergreen tree as well as you can. A black bear can climb any tree faster than a human. A loud,

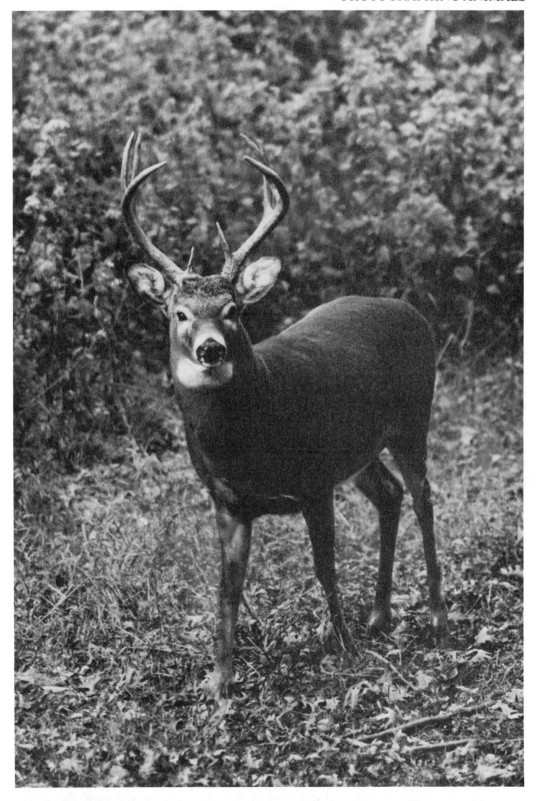

The white-tailed deer is found in all of the 48 contiguous states. This is a really fine buck.

sharp noise may deter a threatening bear. I always wear a Little Thunderer police whistle around my neck when I'm in wild country. It's great for signaling, can be used if you get lost, and may stop a bear from attacking.

With any large, dangerous animal, unless you can reach shelter or safety quickly, do not run. Running from a threatening animal may stimulate an attack. Stand your ground, face the animal, and make noise. I also pray a lot. By following my own advice, I have stopped an oncoming elk and bear.

I don't know if I could follow the advice I am about to give, but what I'm passing on is the advice of experts. If you are actually attacked by a bear, play dead. Fall to the ground on your stomach, and lock your hands behind your head to protect your neck. Bears don't usually eat people, but they often maul them. If the bear thinks you are dead, it may lose all interest in you and leave. But don't move till you are sure the bear is gone. Better yet, use long lenses and stay away from bears.

The majority of people visit the national parks in June, July, and August because most get their vacations in those months and their children are home from school. It is also the poorest time of the year to photograph or even see wildlife. In hot weather, the animals cool off in the shade or seek relief from the hordes of stinging, blood-sucking insects by going to higher elevations.

September brings relief for the animals from the heat and from the insects. Park attendance drops dramatically. The weather is usually good, and the out-of-doors arrays itself in its most flaming, beautiful colors. September also brings on the rutting, or breeding, season for both the elk and the moose. This is the time of year to photograph these magnificent animals. They are in their finest physical condition. The velvet has peeled from their antlers, and their necks have become swollen. Each of the adult males epitomizes maleness; each is the end product of eons of evolution. This is also the time of the year that the elk and moose are most dangerous. Most park animals have lost their fear of human beings because of the protection afforded them by the park and by their constant exposure to humans and their activities. During the rutting season, the males are ready, willing, and able to do battle with one another or with anything else that gets in their way. Rutting moose have been known to attack people, cars, trucks, a bulldozer, and even a train.

Most animals betray their emotions by their actions. They telegraph their punch. By knowing what an animal is about to do, you can save yourself grief and perhaps your life. Everyone knows that a dog that erects the hair on its neck; curls its lips in a snarl, exposing its canine teeth; and growls is a dangerous dog about to attack. Wild animals display similar warning signs. Usually these signs occur in a progression, each one showing a succeeding intensity of emotion.

A bull elk that slashes at saplings and brush with his antlers is an angry, frustrated animal. He may tear up the turf with his antlers and toss grass and sod in the air. When the hair on his neck is erected, and he raises his head and curls his upper lip like a dog, snarling, he has reached the end of his fuse, A charge is imminent.

Moose usually raise the hair of their manes as a first sign, following by the laying back of their ears. If a bull moose is near brush, he may slash the bush with his antlers. If these signs are followed by the moose opening his mouth and extending his tongue, you are in big trouble.

Although cow elk and moose do not have antlers, they also can become aggressive, particularly in defense of their young. They go through all the same signs as the bulls, except for the raking of the brush and trees. When they attack, they do so by striking out with their hooves. An attacking cow moose weighing 800 pounds is a deadly adversary.

A big bison bull can weigh up to 2400 pounds. These animals are large, and they can be dangerous. A man was killed by a big bull in Yellowstone several years ago when the man kicked the bison to make it stand up. The bison jumped to its feet, whirled about, and killed the man. The bison had no time to give any warning signs; it just felt it was being attacked.

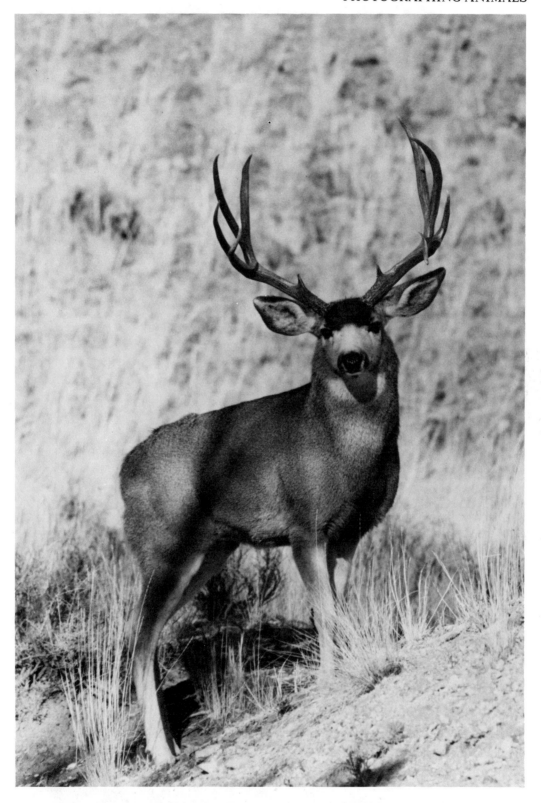

Mule deer bucks have larger antlers than the white-tailed deer. Photo by Irene Vandermolen

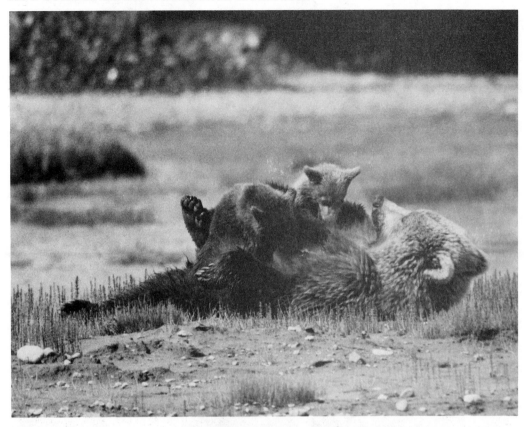

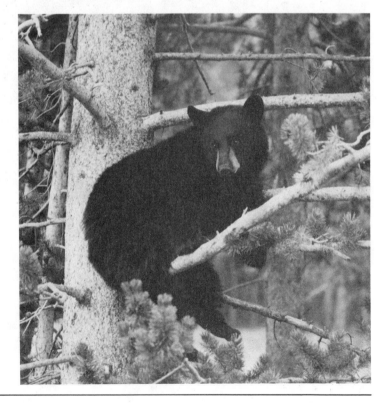

Top An Alaskan brown bear nursing her cubs. A mother bear with cubs is a dangerous hazard in the out-of-doors.
Bottom Black bears can climb up trees faster than humans can fall out of them.

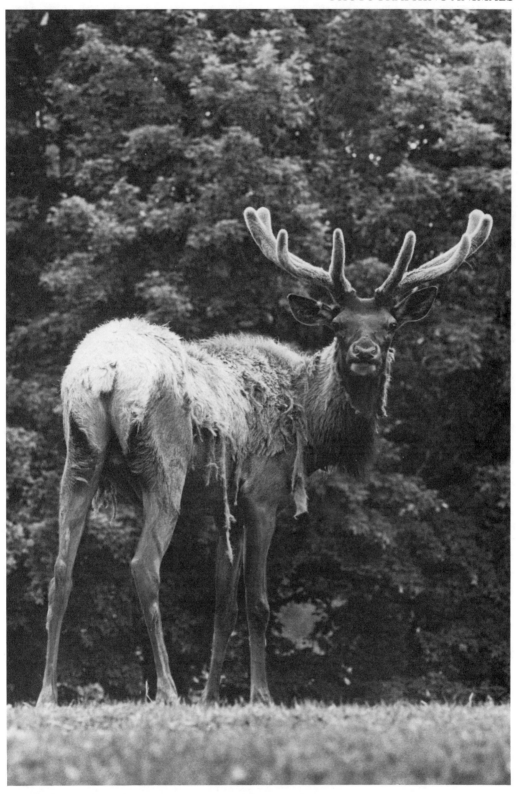

This bull elk is shedding his winter hair, and his antlers are in velvet.

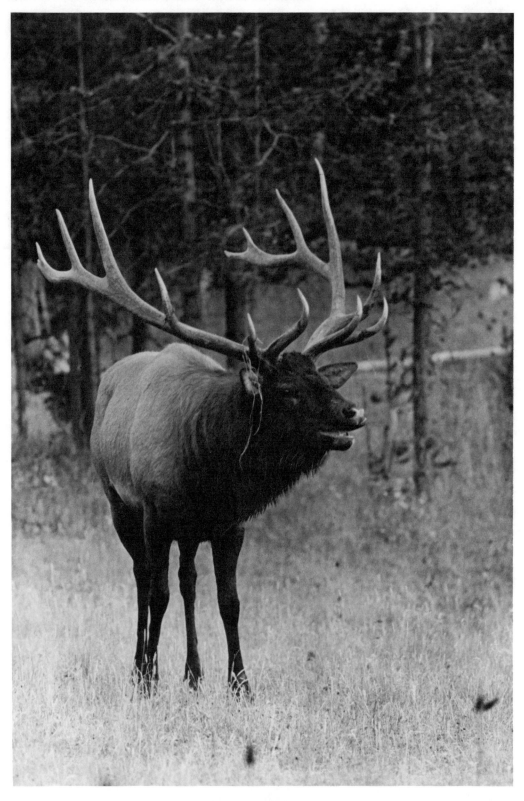

Bull elk are in their finest physical condition in September. Photo by Len Rue, Jr.

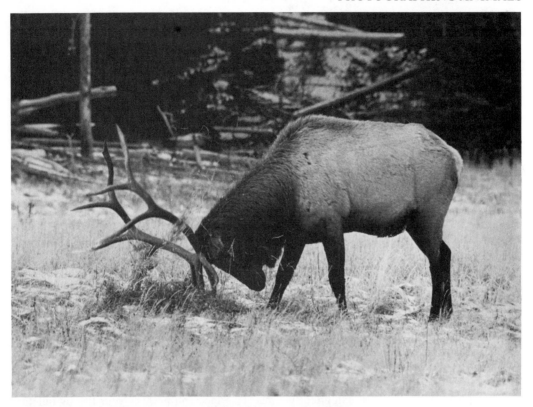

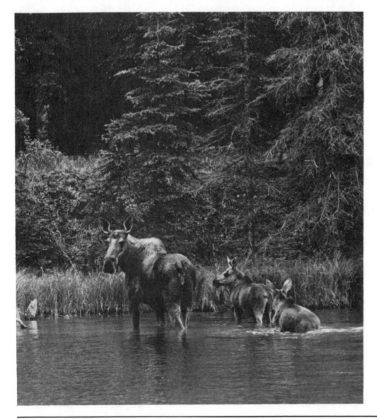

Top A bull elk tears up the ground in frustrated rage. Photo by Len Rue, Jr.
Bottom A cow moose with calves can also be dangerous.

A bison generally shows its displeasure by first rolling its eyes so that the dark pupils all but disappear and only the bloodshot whites of the eyes can be seen. Domestic bulls give this same sign of aggression. Then the bison's back arches even higher than normal. It may or may not paw the ground with its forefeet. The final sign is that the tail is lifted high. When all these signs are evident, the bison is usually thundering your way.

Most people respect elk, moose, and bison because of their sheer mass and size. They usually have no fear of the much smaller deer. "Bambi" was never a threat to anyone. I specialize in deer photography, so please, take it from me: Deer can be among the most deadly of adversaries. This is particularly true of deer in captivity, but many people have also been attacked in the wild.

The average white-tailed buck deer weighs between 125 and 175 pounds, but most of that is muscle; deer have larger, stronger muscles than we have. A deer can jump 9 feet vertically and 27 feet horizontally, and can run at a speed of 35 to 40 miles per hour. We can't. When a buck begins to paw the ground, lay his ears back along his neck, erect all the hair on his entire body, tuck in his chin, emit a high-pitched whine, open his mouth and flick his tongue up his nose, you are confronted with potential death and destruction. Workers at the deer research station in State College, Pennsylvania, have had bucks run their antlers through ¼-inch plywood shields that the men were carrying for protection.

Wild sheep, goats, pronghorn, and caribou seldom show signs of aggression to humans. I have never known javelinas or peccaries to charge, as they are so often reported to do. Nevertheless, I treat all wild creatures with respect.

I'm not saying all this to scare you. I'm relating it for your education and safety. You may not have time to learn these signs of aggression in the field, as I did. By using telephoto lenses, you can avoid "pushing" an animal or invading its personal territory. By knowing the signs of aggression when they are first exhibited, you can save face and perhaps your life by quietly backing away from what could turn into a dangerous situation.

How to Photograph Animals

You cannot just pick up a camera and walk out through the fields or woodlands and take animal photos. Almost every shot must be planned. By experience, you can train yourself to take advantage of the unexpected opportunity when it occurs.

You are much more likely to encounter the unexpected while driving your car. Keep a telephoto lens coupled to your camera, and have it accessible when you drive. I keep the camera, lens, and Gitzo window bracket in the back seat of the car, bedded down on a piece of foam to protect the equipment against bumps. I cover all the equipment with a blanket to protect it from dust and sunshine, and to keep it out of sight of the prying eyes and itchy fingers of potential thieves. "Lead them not into temptation."

Many shots can be taken from the car, and they should be taken from the car if the subject is within range. I keep a tripod on the floor of the car in case I have to get out of the car and approach a distant subject closer. But be prepared. Don't have to unpack everything, or the opportunity may be lost.

Wildlife outside a park or refuge will probably have to be stalked; wildlife in a park should not be.

Most animals' sense of smell, hearing, and eyesight are far more keen than those of humans. In many instances, we cannot even comprehend what they can deduct from these senses. I also firmly believe, based on many years of observation and close association with animals, that they have a sixth sense, as we do, a psychic ability to respond to stimuli that are beyond the five normal senses.

In stalking an animal, it is important that you are not seen, that you move cautiously and silently by taking advantage of every bit of existing cover. This is often difficult to do. What is

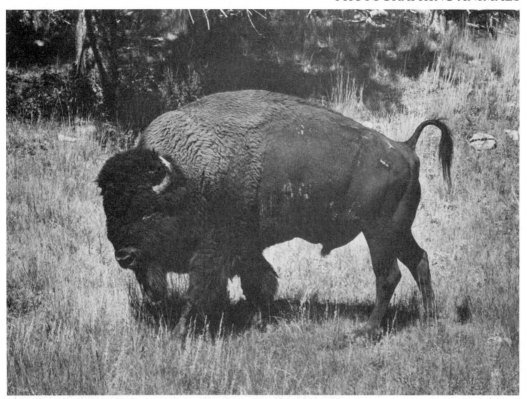

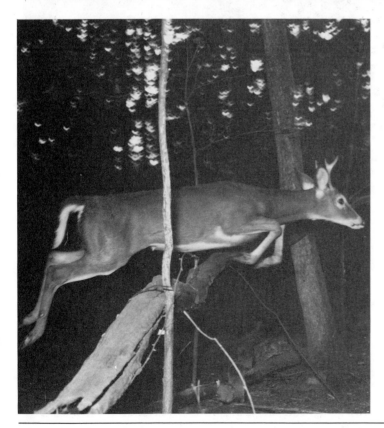

Top The raised tail position of this bison bull shows that he is about to charge. *Bottom* The white-tailed deer is a forest animal and an excellent jumper.

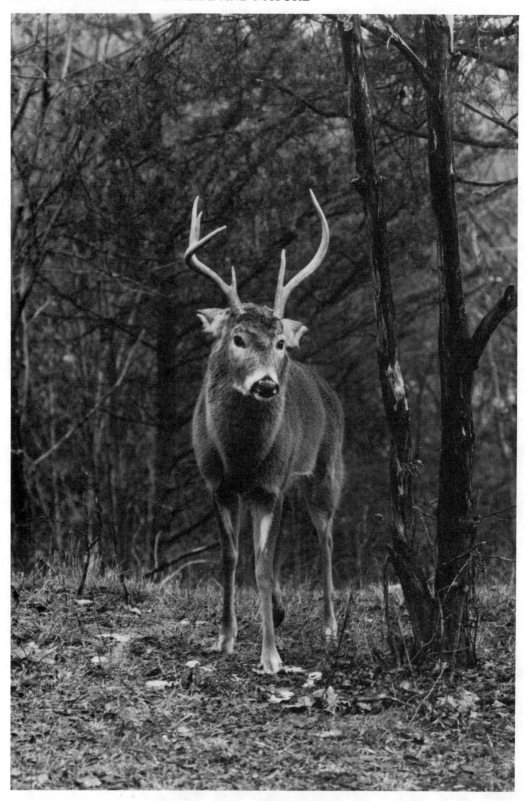

The erected body hair and flattened ears show that this white-tailed buck is about to charge.

even more important is that with most animals, the stalk must also be made with the wind blowing away from the animal and toward you. The wind can be quartering, but you have no chance of success if the wind is blowing from you to your subject.

As I mentioned, I usually wear camouflage clothing. In stalking animals, it is imperative that you do so. I also always carry a camouflage face mask. Most people have no idea of the tremendous amount of light that is flared and reflected from a human face. I have a full beard, and that helps to break up the flare and outline my face. People with swarthy or black skin have a natural camouflage. Camouflage grease paint can be used, but it is messy. It is a lot cooler to wear in the summer, though, when a face mask is hot. But a face mask also gives some protection against stinging insects.

Very thin mesh camo gloves will mask the movement of your hands.

I prefer to wear the standard green, brown, and black camouflage in spring and summer. The brown and black camo is best in autumn. I have found that the new Trebark camo is the best for photography in the woods when the leaves are off the trees. I am trying to get some of the light tan and brown camouflaged clothing that the army is now using for desert or sandy soil situations. White camo clothing should be worn when there is snow on the ground. Industrial coveralls, pants and jackets made for painters and bakers, work very well. In an emergency, you can use an old bedsheet. Sheets work best against a pure white background.

Commercial white and black camo outfits are available that work very well and are insulated against the cold. Black and white camo is effective in a forest when the snow lies between the black tree trunks. A hunter wearing all white would be conspicuous. It is important to wear camouflage clothing that most clearly matches the habitat you are using it in. Camouflage that doesn't match is the same as none at all.

Most grazing and browsing animals feed into the wind. This allows them to detect the scent of any predator upwind of them. They move frequently, which puts more space between themselves and any predator stalking them upwind. The predator also has to constantly move, to keep up with or get closer to the prey. As a photographer, you are regarded as a predator, although you only want to take your subjects' pictures, not their lives.

In stalking animals, remember that all rodents and hooved animals are classified as prey animals and have eyes on the side of their heads, providing them with monocular vision. Most can see about 310 degrees of a circle; some can see even more. This means they can see backward as well as forward. Human predators have eyes on the front of their heads. We have binocular vision that covers about 80 to 100 degrees of a circle. We have better depth perception than our prey.

When stalking, it is best to move only while the animal is actually feeding or is otherwise distracted. Most animals, and deer in particular, invariably move their tails before they raise their heads. When you see the tail twitch, stand still. When the animal's head goes back down, advance cautiously. Deer also flick their ears back and forth and stamp their feet when nervous. Marmots, woodchucks, and ground squirrels usually sit upright on their haunches, five to seven times per minute, to look around for danger. When you see them move, stand still.

Instead of stalking after a subject, it is better to anticipate the general direction in which it is traveling. Then, keeping out of sight but watching the wind direction, make a large semicircle around your subject, getting ahead of it but being off to one side so that it cannot smell you. Then sit still and allow the subject to move within range. There is far less chance of being detected if you remain motionless and allow the subject to move toward you.

If you plan to do a great deal of stalking, you should wear lightweight rubber-soled shoes rather than stiff-soled hiking boots. Avoid stepping on sticks that might crack. Step over logs so that you don't slip on wet ones. Dry leaves cannot be walked on quietly, but damp ones muffle sound. Soft, wet snow absorbs sound. Cold, dry snow squeaks as the crystalline edges grind against one another when compressed. You cannot wear hard-surfaced clothing, such as

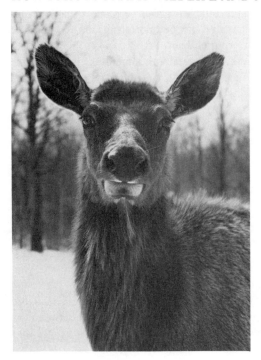
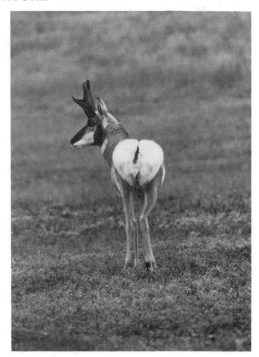

Left The large ears of this cow elk funnel in any dangerous sound.
Right Pronghorn antelope have excellent eyesight. This buck is alarmed by what he sees, as is shown by his erected rump hair.

twill and denim, for stalking because twigs or stiff grass will rasp on the hard surface. I used to wear wool in cold weather, but now I use the soft camouflaged outfits knitted by Winona Mills and Trebark. These are warm, soft, and noiseless.

In national parks, where the animals do not fear humans and are accustomed to their activities, stalking is likely to scare animals off. In fact, as you approach a park animal, do everything possible to let it keep you in sight. If you inadvertently walk down an intervening hollow, the animal may think it is being stalked when it can no longer see you. Then, when you reappear at closer range, the animal will probably take off. Whereas, in stalking, you may have had to take a longer route to stay out of sight, in the park you may have to walk a longer route to make sure you stay in sight so that the animal can see you at all times.

When attempting to "walk up" to an animal, don't hurry. Take it easy, and don't walk directly toward the animal. Don't even look directly at the animal; be interested in everything else around you, but seemingly pay no attention to the animal you want to photograph.

Prey animals instinctively know whether a predator is hunting or whether he is merely moving about. A hunting predator walks with directness, purposefully, and alertly, and this is transmitted as much by posture as by action. Man's actions are read by wild creatures in the exact same way.

I usually walk on an oblique angle to the animal I want to photograph, circling to get, or to keep, the sun behind me. I may even stop, look around in other directions, or just fiddle around.

When I am walking up to an animal, if it is a really fine specimen, I begin to take photos long before I reach the desired range. Don't make a big production out of it, but grab a few shots as you advance. You can never be absolutely sure how long the animal will stay in the area. Take some shots and then meander on your way, slowly but steadily shortening the distance between you and your subject. Then shoot some more. If you are in luck, your subject

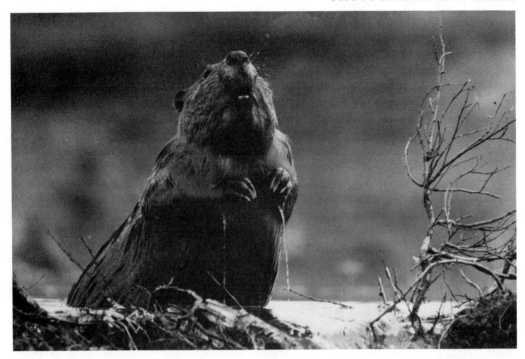

Many animals depend primarily on their sense of smell to detect danger, as this beaver is doing. Photo by Len Rue, Jr.

may hold still, and you may finally arrive at the distance you desire. The photos you take at the desired spot will undoubtedly be so much better than your grab shots that you will not use the first ones. If the animal suddenly dashes off, however, the grab shots may be all you will ever get.

If you have a lot of shots of the subject you are walking up to, don't bother with grab shots. But don't neglect to take them just to save film. Film is the cheapest part of any photographic trip. Your time and the expense of getting in the field are the real killers. So, when you are in the field, shoot, shoot, and shoot some more. The more photos you take, the more choices you have, and the better chances are that some may really be superb. The laws of chance favor the photographer who exposes a lot of film.

In walking up on sheep, I often stop in plain view, and perhaps eat part of my lunch. I try to avoid bending over or sitting down because the animal may be frightened when you straighten up or get up. If the animal is bedded down, then you can sit down very slowly. After the animal arises, you can do the same, very slowly and without sudden moves.

I like to let every animal become accustomed to me. I want to get it to accept me, or at least to accept the fact that it can't get rid of me but that I am harmless.

I constantly talk to wildlife—all wildlife. Anyone working with domestic animals talks to them to calm them. I did this on the farm as a boy, and I do it now with wildlife. It doesn't matter what you say to the wildlife, just so long as you speak in a soft tone; preferably in a monotone. I don't want a wild animal to be caught by surprise, and so I often talk to it before it can actually see me but when I know it is in the area.

Get up and be out early; wildlife is. Locate wildlife before you can take photographs so that the animals have a chance to get accustomed to you. Get out early before the tourists blunder on the scene and cause the wildlife to take off. Beat the competition, and get the photos they won't get. As incomprehensible as it is to me, I meet wildlife photographers who do not like to

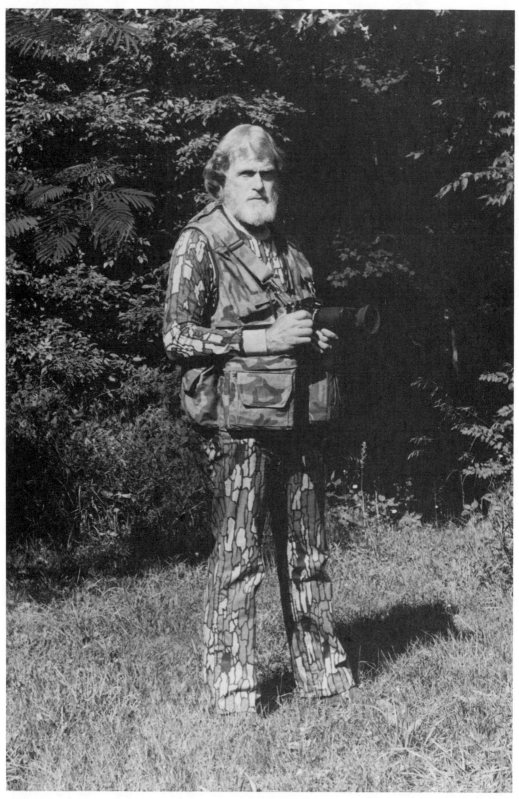

Trebark camouflage is new, but it is the most effective when the leaves are off the trees.

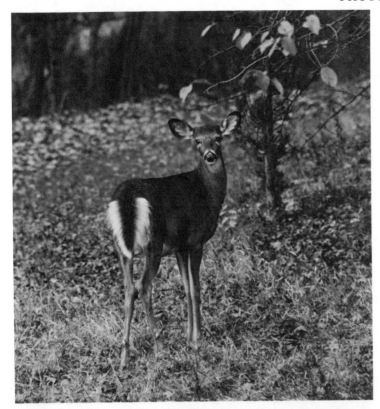

Top The flared tail of this white-tailed "button" buck shows that he is alarmed. *Bottom* Suspecting danger, this white-tailed doe nervously stamps her foot.

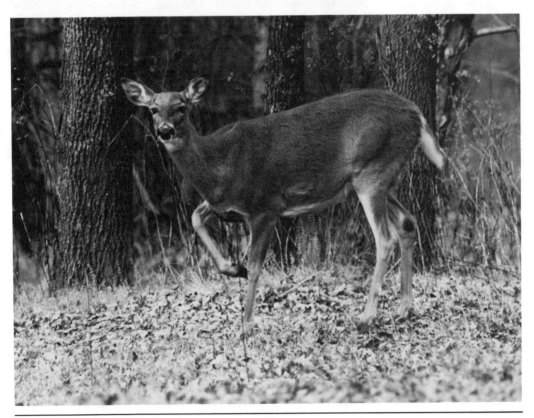

get up in the morning. Wild creatures are most active early in the morning and late in the afternoon, and to photograph them you have to be ready when they are. Most wildlife takes it easy in the middle of the day, and, like the animals, I often take a short nap at that time myself.

I worked on red foxes in Alaska one summer so constantly that they accepted me and would lie down and go to sleep within 8 feet of me. When they dozed, I dozed, although I dozed for a shorter time because I did not want them to wander off while I slept. When they got up and hunted, I would drop behind so as not to spoil their hunt. I have great photos of them stalking prey, carrying it, eating it, and caching it or feeding it to the pups. Those foxes got to believe that my being with them was as inevitable as death and taxes.

In the winter, or in cool weather, wildlife may be more active in the daytime than it ordinarily would be. Winter light is favorable in the middle of the day because the angle of the sun is low on the horizon. In the summer, the sun is at its best angles in the early morning and late in the afternoon when the animals are active. The light angles of the overhead sun at a summer noontime create extremely harsh shadows and high contrasts.

Another little known facet of animal behavior is that except for mice and rats, and the predators that feed on them, most animals prefer to feed in the daytime. Many animals, particularly where they are heavily hunted, have become strictly nocturnal, but they have done so only because they are safer moving about after dark. In areas where they are protected, these same animals revert back to being crepuscular, feeding and moving about primarily at dawn and dusk.

Always pay close attention to any animal in the area in which you are working. When an animal becomes alert and stares in one direction, you had better stare there too. Something has caught the animal's attention. A wild animal will spot another animal long before you are aware of it. An animal will not pay that much attention to the movement of some small animal; what it looks at is something of importance to that animal. A hooved animal may have spotted a prey species. Or another of its own kind. In the rutting season, it could mean the appearance of a bigger and better animal. If you are watching a small bear, and it suddenly dashes off, you know that a big bear is coming. Big bears may kill smaller bears, and the little bears know it. At all times, it pays to pay attention when the wildlife pays attention.

In order not to leave out something that may be of great value to you, I am next going to go down the general list of animal groups and tell you just how I work with each group.

Opossums are almost strictly nocturnal, although they will venture forth late in the day on overcast days in late fall or early spring. Opossums are usually caught in box traps, or picked up carefully by their tails at night and then released in favorable locations during the day. Opossums seldom "play possum"; most of them will readily scramble up a tree if given the opportunity. Make sure to release opossums up saplings and not mature trees, or they will climb too high to be photographed.

Mole photos are gotten mostly by luck. The tunnels that moles make on the top of the earth are easily seen, and if everything is absolutely quiet, you may actually see moles dig them. You can also flatten mole tunnels with your feet, and as the moles go through the tunnels, the earth will be pushed back up. Dig the mole out and turn it loose and then photograph it as it digs back under.

Shrews have voracious appetites and are active right around the clock. They feed mainly on insects and earthworms, but they can be baited with scraps of meat. Either bait them or capture them and shoot them in a studio—but remember to keep an ample supply of food available to them at all times. Because of their extremely high metabolic rate, shrews eat three times their weight in food every 24 hours.

Most flight pictures of bats are taken under controlled conditions in a laboratory because, usually, AC current is needed to power the big electronic flash units with which most bat pictures are taken. Photos of bats in the wild are taken with flash in caves, hollow trees, or

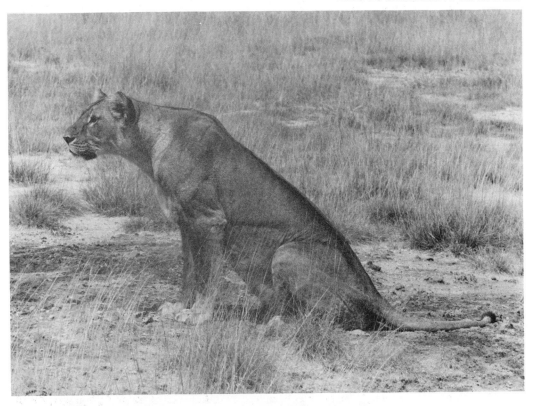

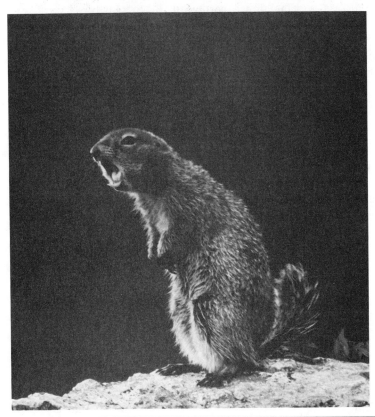

Top The alertness and posture of this African lioness relays a danger signal to all her prey. *Bottom* Standing erect, this Arctic ground squirrel sends forth a scolding alarm note.

attics where bats sleep during the day. Never handle bats with your bare hands; they will all try to bite, and a few bats are rabid. When there are large colonies of bats, you can contract rabies if infected bat urine is sprayed on you from the ceiling.

Most bear photos are taken by the use of natural food or by baits or at dumps. Bears are extremely intelligent animals and can easily avoid being seen, despite their size, if they are not attracted by food. They can be attracted by almost anything edible. They are particularly fond of honey.

Bears, when they are seen in parks, are attracted by the food that tourists give them. It is illegal to feed wildlife in a national park. Don't do it. Outside the park, food is the key to success for bear photographs.

The McNeil River is the most famous spot for brown bears, but most of the rivers and streams in Alaska that have salmon runs will have black, brown, and grizzly bears feeding in them. When working on fishing bears outside the parks and refuges, I definitely recommend that you carry a high-powered rifle or large-bore shotgun for your protection.

When photographing bears that are attracted to a dump, don't take photos in the dump. Take them on the trail going to the dump.

Raccoons are usually nocturnal, but in protected areas, especially campgrounds, they are frequently seen about in the daylight hours. Flash will often have to be used to take raccoon photos. Most raccoon photos are taken of pet animals. I have raised raccoons all my life and have a state license that enables me to do so. I have taken thousands of photos of my raccoons. I want to add one word of caution here: No wild animal makes a good pet. Sooner or later the animal will turn on you and bite and claw you. Female raccoons usually remain docile till about one year of age, the males till they are two years of age. For every story you can tell me of a raccoon that was tame all its life, I can tell you of a hundred that weren't.

Another word of caution: There have been recent outbreaks of rabies throughout the southeastern states, and the disease is being spread northward. Be extremely wary of any smaller wild animals that do not act wild. Animals that are wandering about in the middle of the daytime, that allow you to approach closely, or that try to approach you are undoubtedly sick. They may be rabid or suffering from encephalitis. If they bite you, you will need injections for rabies or an infection. The encephalitis cannot be transmitted to humans, but can kill your dogs or cats if they get near the infected animal. Encephalitis is carried by raccoons, skunks, and foxes. Any suspicious animal should be reported at once to your game department, health department or state police. Always make sure that your dogs and cats have their rabies inoculations.

The various members of the weasel family are seldom seen, but they may be abroad at any hour of the day or night. They may be hard to find, but they are comparatively easy to photograph when found because weasels and mink seem to be absolutely fearless. They are also very curious and are just as anxious to see what you are doing as you are to see them. They are not plentiful anywhere and will be encountered much more often in true wilderness. All members of the weasel family can be called by making a squeaking sound.

At some campgrounds the martens have become a nuisance to backpackers. They raid packs for food at every opportunity. Martens have a sweet tooth and can easily be baited with blueberry or raspberry jam into posing for your camera.

The slides made by river otters, in either mud or snow, advertise their presence. They may be baited with fish, or perhaps you can find where they are catching fish on their own.

Thankfully, sea otter populations have increased in both numbers and range so that they are now found all along the Pacific coast from California to Alaska. Their numbers have decreased a bit in California, and the decline is thought to be caused by overuse of the abalone shellfish and by oil pollution, to which these otters are particularly susceptible. Oil causes the otter's fur to mat so that it loses its insulating qualities, and the otter dies from exposure.

The best way to find fox dens is to track them in the snow in winter. In January and

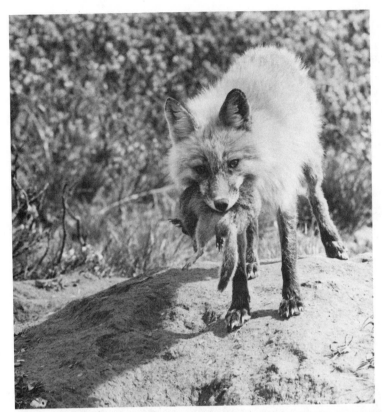

Top The results of a successful hunt. An Arctic ground squirrel is brought back to feed the pups by the female red fox.
Bottom This red fox accepted me to a point where it would sleep when I was sitting just 8 feet away.

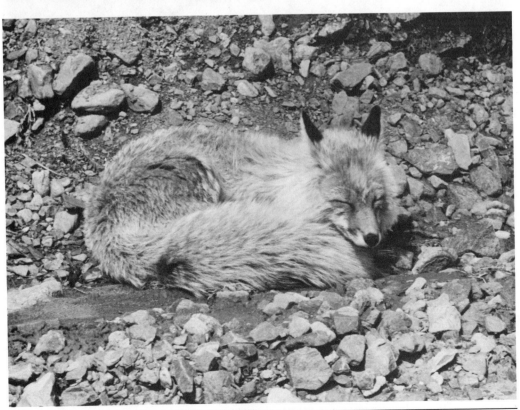

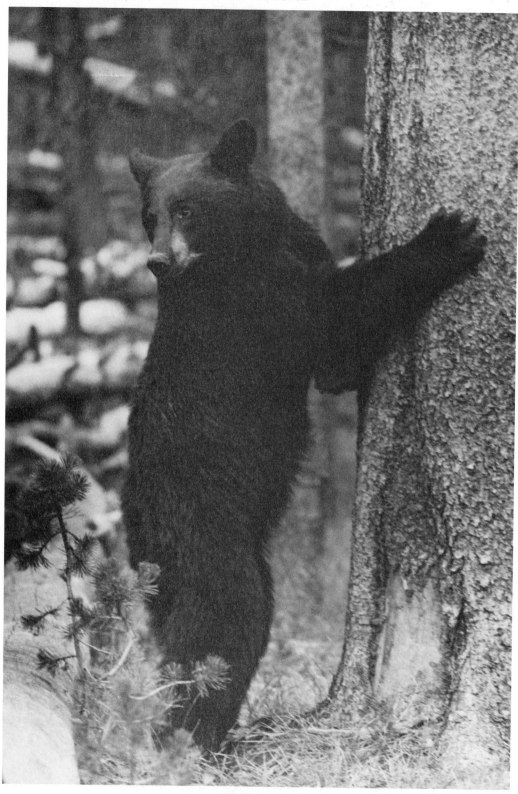

This young black bear nervously watches the approach of a bigger bear.

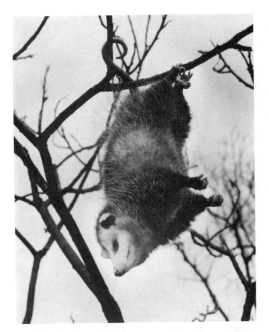

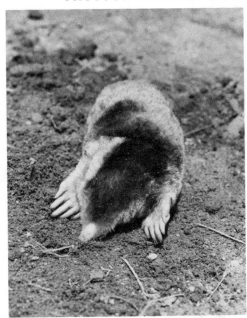

Left Opossums don't hang by their tails. Note how this one is holding on with its hind feet with some support from its tail.
Right Common moles spend about 98 percent of their time tunneling beneath the surface of the earth.

February, foxes clean out the dens they have selected to use for their pups. A blind should be worked into the area gradually, but make sure that the prevailing wind blows from the den to the blind. Fox pups begin to play outside the den at the age of six weeks. In Alaska I have sat in fox blinds for all but two hours of the day. I have taken notes of the animals' activities when not getting fantastic behaviorial photographs.

If your blind alarms the foxes, the female will move the pups at once to another den. I have also had this happen several times.

In parks and refuges, even coyotes occasionally become tolerant of humans. The rougher the weather and the deeper the snow, the more tolerant they become, because they have to hunt harder and longer for food. Toward the end of winter and in early spring, deep snow is advantageous to the coyotes because many deer and elk will die of starvation. If you can locate a deer or elk carcass, you will be assured of getting coyote photographs. These scavengers are alerted to the location of a dead animal by the actions of the magpies and ravens, and the coyotes are quick to take advantage of it. Four coyotes were feeding on a dead bison the last time I was in Yellowstone. Bears also will look for carcasses as soon as they leave their winter dens.

Although I have had no success with predator calls, a number of my friends have gotten excellent action shots of coyotes by using these calls. After my friends conceal themselves, and with both wind and sunlight favorable, they have used a call that sounds like a dying rabbit. In areas where foxes, coyotes, and even bobcats have not been hunted or trapped, all three animals have responded readily to the call. On occasion, bears and cougars have also responded, so be sure you are ready for everything before you start to call. Sitting against a tree or a huge rock will not only help camouflage you but also will prevent you from being mistaken for prey and being attacked from the rear.

The best wolf photos are taken in northern wilderness areas where wolves have not been hunted or in protected areas such as parks and refuges. Most wolf photos result from a chance

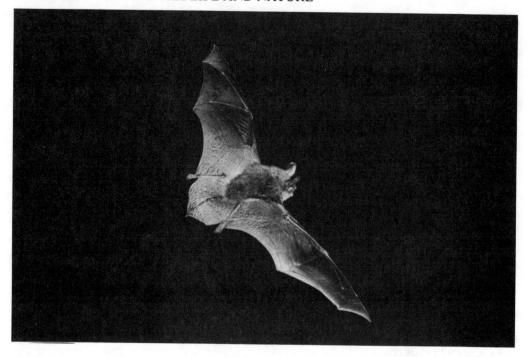

The speed of the electronic flash that stopped the action of this little brown bat was 1/40,000 of a second.

encounter, not from planning. I saw a number of wolves in British Columbia, but they usually saw me first and left me with only the memory. The biologists on Isle Royale, Michigan, have taken superb wolf photographs, but they worked with the animals for years, and the wolves were never molested.

Members of the cat family are even harder to photograph because they are much more furtive and secretive than wild members of the dog family. I am willing to bet that 99 percent of all photographs of mountain lions—including mine—are taken of tamed or captive animals. (The photographer goes to his local rent-a-cougar shop!) The exception is when these big cats are run by dogs and are treed and then photographed. Cougars will snarl and growl and look ferocious, but they almost never attempt to attack photographers. Many people live their entire lives in areas that have mountain lions, yet they never see or hear the cat and know of its existence only by its tracks. These big cats lay up for only a day or two during the worst snowstorm. Then they are out and hunting, leaving their tracks as their signature.

Sea lions are found only on the west coast and are comparatively easy to photograph because they are protected. Spots such as Seal Rock in California and the Sea Lion Caves in Oregon are famed for sea lion populations. Although sea lions may feed, and be gone from the rocks, at any time of day, they usually feed most heavily just before and during high tide. Plan your picture taking accordingly.

The same feeding schedule applies to harbor seals. Harbor seals are found on both the east and west coasts, however, giving eastern photographers a chance to score. Harbor seals also become very tame when protected, but they are exceedingly wary in Alaska, where they are hunted.

The huge elephant seals were almost annihilated for their oil. Thankfully, with complete protection, their populations are rebuilding nicely. They can be photographed on a number of islands off Baja California and on California's Channel Islands. I have not worked on these marine monsters, but my son spent five days photographing them for me.

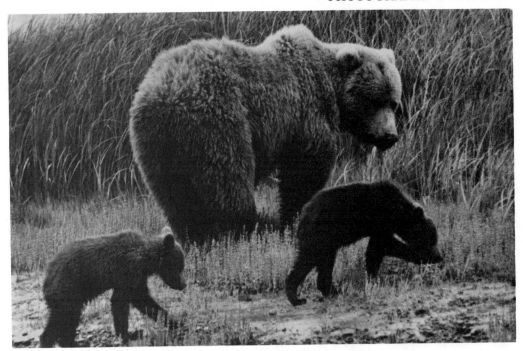

The McNeil River in Alaska, where this brown bear and her five-month-old cubs were photographed, has the largest concentration of bears in the world.

I have not photographed any Atlantic walrus but have worked on their Pacific counterparts on two different trips. I have not photographed the cow and calf walrus, for they usually stay up on the Arctic ice. But each year, in July, thousands of big bull walrus come down into Alaska's Bristol Bay and haul out on the beaches of Round Island. The island can be reached by boat from Togiak or Dillingham and by plane from King Salmon. I have used both routes. All the photos you have ever seen of huge packs of walrus are taken on this one island. The weather on the Alaskan coast can be bad, but some bright sunshine can be expected at that time. The walrus can be approached quite closely. Use your long lens for portraits, and move slowly so as not to alarm them. Do not allow yourself to be silhouetted against the skyline because this frightens them. Keep low and crawl among the rocks, then you can set up and shoot in the midst of them.

Woodchucks, marmots, and ground squirrels are among the easiest subjects to photograph. Their mounds and burrows are conspicuous and easy to locate. These creatures are strictly diurnal, and most are active throughout the entire day. Woodchucks, in particular, are easy to photograph because so many are found in farm country, and they are used to machines. Your car or truck can be used as a blind, or a blind can easily be set up and will be accepted. In a hayfield, a couple of bales of hay can serve as a blind. Woodchucks in a hayfield have to be photographed shortly after the hay is cut; otherwise, the grass will be so high that the woodchucks will be hidden. I like to shoot early in the spring before the hay grows high the first time. The woodchucks are also hungrier after coming out of hibernation in the spring and feed longer.

All woodchucks and marmots and most ground squirrels and chipmunks hibernate. They spend the entire winter sleeping with their body temperatures hovering just above freezing. The length of time that the various species spend in hibernation depends on the latitude and the elevation where the particular species is found. The time spent in hibernation may vary from 3 to 4 months for woodchucks up to 7 or 8 months for northern marmots and ground

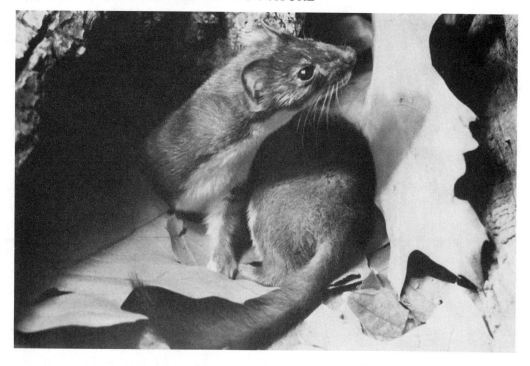

Weasels are fearless little animals that depend on their speed for safety.

squirrels. So there is no point in planning to photograph these creatures in the winter; they won't be seen. Prairie dogs don't hibernate, but they stay in their burrows during protracted cold weather.

A little-known fact about most chipmunks is that in hot weather many of them retire into their dens to escape the heat. This is called estivation. This explains why, during August, the chipmunks seen yesterday may not be out today.

With most ground squirrels and marmots, I use my pocket blind rather than set up a large rigid blind. In parks these animals are accustomed to people, but they will often retreat into their burrows if approached. By slipping on my portable blind, I'm ready to shoot in a few minutes, hidden from sight.

A fact to remember when working with animals that have dens or burrows is that wildlife has all the time in the world; time means absolutely nothing to them. You want them to come out as soon as possible, but that does not mean that they will. They may retire and curl up and go to sleep and not come out again until tomorrow. Although burrowing animals are easy to photograph, you may not get the photographs you want when you want them.

Prairie dogs are easy to work with—when you can locate them. Because prairie dogs create "towns," that is, large colonies of burrows in one area, there are concentrations of these animals. They are grass eaters and consume most of the grass in their areas. As a result of these two situations, they have been relentlessly persecuted by ranchers and farmers in the West. The government has aided the ranchers and farmers in the past with massive poison campaigns that have extirpated the prairie dogs from about 98 percent of their former ranges. Good colonies are left in national parks and in refuges such as Devils' Tower in Wyoming. They are now making a comeback in other areas.

Tree squirrels, such as the gray, the red, and the fox, are easily photographed by baiting. Although I have never done it, each time I get near New York City's Central Park, I always plan to come back to photograph the gray squirrels there. Almost every city park is overrun

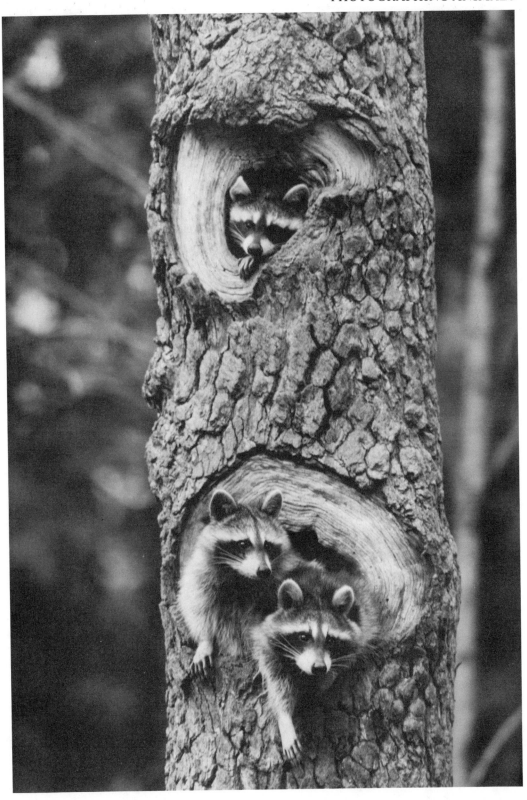

These young raccoons were born and raised in this hollow gum tree. Photo by Irene Vandermolen

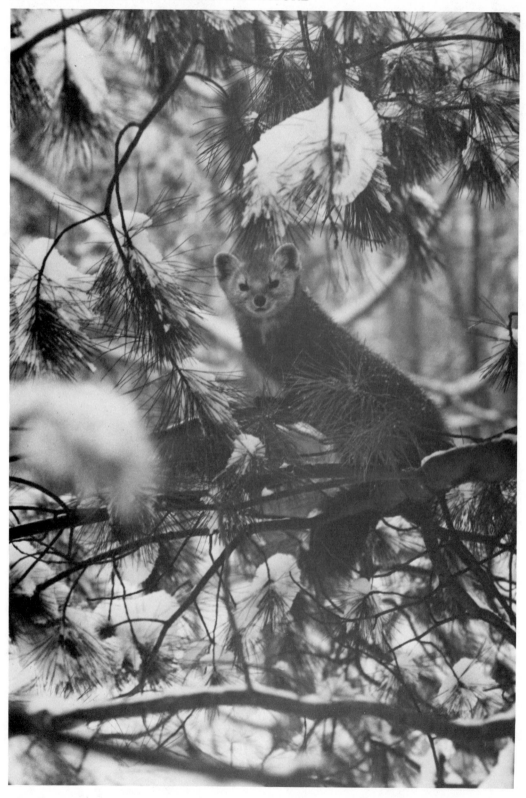

The marten is again being seen in many mountainous areas of the northeastern states.

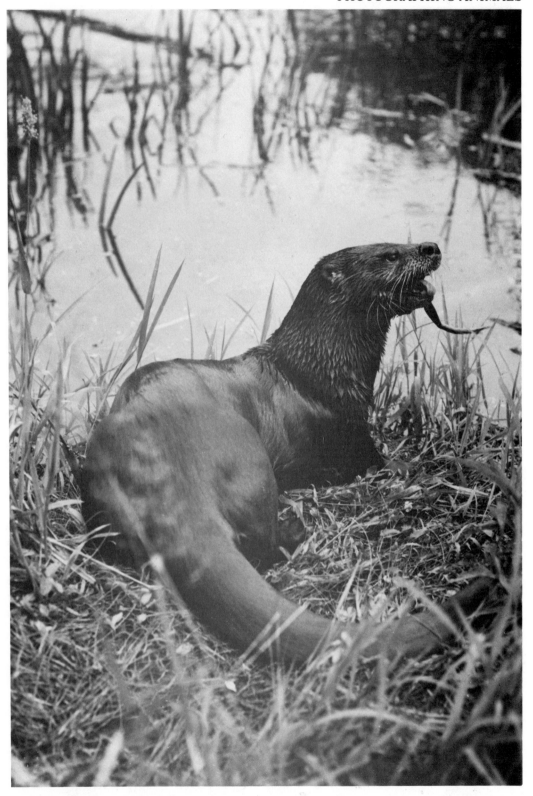

The river otter feeds primarily in and around water. This one is eating a frog it has just caught.

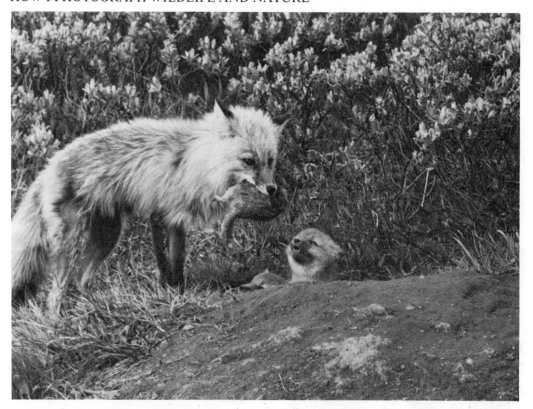

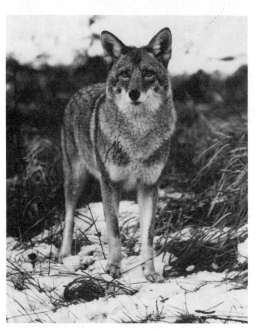

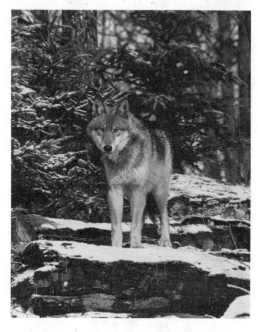

Top This photo of a red fox bringing a ground squirrel to her pups was shot from a blind about 30 feet from the den.
Bottom left This coyote came in to a predator call but stopped when it became suspicious. Photo by Len Rue, Jr.
Bottom right Wolves are common in most sections of Canada and Alaska.

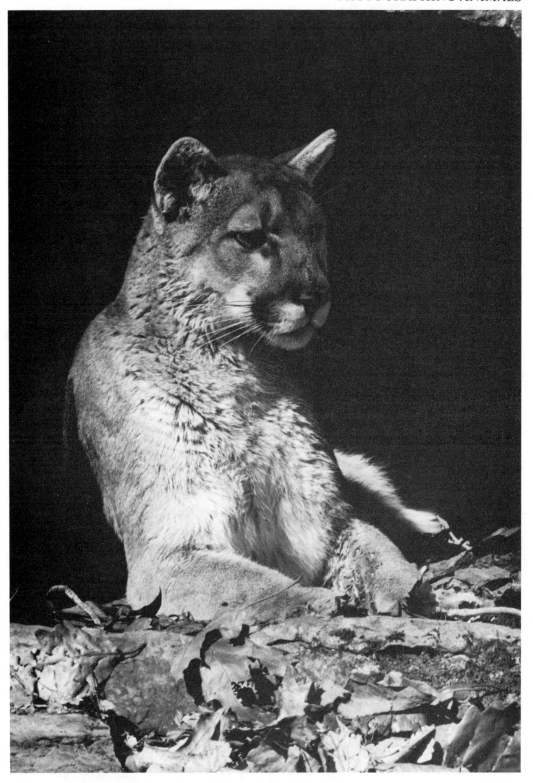

The mountain lion, or cougar, is again being found in the eastern half of the United States, where it had been almost wiped out.

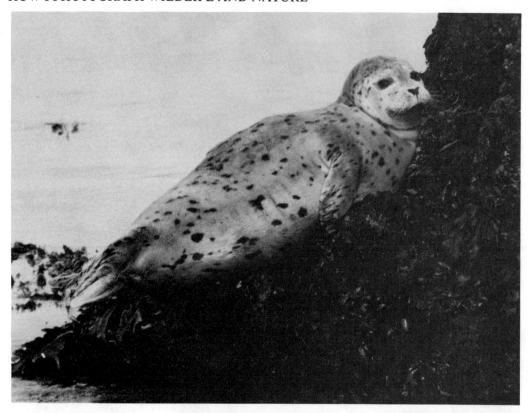

Top Harbor seals come in several different colors and can be found on both the Atlantic and Pacific coasts. *Bottom* Sea lions are commonly seen along the Pacific coast. Photo by Len Rue, Jr.

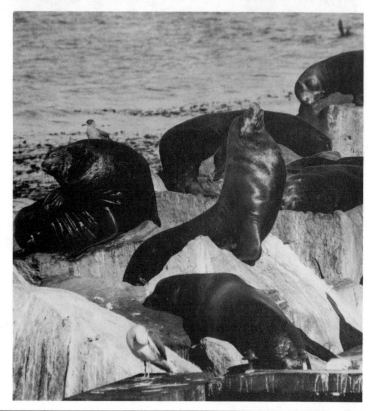

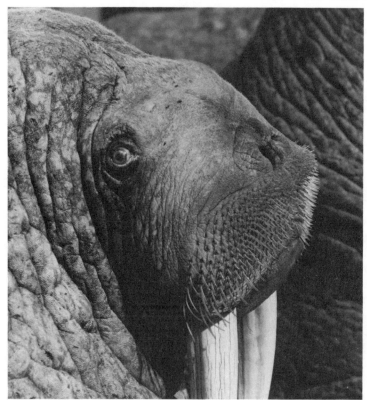

Top Most photographs of Pacific walrus bulls are taken on Round Island in Alaska's Bristol Bay.
Bottom By being very careful, I was able to work my way in among the walrus without awakening them. Photo by Jim Balog

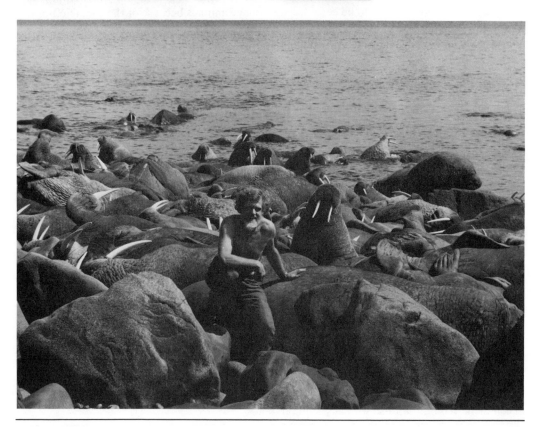

with these bushy-tailed panhandlers. Although I have dozens of gray squirrels around my home and some are fairly tame, in the cities hundreds of them are very tame. The editor of a hunting magazine who needs photos of gray squirrels to illustrate an article doesn't care where the photos are taken. Just make sure that your camera angle excludes every evidence of man and his buildings. Why work on wary wild squirrels when you can work on photogenic tame ones? Make sure not to photograph the squirrel eating a peanut or other nontypical wild food. You can gather hickory nuts, walnuts, and in the South pecans to bait the squirrel and photograph it using natural food.

Flying squirrels are strictly nocturnal. Unless their den is disturbed, they never venture out during daylight hours. Flash has to be used.

My series of flying squirrel photos, taken 30 years ago, probably did as much to get my work noticed all over the world as anything I had done to that time. I had a custom-built speed light that had a flash duration of 1/40,000 of a second.

I discovered that flying squirrels were coming to my bird feeders at night. To get to the feeder, they zoomed in and landed on a particular tree in my backyard. I set up my camera and strobes and began to shoot. I took several hundred photos, many of which were misses because I was tripping the camera manually, not with an electric beam, and my reaction time varied. The photos, as published, always looked like a sequence, although they were not stroboscopic but separate shots. Baiting with sunflower seeds is the best method I know of to work with flying squirrels, which do not fly but glide.

The burrows and "plug" mounds of the western gopher are very common and in some areas cause considerable damage. I have never seen a gopher. They are strictly nocturnal.

I have always been particularly interested in beavers, and 20 years ago I wrote a book about them. After having been extirpated from most of their original range by 1850, beavers have scored a tremendous comeback. In some areas, for example Alabama and Mississippi, they have become so numerous as to be considered nuisance animals because of the valuable timber they kill by cutting or flooding. No one should have any trouble finding beavers to work on. A phone call to your state game agency will help you locate an active colony.

Beaver that are harassed are strictly nocturnal; in parks and refuges they are not. Under normal conditions, beavers come out in the early evening. In late summer and early fall they become "workaholics," storing several tons of branches in the mud at the bottom of their pond, near their den or lodge, to be used as food when the surface water is turned into a solid covering of ice. I have found that beavers are very punctual. When you find them coming out of their lodge at a certain time, or doing something daily at a certain time, they will usually do it each day at that particular time.

I had been working on beavers for several weeks in Horseshoe Lake, Alaska, when an elderly couple came to the lake one day about 3:00 P.M. and asked if I thought they would see beavers. I told them where to sit and said that a female beaver would come over a small dam at 4:20 that afternoon. The beaver would swim to a certain point of land and cut down a small aspen tree and drag it into the water and carry it away. The couple were amazed when the beaver did just as I had said it would do. I cannot guarantee that any wild creature will do anything on cue, but that beaver followed that sequence of action for a week. I have lots of photos to prove it.

The New Jersey beavers I worked on for my book would come out only at night, so I had to use flash. At first I worked only on nights when the moon was full so that I had enough light to see when they were in the prefocused area. What headaches that eye-straining job produced. Then I read somewhere that animals cannot see red light, so I used an old railroad lantern that had a red glass shade. I could leave this lit and hung above the beaver activity spot, and the beavers paid no attention to it. Now I have headlights and flash lights with red filters for use at night, and these work very well. I get mine from Burnham Brothers in Texas. I strongly recommend red light for use with any night animal.

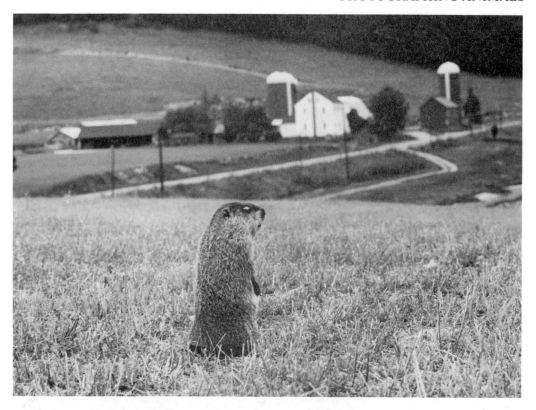

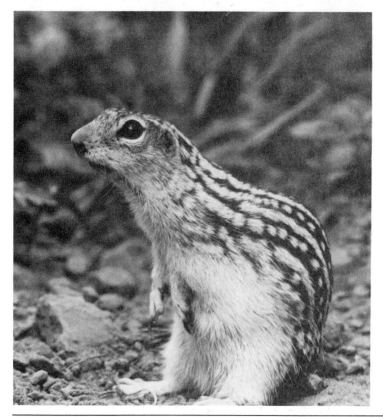

Top This woodchuck is looking over my neighbor's farm fields in northwestern New Jersey.
Bottom Unlike most animals, the 13-lined ground squirrel remains active even during the heat of the day.

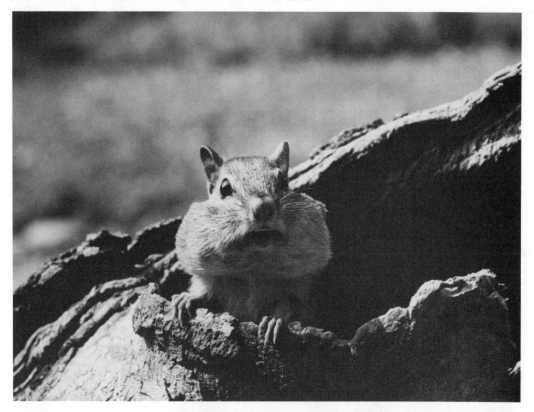

Top With its cheek pouches stuffed full, the eastern chipmunk is ready to carry food to its underground cache.
Bottom This red squirrel was easily baited to sit on top of this stump by using sunflower seeds.

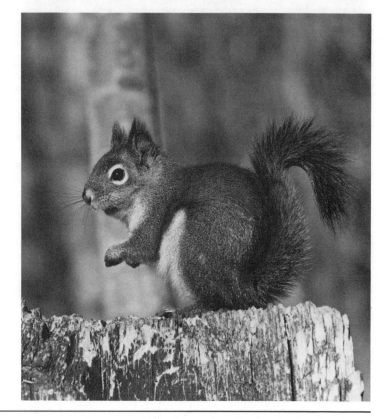

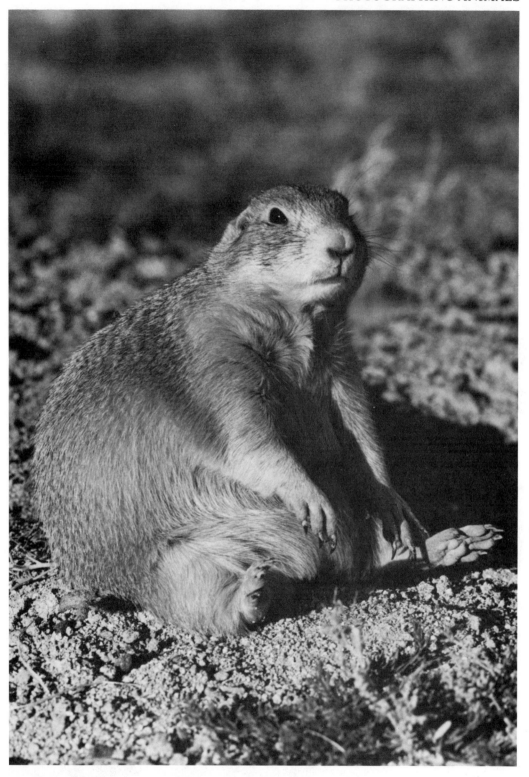

Although black-tailed prairie dogs do not really hibernate, they do not come out unless the winter weather moderates, and so they need their layer of fat which can be converted to food.

This set of flying squirrel photographs has been my most published work; it has appeared in several hundred publications. The photos were taken at 1/40,000 of a second.

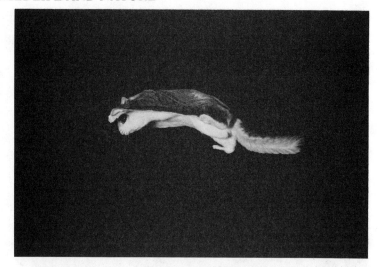

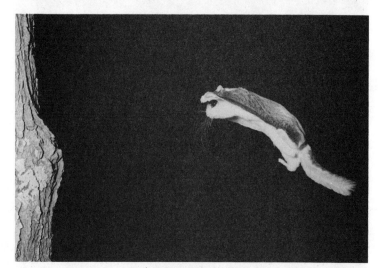

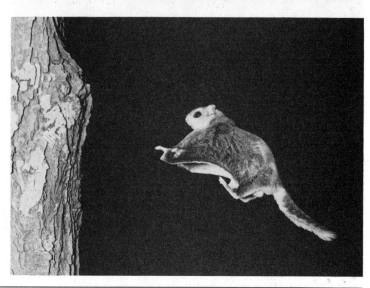

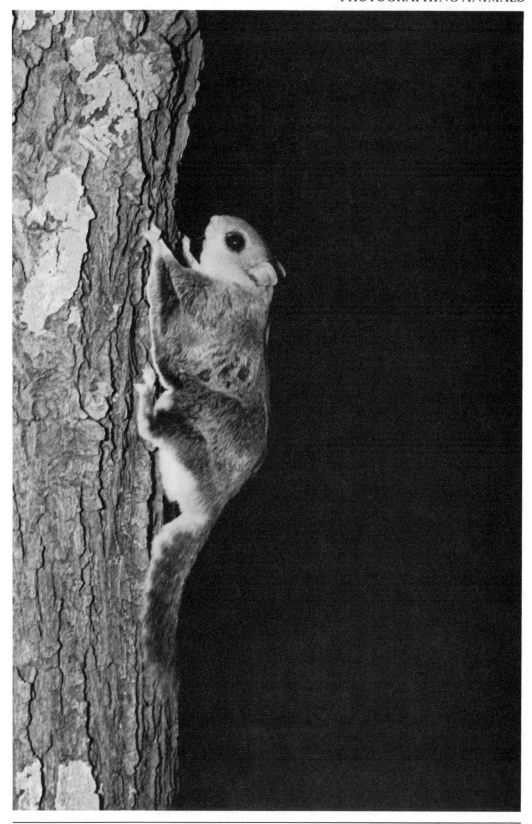

Beavers have specific spots where they leave the pond and where they cross their dam, and these trails are so conspicuous that they cannot be missed. You can set up your cameras to prefocus on these sites. To float larger pieces of wood back to their ponds, beavers often dig canals; these are great spots for pictures. Each fall the beavers coat their lodges with a layer of mud; and this makes for good photo opportunities. Beavers can be lured to a certain spot by the use of scents used for trapping that contain castoreum. For years I have used the various animal scents put out by S. Stanley Hawbaker. Apples and corn can be used to bait a beaver, but I prefer to use native aspen because the beaver can be photographed eating the aspen. I would not take pictures of beavers eating the other baits.

Where they are not molested, muskrats and nutria also come out during daylight hours. My writing desk is near a large picture window in my library that overlooks my small pond below. Every day, at any time of the day since the ice melted, I see the V-shaped ripples of swimming muskrats in that pond. I've got to get this book finished, and I have lots of muskrat photos; otherwise I'd go down and set up my blind and shoot. Muskrats can be baited to a particular spot with apples or parsnips, a favorite food. The parsnip is a root plant and muskrats feed heavily on roots, and so they can be photographed feeding on it.

Almost all rats, mice, and voles are photographed in a studio setup. Some of these animals can be baited to a particular spot, but as they are all nocturnal, you will have to use flash anyway. Most photographers use live traps to catch them, photograph them in a setup, and let them go. Sunflower seeds, peanut butter, and oatmeal and cheese are all good baits that work well. In fact, almost anything edible will work, but the first baits work best.

Porcupines are easy to photograph, if you can find them in the wooded areas they inhabit. They usually go lumbering along, paying no attention to anything but their stomachs. They are easily found in the winter by noticing all the dropped tree bark lying on top of the snow. The porcupine doesn't want to eat the rough, dead, tasteless outer layer of bark; it wants to eat the sweet inner layer of cambium bark. So, it peels off the outside layer and drops it. A porcupine feeding in the treetops eats all the bark because the tops are all tender. No matter where the porcupine girdles the tree, the white, debarked trunk will stand out conspicuously against the otherwise dark forest.

If the porcupine is in a small tree, or is low enough on a large tree to be photographed where it is, you have no problem. If it is too high or there is too much intervening brush, then you will have to climb up to photograph it. At first the porky will be disturbed, but if you just sit still for 15 or 20 minutes, you will be forgotten. The porky will go on eating or whatever else it was doing. Whatever it does, it does in slow motion.

Porcupines cannot throw their quills, but they do lash out with their strong tails. The quills will not go through a pair of stout boots or heavy gloves. If you want to move a porcupine, put your foot on the porky's back and gently pin it to the earth. Then, with your glove, push all the quills on the tail toward the tip and pick it up. You can then turn the porky loose in a small tree where it can be photographed.

Pikas live in the high-altitude talus slopes of our western and Alaskan mountains. They usually betray their presence by their sharp-whistled alarm notes. Or you may see their small grayish-brown bodies scampering away among the rocks. If you watch from a distance for a while, you will note that although pikas can disappear almost anywhere in the jumbled rock, they have favorite spots that lead directly to their dens. Just set your camera up there and wait them out. Although a blind is usually not needed, the use of a pocket blind does help shorten the waiting time. Pikas can be baited to a particular rock by placing some of the fresh-picked grasses that abound in the area. These grasses should be placed near the pika's den entrance so that it does not have to go very far. The pika then may eat the grass or carry it away to be dried and stored in its cache of hay. This hay cache is what the pika eats during the winter when the mountain is blanketed with snow. Find a hay cache up under some rock, and you've found the pika.

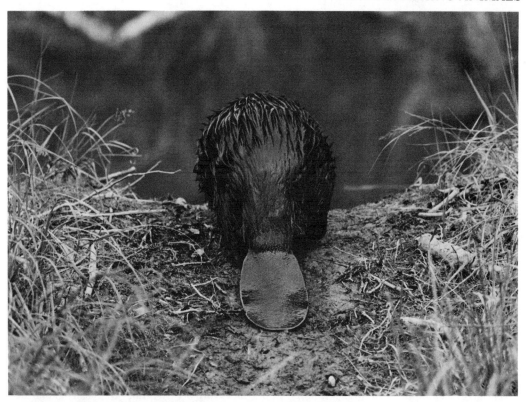

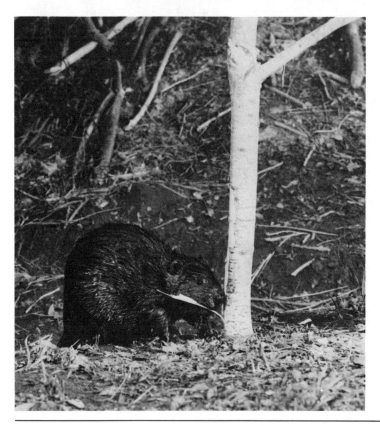

Top Beavers have well-worn paths that they use consistently, making it easy to photograph them.
Bottom One of the first flash photographs I took 20 years ago of beavers at work at night.

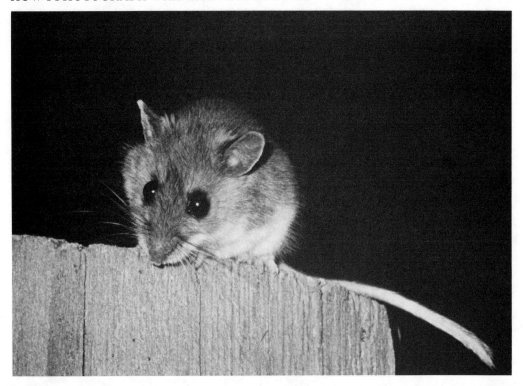

The snowshoe rabbit, and all jackrabbits, sit out in a "form" throughout the year, no matter how bad the weather. For maximum warmth, these forms are usually in dense brush or high grass on a south-facing slope in winter. They may be beside a large boulder or on the side of a gully, with both boulder and gully acting as windbreaks. In the summer, jackrabbits stretch out in the shade of a cactus or dense brush, trying to beat the heat.

In winter, look for the animal's tracks in the snow; in summer, look for tracks in the dust or sand. By walking along carefully, you can often spot the animal's dark, shoe-button eyes before you actually see the rabbit. If you make no sudden moves, you may be able to get a number of photos as you move up slowly. When hares break cover and dash off, note where they are going. Wait a while, give them a chance to settle down, then try to walk up on them again. Sometimes you can do it, at other times they will keep moving out ahead of you. In the hot, semidesert country in Texas, jackrabbits don't want to run at all; they will move no farther than the next large clump of shade, then they will flop down again.

The white-tailed jackrabbit and the snowshow rabbit (both animals are really hares) turn white in the winter and brown again in the summer. Photographs of these animals in their various color phases make for very salable sequences.

I do most of my cottontail rabbit photography right in my backyard. I have several long, narrow pieces of lawn surrounding my house. Every 75 feet or so, at the edge of the woods surrounding the lawn, I continually pile heaps of brush. These brush heaps rot down every three or four years, and I constantly replenish them. Each brush heap is a potential rabbit's home. I have provided the rabbits with shelter, in the form of the brush heaps, and food in the form of my lawn. And I let the lawn grow quite high. I have made this a rabbit's idea of heaven, and rabbits have provided me with hundreds of photographs each year.

I ordinarily have six to eight rabbits of different sizes in the yard every evening and early morning. If it has rained through the night and cleared, the rabbits will be out in good sunlight much later in the morning because they will not have moved while it rained. Their fur is not waterproof and they hate to get wet.

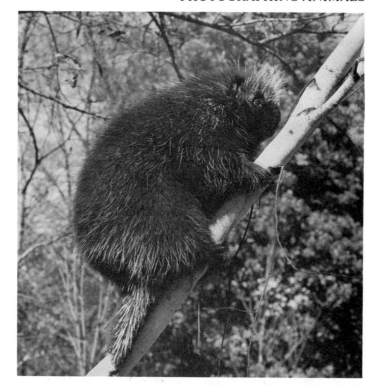

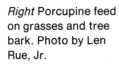
Right Porcupine feed on grasses and tree bark. Photo by Len Rue, Jr.

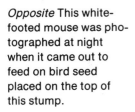
Opposite This white-footed mouse was photographed at night when it came out to feed on bird seed placed on the top of this stump.

Every time I see the rabbits, whenever I see them, I walk slowly past them and talk to them constantly. Then, when I have a good morning for photography, they are accustomed to me. I have taken lots of great behavioral photos.

I have noticed that I can work with cottontails through June, July, and part of August. By mid-August, they are just not seen as often, nor will they allow me to approach as before. I have discerned this pattern year after year and can only relate it to their diminishing numbers by increased predation by neighbors' dogs and cats.

Peccaries are usually skittish. I have taken photos from the car, and I have walked up on some in the Big Bend country of Texas. At the Desert Museum in Tucson, I got some photos at their famous waterhole blind. Food is usually plentiful for the peccaries, so food baiting is not all that successful. Water is usually scarce in the dry areas they inhabit, and I believe a blind situated at a waterhole, or by a stock tank overflow, will produce the best results. I am not really all that satisfied with the peccary photos I have taken because I was always pressed for time. I plan to sit at waterholes for them.

Any year that I am not in Yellowstone National Park in September to photograph the elk, I get homesick. I love Yellowstone at any time of the year, but particularly in September, and I love to photograph elk. It's like a gathering of the clan. In any week, of any year, that I get to spend there, I meet with about two-thirds of all the big-name professional wildlife photographers in the country. The competition is fierce, but it's friendly competition; they are all friends of mine. When the elk have bedded down for the day, most wildlife photographers spend much of their time talking to other wildlife photographers.

What we pray for is an early September snowstorm. If the month is warm, you might just as well stay home because the elk will stay high in the mountains where they are exceedingly hard to get to. An early snow pushes the elk down and then everyone rides the roads and scans with their binoculars all the meadows between the park headquarters at Mammoth and the West Yellowstone entrance along the Madison River. Elk may also be seen at Junction Butte and in Lamar Valley. However, I have always found the elk in Lamar to be extremely skittish.

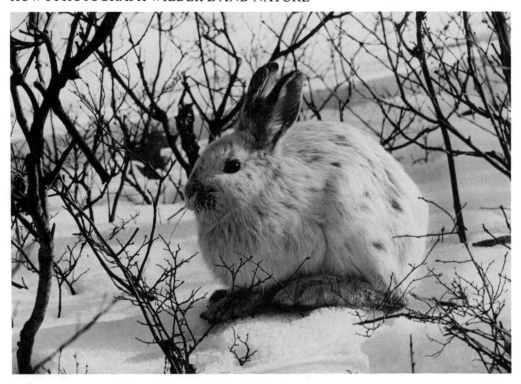

The snowshoe, or varying, hare is white in the winter and brown in the summer.

The elk can usually be walked; do not try stalking them. Use extreme caution not to get too close to either the big bull or his harem out in the open; use your telephoto lens. When working with either elk or moose, always have an escape route picked out in advance. If possible, know which is the closest tree that can be climbed, and don't hesitate to climb it if you have to.

Both elk and moose can run at speeds of up to 35 miles per hour, that is, 3080 feet per minute. If an angry bull elk charges you from 100 feet, he can be where you were in less than 2 seconds. How far can you be from where you were in that length of time? You had better have some idea, and you had better go in the right direction. As I said, always have an escape route picked out when working with potentially dangerous animals.

Although most professional wildlife photographers would prefer to have a beautiful big bull elk or moose all to themselves, they usually have to share it. There is safety in numbers. Neither animal is as apt to charge a small group of three or four as it would the lone photographer. If it does charge a group, it cannot be as decisive; a charging elk seldom has one figure in the group picked out as a target. Herding always works to the herd animal's advantage over the predator, and when an elk or moose charges, it temporarily is the predator, and the photographers are the herd animals. Having been in a group scattered by a charging elk or moose many times, I think I know why the animal never caught any of us. It was probably too busy laughing. It is a comic sight to see four or five photographers scattering through the trees like a covey of quail, their cameras and tripods banging on everything.

I would rate the bull moose as more truculent and dangerous than the bull elk in the rutting season. The moose is a lot bigger, standing 6 to 7 feet high at the shoulder. The moose can go over the top of a lot of bushes that will only slow you down. During late spring and through the summer, give a wide berth to cow elk or moose with young. They will not hesitate to attack if they feel the young are threatened. Use your telephoto lens on these animals.

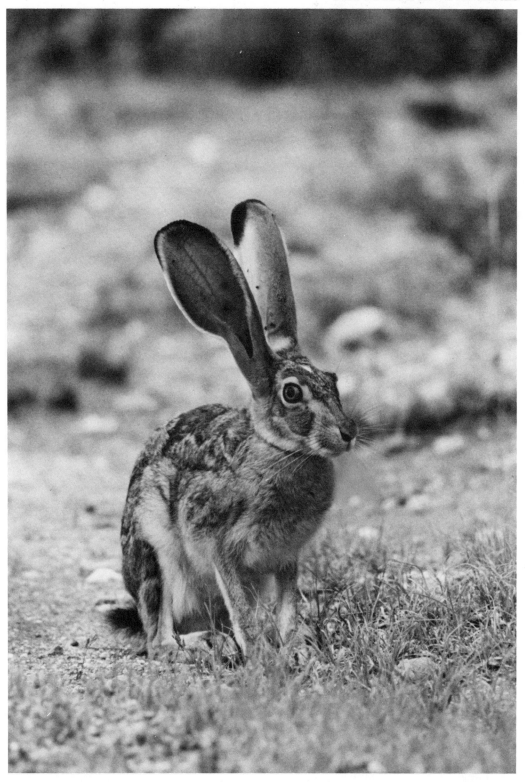

The large ears of the black-tailed jackrabbit allows its blood to cool down; they also act as thermoregulators.

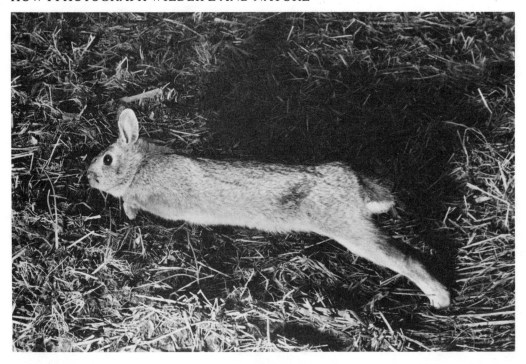

A high-speed flash "froze" the leap of this cottontail rabbit.

During the late fall, after the rut, or during the winter when their antlers have been shed, or in the summer when their velvet-encased antlers are still growing, both elk and moose are comparatively docile. Except for some life history behavior shots, it doesn't pay to photograph either animal under these conditions. The photos just don't sell.

Caribou are beautiful big animals in the rutting season, and I have never known them to be aggressive toward humans. A caribou just floats away across the tundra from anything that it feels is a threat.

Caribou are unpredictable. I have seen a herd that was lying down jump to its feet and dash off as soon as I stopped my car. At other times, I have worked with caribou in willow thickets and have gotten within 10 or 12 feet of them. I have had to back up in order to use the normal lens.

Most caribou are photographed in McKinley National Park because it is one of the few places where they can be photographed from the road. The McKinley herd has declined drastically in numbers, and as caribou are migratory, you just have to take your chances on finding and photographing a herd. No longer do big herds pass through the park, but some very good bulls are still to be found there. Ride the bus till you spot the animal you want to photograph. Then just get out and try to walk up on the caribou you have selected. Don't push the animals, and don't walk directly at them. If the caribou bull takes off in high gear, forget him. You cannot follow a caribou across the boggy tundra.

There are still many large herds of caribou in Alaska and Canada, although their populations have declined drastically all over North America. These herds can be reached only by plane, and in the north that gets to be a very expensive proposition.

I have probably taken more deer photographs, over the years, than any other photographer. And I'm just as excited about taking my next one.

Deer are such creatures of habit that, after you have studied their activities for a while, you know just where to put your blind. Whitetails have favorite alfalfa fields where they come out

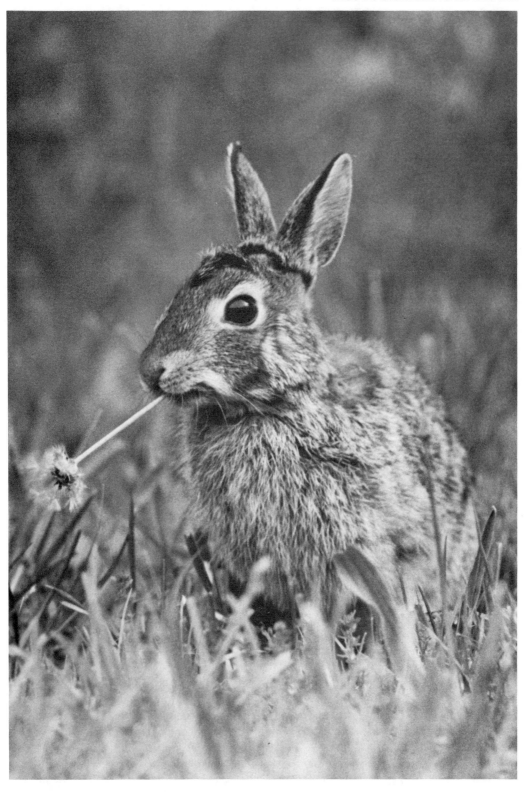

I photographed this dandelion-eating cottontail rabbit from a very low angle.

in the late afternoon to feed. They have favorite oak forests where they feed on acorns. In the fall they regularly check out every old orchard to feed on the apples that have fallen from the trees. A windstorm provides a bonanza for them. If the apple crop is poor, you can bait them to the area by bringing in apples. Don't handle the apples with your hands, even if they were hand picked.

You want the sun in your favor, but you must have the wind in your favor. Most animals, but particularly deer, depend primarily on their sense of smell. You don't want the deer to smell you, but you can mask your scent, and you can bring them to a desired spot by using scents. I have used scents to attract wildlife all my life. Not satisfied with some of the available commercial scents used for deer, a year ago a group of us pooled our talents and started to produce commercial scents for deer. Unlike hunters, who use our scents to attract deer right to them, I use the scents as a diversion. I squirt some of our Hunter Pro Pack sex scent on a tree, about 8 feet off the ground, in the general area in which I want to photograph the deer. This scent, used during the rutting season, attracts both does and bucks.

Mule deer and black-tailed deer are usually photographed in western national parks. Many of the park deer have little fear of humans and can be followed as one would follow elk. They do not travel over as large an area in a day as the elk do, so it makes the job a little easier. Our sex scent used on these deer also helps keep them in one area.

The pronghorn antelope is the fastest land animal in North America, but I have had very good luck with it by just patiently following after a single group hour after hour. In August, just prior to the breeding season in September and October, dominant buck pronghorns select the territory they will claim as a breeding range. Once the bucks are on their territory, they will not leave it, nor will they allow any of the does and their young to leave it. Carry water and your lunch with you; it could be a long day.

I found a good herd just north of the Yellowstone Park gate at 6:00 A.M. one day. I slowly followed the herd for 5 hours, never getting close enough to get good photos. The pronghorns would move off a half mile or so, and I would sit down or slowly walk after them, getting them accustomed to me. By eleven o'clock, they all but forgot me and allowed me to get close enough to shoot frame-filling photographs with a 200 mm lens; I got hundreds of photographs. The key to my success was in not pushing the animals and having the patience to wait them out. You cannot hurry wildlife photographs.

Bison are also creatures of the wide-open spaces. Whereas a pronghorn will not attack a human, a bison may. Herds of bison can be found in the Lamar Valley in Yellowstone, and some old "loner" bulls can usually be seen along the Firehole River. The latter area has a number of trees, allowing a closer approach to the big bulls. The National Bison Range in Montana is comparatively open country, as is Neobrara in Nebraska. Safety demands that long lenses be used at the latter locations.

It would be next to impossible to photograph wild sheep where they are heavily hunted because such pressure has made them among the wariest of animals. The bighorns in Yellowstone and Banff and Jasper, and the Dall's in McKinley and Kulane, are almost tame. That doesn't guarantee photographs. First you have to locate the sheep. This is most easily done by driving roads and glassing the likely spots. A trait of sheep that the photographer can take advantage of is their reluctance to move at night. If you locate sheep in the evening, you can almost be sure of finding them in the same area early the next morning and I do mean early. Sheep are up and feeding at dawn. I have had sheep in these areas allow me to get close, but at other times they have taken off before I ever got within camera range. You have to expect the unexpected.

If you were hunting sheep, you would want to get above them because sheep seldom look up. They expect danger to be below them. In photographing sheep, it is better to come up from below so that they can see you at all times. If you attempt to come down on them, they will invariably take off for the next mountain. And it doesn't take them long to get there. The

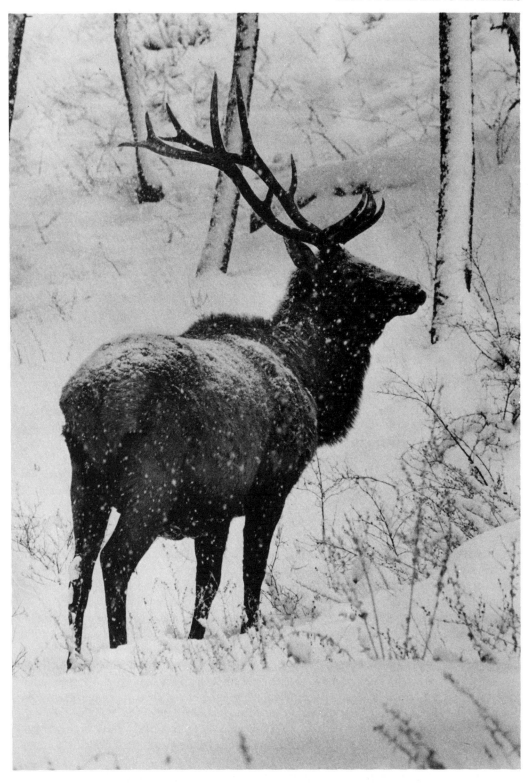

Snow is needed to drive the elk down from the high mountain meadows where they spend the summer.

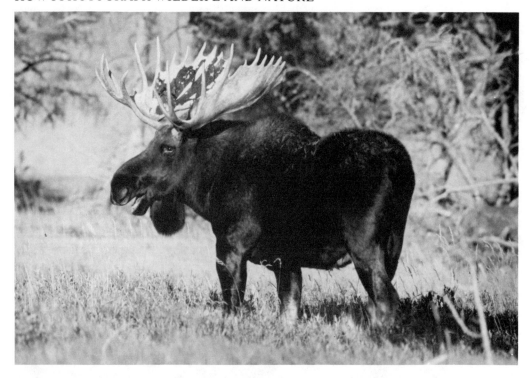

The remnants of velvet on this moose's antlers show that the photograph was taken in early September, prior to the breeding season. Photo by James Keith Rue

ground they can cover in 10 minutes will take you an hour, at least, and because of the steep slopes of some of the mountains, you may not be able to follow at all.

Whenever you are walking in the mountains, follow the trails laid out by the sheep and other animals. The grade will be the most gradual, although considerably longer than going straight up. Go the long way. You will gain the top in better shape and probably in the same amount of time. Most of the mountainsides are covered with loose talus rock, and if you try to walk straight up to the ridge, the talus will slide and may take you down the mountain with it. It's like coal running down a chute.

I always try to get below the sheep so that I can silhouette them against the sky. It does not look natural to photograph down on sheep. Everyone's concept of sheep is that they are creatures of the high country, which they are, so get below them and shoot up at them. When possible, shoot them against a good blue background; blue really enhances a photograph. A great deal of the time, I do not carry my 600 mm lens in the mountains. I take my 55 mm macro in case I want to photograph alpine flowers, sheep tracks, and so on. I take the 80 to 200 mm zoom because you often can get within that range of the sheep. I do most of the work with the 400 mm, which is my main lens for wildlife work. I carry 1.4x and 2x doublers, effectively giving me 560 mm and 800 mm lenses when I need the extreme magnification. I have found that the 600 mm is just too great a magnification for most of the shots taken on sheep. You often have to back away from your subject to be able to include some of the environment.

If I am in the mountains when I expect to get sheep fighting pictures, I carry my 50 to 300 zoom lens. Only a zoom lens allows you to quickly change from portraiture to wide field action without changing the position from which you are photographing.

I carry all my gear in a Lowe Pro Quantum pack. I still have plenty of space for food, water, and a few survival items.

Sheep are excellent rock-climbing animals, but mountain goats are better. The goats can go

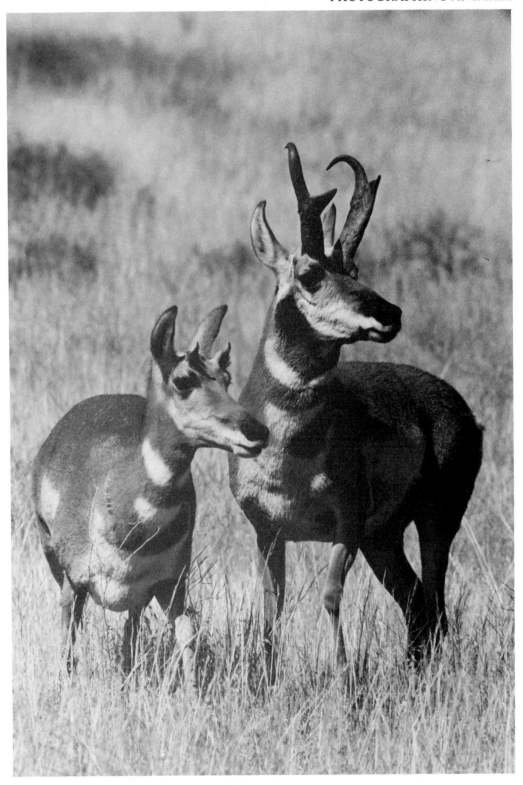

These antelope finally accepted me and allowed me to take hundreds of photographs at close range.

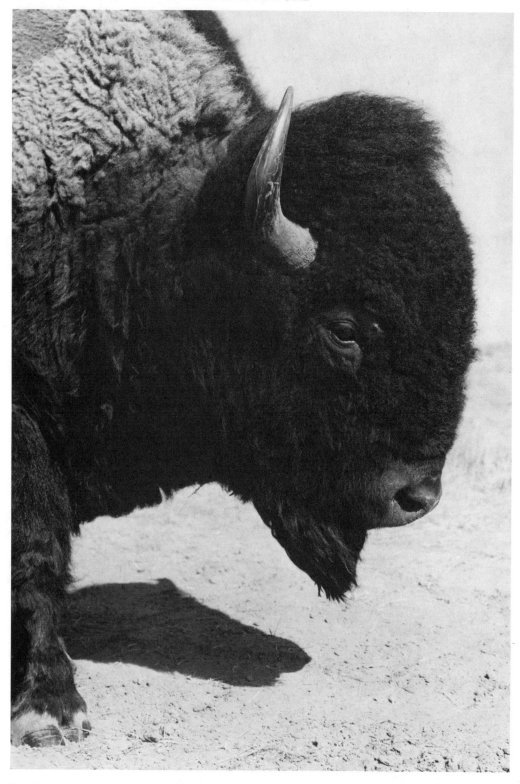

The "loner" bison bulls are usually the largest of the bison. Because of their age, they are driven out of the herd by younger bulls.

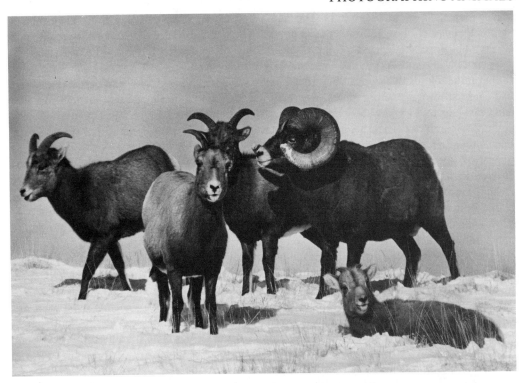

This is one of the finest bighorn sheep "family" photos I have ever taken.

where the sheep cannot, and because of this, goats climb much more deliberately than sheep do. I found the same contrast in Europe. The chamois compares to our mountain goat, and the ibex is similar to the sheep. I can follow a sheep over three-quarters of its terrain; with a goat, I can follow only about one-quarter of the time.

Glacier National Park is the source of most of my mountain goat photos. Good herds can usually be found at Sperry Glacier, Brown's Peak, or in Gunsight Pass. Most photographers rent horses and ride up to the glacier and then work on the goats.

Under ordinary conditions, neither goats nor sheep are a threat to humans, but don't dispute their right of way when they want to use a certain trail. A friend and I were photographing sheep in Yellowstone. We were following two different sheep trails on a very steep talus slope; I was on the lower trail. Suddenly a big ram came around the mountainside on the same trail that my friend was on. The ram never hesitated. He lowered his head and charged. My friend did the only sensible thing; he jumped off the trail and crashed onto the talus below. Luckily, neither my friend nor any of his equipment was broken. The sheep, with the track now cleared, dashed along the trail and disappeared. Perhaps I should not say that the sheep charged. He just lowered his head as he ran, fully intending to use the path he was following, no matter what was in the way.

Musk-oxen were introduced to Nunivak Island, Alaska, in 1935 and 1936 from animals captured in Greenland. The population of these animals in Greenland is approximately 15,000. It is the best place in the world to photograph them in the wild. The herd of musk-oxen on Nunivak Island is held to 800 animals to prevent deterioration of the range. Although Nunivak is about 40 miles square, the musk-oxen are forced by the deep snow to feed along sea beaches in the winter, and overgrazing occurs. It was along these sea beaches that I took my photos of musk-oxen in 1969.

Charlie Travers and I had hired an Eskimo to guide us. When the musk-oxen spotted us, they galloped down to the beach. The adult bulls, cows, and calves formed their famed "protective circle." We just walked outside their circle at a distance of about 100 feet and took all the photos we wanted. As we got no nearer and presented no threat to the animals, they were content to stand. At no time did they show any aggression.

Our guide told us that one old bull that usually stayed by himself was very cantankerous and had charged several photographers, who had escaped only by dashing back to their boat. An adult musk-ox bull weighs about 750 pounds. There are no trees on Nunivak Island, so there is nothing to climb or to hide behind once you leave your boat. Again, I stress that you use your telephoto lenses, and don't push the animal.

At first appearance, an armadillo seems quite sluggish. Its body, except for its belly, is covered with a thick, scaly skin. The armadillo is an insect eater that feeds mainly on ants. It meanders about digging up anthills and slurping up the denizens thereof with its sticky tongue.

The first one I saw was outside Okeefenokee Swamp in southern Georgia. The lighting was good, and while the armadillo was interested in getting its dinner, I was interested in getting its photograph. Which I did.

After a short time, the armadillo moved off into some dense brush. I wanted more photos. I know that armadillos cannot bite; they have only a few rudimentary teeth in the back of their mouths. They do have long powerful claws that they use for digging but not as offensive weapons. I decided to carry the armadillo by its tail to a more open spot. That's when my knowledge of these critters increased dramatically.

When I grabbed the armadillo's tail, the animal, using its powerful hind legs, jumped about 4 feet up in the air and ran away. It scooted in under bushes that I had to go around. I lost it when it disappeared down its burrow in the earth.

I have caught a number of armadillos in Texas. One walked right between my legs as I was standing still in the path it was following. I have found that to get their picture, it is best to just move up on one, slowly, while it is feeding. It will probably continue its activities. If you catch one and put it down in an open area, it will run off. When you find an armadillo, walk up carefully and start snapping photos.

I have not as yet photographed a Florida manatee, although I sure plan to do it. These gentle creatures can be found in many freshwater springs in Florida. Unfortunately, many of them are badly scarred from being cut by the propellers of motorboats. They can be photographed best if you use either snorkel or diving gear.

I have done no whale photography because photos of these behemoths are best taken under water. If photographs of just their heads, fins, or flukes will satisfy you, such photos can be taken from tour boats specializing in whale tours. Tours can be taken from Long Island, New York, from southern California, and to Alaska's Glacier Bay. In Glacier Bay these huge animals sometimes jump entirely out of the water, evidently in exuberance. No one is absolutely sure why whales do this, but Glacier Bay is one of the few areas in the world where they do it consistently.

Taking Action Photos

As I have mentioned so often, all of us miss desirable photos simply because we were not ready when the pose was struck or the action took place.

As you work with a wild animal, you learn to know by its actions, or reactions, what it is going to do. With waterfowl, nervousness is shown by neck craning, holding the neck stiffly erect; in ungulates, it is ear and tail flicking; in the cat family, tail twitching. Hares and rabbits tense their muscles as they set their feet for a fast takeoff. I love to photograph the tenseness in animals because it implies motion even when the creature is standing still, and so fantastically sharp photos can be taken.

There are times that tenseness or even alertness are exceedingly difficult to get when

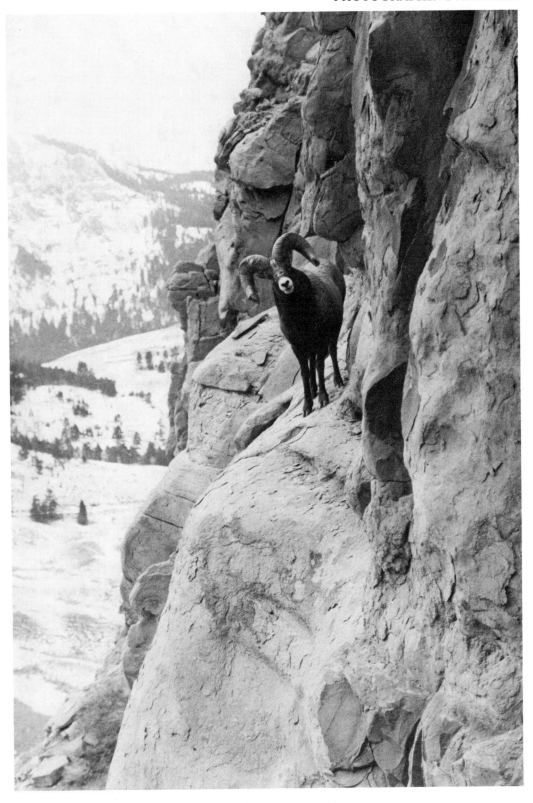

I can usually follow wherever sheep go, but this is where I stopped.

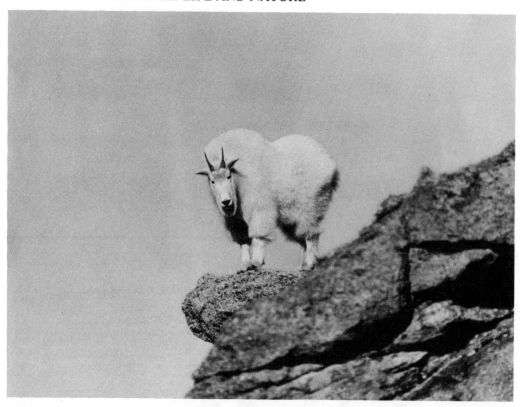

Top Mountain goats are so sure of their climbing ability that they do not run off as quickly as sheep do. *Bottom* This superb male ibex is the counterpart of our sheep; it is found in the Swiss Alps. Photo by Irene Vandermolen

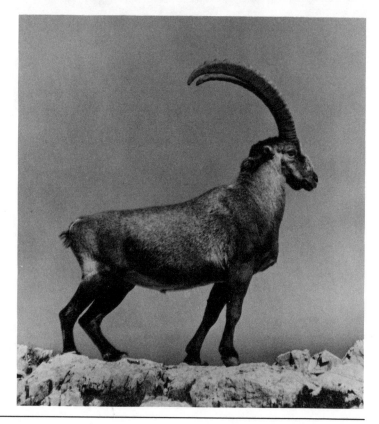

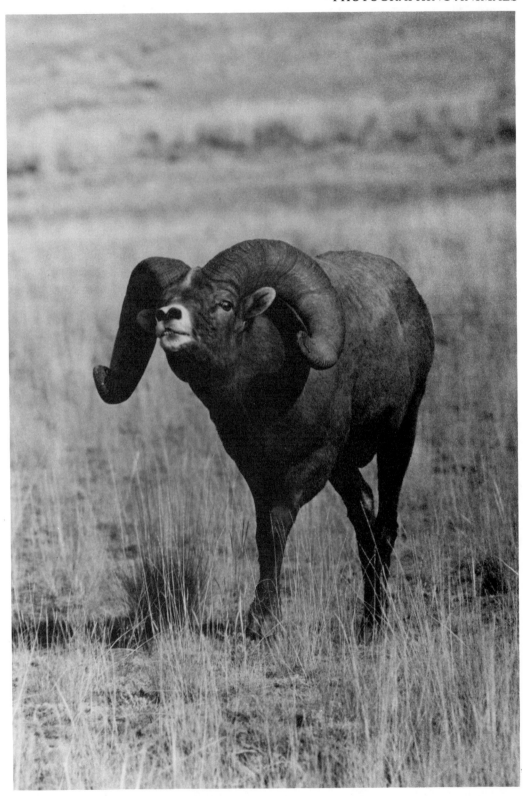

Wild sheep are seldom aggressive; just don't get in their way.

photographing park animals. As I have mentioned, the wildlife in parks is usually accustomed to humans and their activities—too accustomed. Wild animals see so many people so often that they become jaded; they do not look at the photographer or even look up from their feeding. Feeding pictures are all right—they tell a behavioral story—but that's about all they tell.

What editors want to see is an alert animal, one that looks as if it has never seen a human before, and the viewer has just surprised it. I always try to get an eye glint, the sun's sparkling reflection in the creature's eye, because such a highlight makes the creature really look alive.

To get an animal to look alert, to look really alive, is an art in itself. It is usually done by the photographer, or assistant, making a sharp or loud noise or a sudden movement. I may whistle, clap my hands, wave my arms, jump up and down, throw my hat in the air, or duck out of sight and then quickly reappear. Most of the time, one or more of these actions works; but at times, nothing works. Overdo it, and your subject may take off.

In whistling I use my mouth or my little police whistle or even a silent dog whistle. This last works well and can be heard only by the wildlife because of the whistle's exceedingly high pitch. Or I may use a call that imitates the sound made by the creature or a call that would be made by an entirely different species. Nothing works every time, but they are all worth trying.

If you have a buddy or an assistant with you, have him get some distance behind you and walk a semicircle around you. At times I have found that wild creatures pay more attention to a distant moving object than they do to one that is close up.

Many times, I have needed to have the wild animal's head turned slightly in order to get the sun's reflection as an eye glint. By having my assistant walk in the direction I want the animal's head to turn, I can get that eye glint as the animal moves its head to follow the action of the assistant.

I have thrown small stones into bushes or into water to get an animal's attention and get it to turn its head in the proper direction. I have even thought of carrying a slingshot to place the stone more accurately or farther than I could throw it, but a slingshot would be just one more item to carry.

As you approach the animal, have your exposure predetermined and set. Estimate your distance, or actually stop and prefocus. When the animal breaks and dashes off, shoot. Try to keep focusing, but keep shooting. Yes, you will miss a lot of shots if your focus is not sharp, but, with practice, you will get good shots too. All too often, as soon as an animal dashes off, many photographers give up in disgust. If you don't shoot, you will never learn to shoot moving subjects. And if you don't shoot, you don't get pictures. Yes, I miss lots of action shots, but I always try for them.

There are two ways of depicting action with a still camera. You can prefocus on a spot where the subject will pass and shoot with a shutter speed that is slow enough to allow the subject to blur. Or you can focus on the subject and pan your camera at the same speed as the subject, using a shutter speed that is fast enough to freeze the subject and action but allowing the background to blur. Either method will portray action. I prefer the latter method because I want my subject to be as sharp as possible. I have seen photos where both the subject and the background were blurred; one such photo ran as a double-page spread in a major pictorial magazine. I would have thrown that photo out, if it had been mine, but the art director thought it was "very artistic." And let me say this: Art directors are as entitled to their opinion as I am to mine, and they buy the photos. Remember that when some art director rejects what you think are your finest photos and buys something you think is second string.

If, for artistic reasons, you plan to blur both the subject and the background, and you don't want it to look like a mistake, use an extremely slow shutter speed. By shooting at speeds of 1/8, 1/4, or 1/2 second, a panned subject can be blurred to the extent that it is more suggested than depicted.

Panning, and focusing while panning, takes practice, but that's easy to get. Just practice on people walking by, cars on the highway, or any subject that follows a well-defined path.

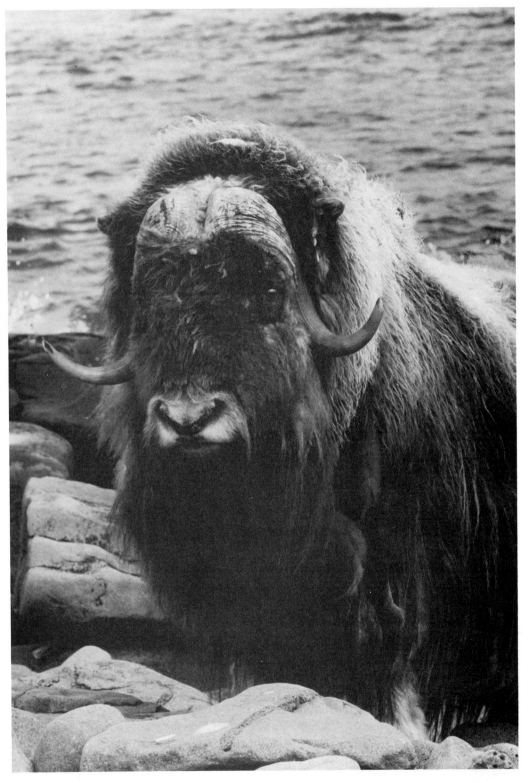

The long, dense coat of hair and wool allows this musk-ox bull to withstand the coldest weather in the world.

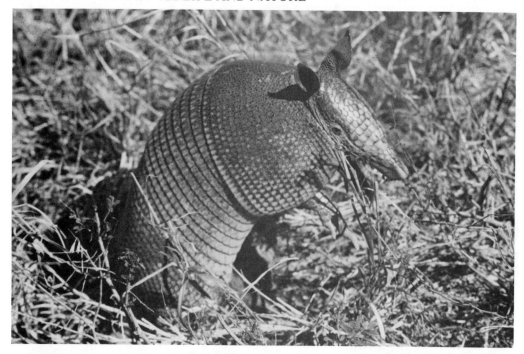

Armadillos often stand erect to get a better look at whatever has disturbed them.

The photographers who shoot with long lenses just with a shoulder pod can get into action faster than I can with my tripod, but any photos I take with the tripod are going to be a lot sharper than those taken with a shoulder pod. Let me clarify that. I do not use a tripod on lenses shorter than 300 mm, but always use it on lenses of 400 mm and up. I do use a Leitz shoulder pod whenever I can on lenses up to 300 mm because it definitely allows me to hold them steadier. I don't want you to meet me out in the field someday shooting with my shoulder pod after reading that I use only a tripod. I use the shoulder pod on shorter lenses, and it is a great help. I just cannot hold the big lenses steady with it.

In the chapter on birds, I mentioned that I sometimes used a gyroscope on my camera and lens because it allowed me to hold longer lenses without the use of a tripod. The gyroscope works well with birds, but does not work well with animals because they can hear the high-pitched whine at a long distance. It alarms them.

Although I always use a motor drive on my cameras, many photographers do not. Many situations do not require a motor drive, but for action photographs, they are a must. There are motor drives and motor winders; the former are battery powered and the latter are spring wound.

Using my Nikon motor drive, I am able to take five frames per second (FPS). The motor winder takes about two FPS. I cannot afford to use the motor winder, I would be missing too many shots. Even five frames per second is not fast enough, nor is the six frames per second gotten with the Nikon 3 motor drive.

Let me explain why. I had the opportunity to photograph two white-tailed bucks running across an open field. I had good sunshine and was using black and white film, so I was able to set my camera at 1/2000 of a second at $f/9$. That was fast enough to stop most motion. I held the release button down and let the film roll, visualizing all the different body positions I was going to get. To my amazement, frames 1, 3, 5, 7, 9, and 11 were identical; and frames 2, 4, 6, 8, 10, and 12 were identical. Instead of getting many different body positions, I got only two. This meant that the deer went through a complete four-footed cycle in just 2/5 of a second.

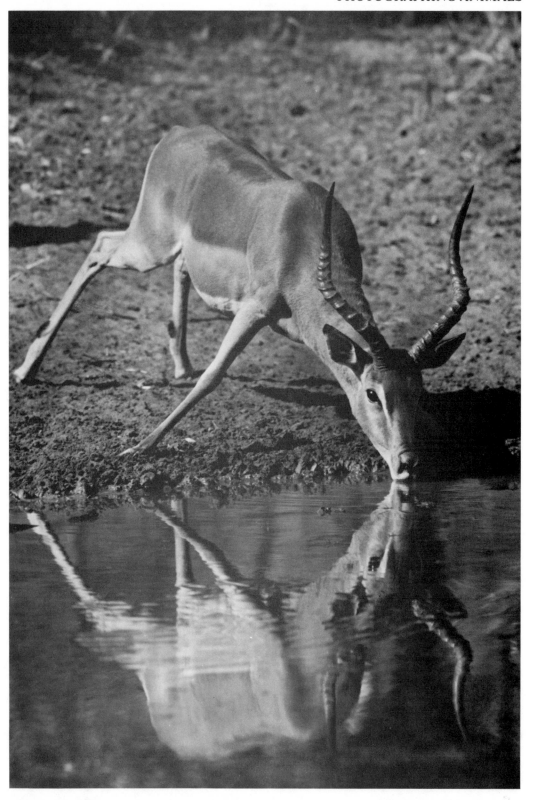

The tension shows in the body of this impala, which has to risk its life to get a drink of water.

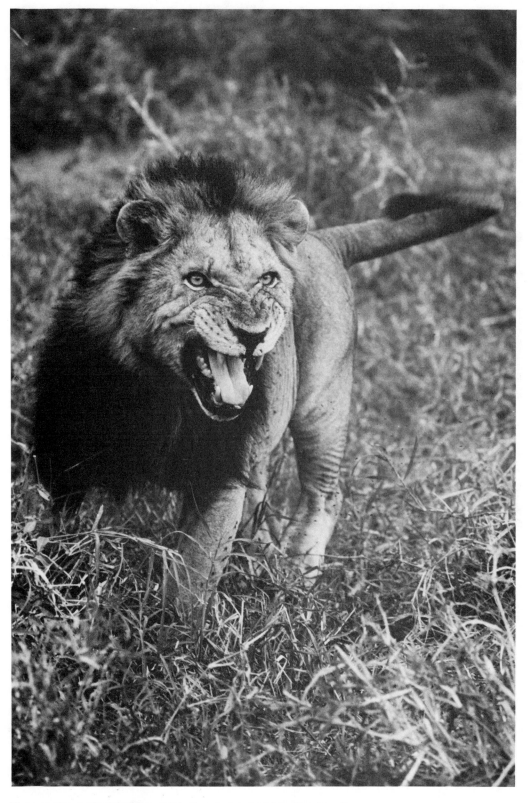

The snarling and tail lashing of this lion shows that it is about to charge.

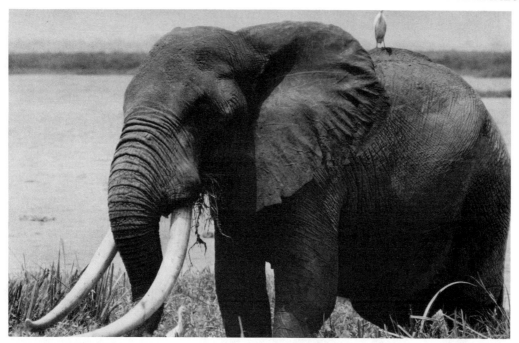

This huge African elephant bull's size and strength made him impervious to all distractions. He simply went on with his feeding.

The bucks were running at a speed of about 35 miles per hour, or 3080 feet per minute, for 51.33 feet per second. They covered over 20 feet, and all four feet touched the ground and vaulted them onward in that 2/5 of a second.

I have photographed a lot of fights between bighorn sheep rams. The rams usually start the fights from about 35 feet apart. They raise up on their hind legs and run forward for several steps, drop to all fours and pour on the speed, turn and counterturn their massive horns for impact, collide, and bounce back.

When I first photographed this action, I was elated thinking about all the photos I was going to get. How many photos do you think I got? Four. I have never gotten more than four photos of any sheep fight, and I have to anticipate the action and shoot at the first movement of the sheep to get even four. Just blink your eyes slowly, and you have missed the entire action. With the Nikon 3, I may get five pictures of the sheep fighting, but it's doubtful.

The pronghorn antelope buck is the fastest land animal in North America and can do 60 miles per hour when he is running flat out. That means he is covering a distance of 88 feet per second.

These examples give you some idea of the speed of wildlife. They should also show why motor drives are used and needed and how, in spite of their usage, photographers still cannot get all the action photos they want.

The distance between the photographer and the subject and the angle the subject is traveling in relation to the photographer have a tremendous bearing on the difficulty of obtaining the action shot.

The easiest subject to focus on is one that is traveling parallel to you. Once the subject is in focus, it will stay in focus for a number of shots. The closer the subject is to the photographer, or the longer the focal length of the lens is, the shorter the depth of field and the more difficult it will be to focus properly or even pick up the subject in the viewfinder. Any time the distance is halved or the focal length is doubled, the speed of the moving subject will apparently be

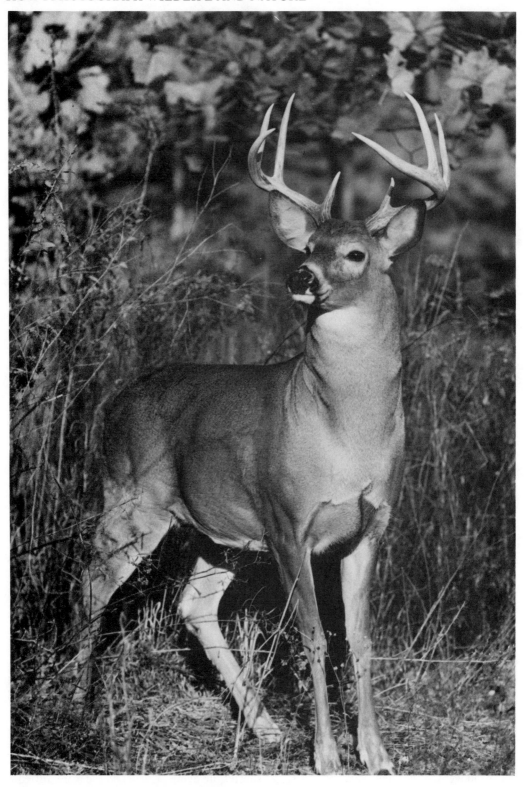

This photograph of a white-tailed buck epitomizes all the alertness, tension, and eyeshine needed for a super portrait. Photo by Irene Vandermolen

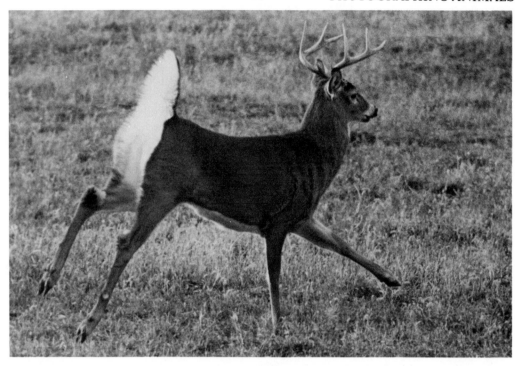

To stop the fast action of this running white-tailed deer, I had to sacrifice the depth of field.

doubled. This illusion of doubled speed is created because the image on the film will also be doubled. The shutter speed needed to stop the action of the parallel subject is determined by both the speed of the subject and the amount of action it takes the subject to move. Panning will stop action at a much slower shutter speed than taking a photo at a fixed point with a stationary camera. The body of a running deer can be stopped with a shutter speed of 1/500 of a second; it takes 1/2000 of a second to freeze the motion of the deer's legs, which are traveling at a much greater individual speed than is the body.

A subject that is moving diagonally to the photographer can be stopped at half the speed needed to stop one moving parallel. Focusing is usually done by constantly refocusing on the subject as it moves in and out of the focused-on range. It is difficult to match your focusing and panning precisely to the movement of the subject, but it can be done.

Proper focusing is difficult when the subject is moving directly toward or away from the photographer because it is more rapidly getting out of the plane of focus. The most successful way is to focus in front of the animal and shoot when it appears sharp. With this method, you usually get only one shot, but the chances of it being sharp are much greater than by any other method for this angle. I would advise pressing your shutter release before the subject moves into the desired spot, and perhaps you will get several shots before it moves out of the area. This is similar to anticipating and stopping peak action. Usually there is one point in most action where the action is stopped by gravity, inertia, or the like. A good example is a ball thrown in the air. The peak action is just as the ball stops going up and before it starts to fall. For a split second, the ball is not moving in space. An animal is moving slowest at the top of its leap.

Capturing the exact peak of the action is better done manually than by firing a burst with the motor drive. Even if you shoot the action as a sequence, you may not capture the peak action because it may occur at the precise moment that the film is being advanced. In a number of those sheep fighting series, I did not get the moment of the actual impact of the

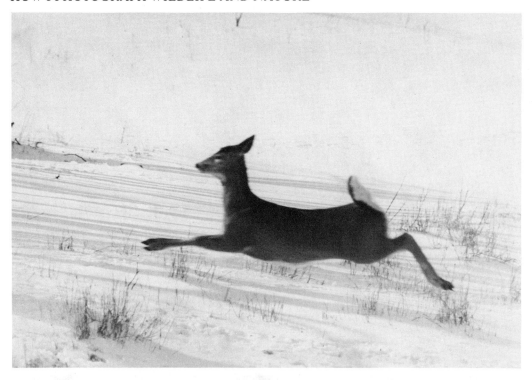

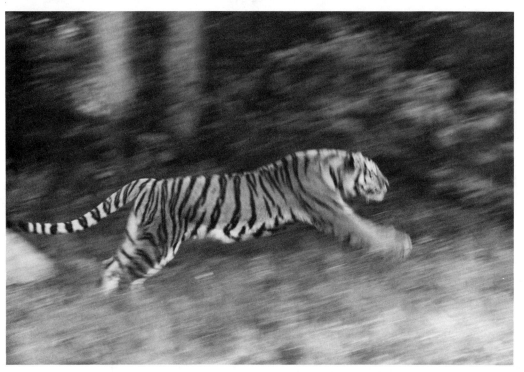

Top To denote action, the camera was panned, blurring the background, but the white-tailed doe is needle sharp.
Bottom An extremely slow shutter speed blurred both the background and the tiger but produced a very "arty" photograph. Photo by Irene Vandermolen

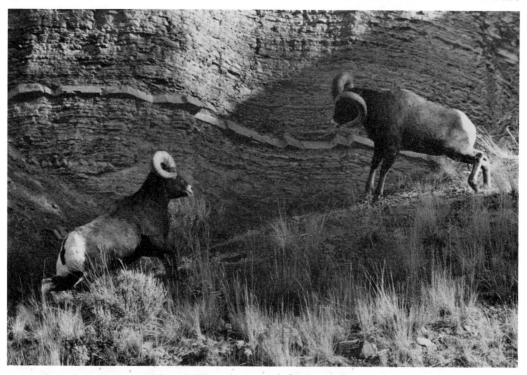

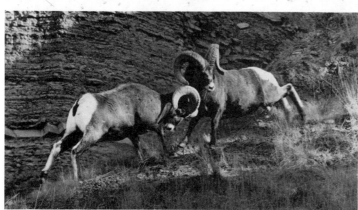

These photos are from three different fights between bighorn sheep. Even the fastest motor drives do not capture all the action needed. Photo by Len Rue, Jr.

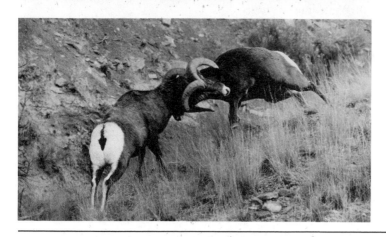

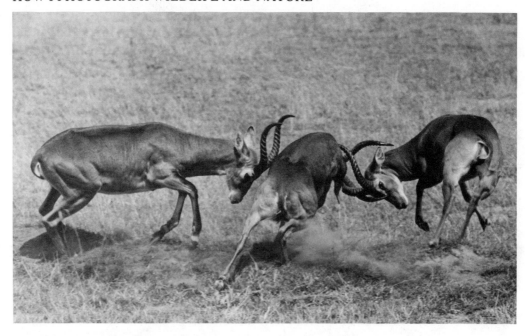

All the action of these fighting Uganda kob was frozen by the photograph being taken at the actual moment of impact.

rams' heads. I got photos of just before the rams hit, and I got them recoiling, but the film was being advanced during the peak of the action. I would have done better to anticipate the collision and then shoot it as a single frame.

Most 35 mm SLR cameras have a focal plane shutter. Even though you pan with your subject, that subject, moving in the opposite direction from the direction of your camera's curtain slit, will be slightly shortened. A subject moving in the same direction as the curtain slit will be slightly lengthened.

Sequences Tell the Story

The major difference between cinematography, which is in reality a series of still photographs, and regular still photography is that by using a motion picture projector the still photos are projected rapidly. The eye and the mind interpret them as moving. The film moves, not the pictures. There is a lesson for still photographers here.

As still photographers, we try to tell the entire story with one picture. This is accomplished in about 90 percent of situations—particularly if the photographer is doing wildlife portraits or is shooting to stop the peak action. The story of wildlife behavior can be told more easily when the photos are used in sequence. We do not really create the illusion that a series of still shots is moving, but the sequence allows us to tell a more complete story.

The use of a motor drive makes the shooting of a sequence easier. There are times, however, that a sequence can be done better with the camera advanced manually or the motor used on the single frame capacity. At times a motor drive will take too many photos of insignificant action or motion. If all motor-drive sequences were shown, it would be as if the action were in slow motion. I'm not saying that you should not use the motor drive to its full capacity. Get all the photographs possible whenever the situation allows this to be done. But there are times when judicious editing of a series tells the same story with greater impact with less photographs.

The Hunter as Photographer

Many hunters carry a camera with them to record on film the trophy they have taken with the gun. Many hunters take wildlife photos just as a sideline. To take good photos while hunting is extremely difficult because the wild animals in hunting areas will always be more wary than those in a protected park. When hunting takes top priority, as it always will do on a hunting trip, any wildlife shots will be grab shots. And they will look it.

When a hunter finds his camera in his hand when he should have had the gun, a transition begins to take place. Many hunters give up hunting and take up photography because they realize that to shoot a good wildlife photo is a greater challenge than shooting an animal with a gun. While almost all hunters eat the meat of the game they hunt, it is the challenge of the hunt that they are really interested in.

A successful hunter has the main prerequisite for being a successful photographer. He knows wildlife. The more you know about any creature or subject, the more successful you will be in coping with it. That's why this book should make you a better photographer.

The hunter who just wants to take photographs of his trophy animals can improve his photographs by utilizing the following suggestions: If the animal you have just taken is truly a trophy, then you may have the basis for a good, salable story. All hunting stories are enhanced by photographs; in many cases, the photographs actually sell the story. Editors expect writers to supply the photographic illustrations.

Many animals, after death, have relaxed their muscles; they will have their tongues sticking out of their mouths. Before taking any photographs, push the animal's tongue back in its mouth. Wipe away any traces of blood from the animal's mouth and nose; you can do this with a handful of grass. If there is blood on the snow, kick clean snow over the spot to cover it. If there is blood on the rocks or ground that cannot be covered, move the animal to a clean spot, if possible. Take your photos as soon after obtaining your trophy as you can before the eyes get their green glaze.

The Boone and Crockett Club is the official scorekeeper for North American trophies. Their certified people do a very meticulous job of measuring horns, antlers, or skulls of trophy animals. You can't fool their tape measures. You can enhance your photographs by judicious placement of the trophy and the hunter. A hunter posed in front of his trophy will cause it to look smaller. When the hunter and the trophy are on the same plane, the size of the trophy will be judged correctly by anyone who knows the hunter. Many sportsmen include their fishing rod with their catch or their guns with their trophies. Both items are great for recording scale, but remember that they will be a basis for exact evaluation. The hunter who sits behind his trophy does not make it a fraction of an inch larger, he just makes it seem larger. And there is nothing wrong with that.

Most hunting photos are taken with the hunter sitting directly behind his trophy, framed by the horns or antlers. If, instead of sitting directly behind the animal's head, the hunter sits by its shoulder or moves back to its flank, the trophy will appear even larger as the hunter's size is diminished.

On any trip, but particularly on a hunting or fishing trip where there is a hope of selling a story, take tons of support photos. Take pictures of the mode of transportation to the area, of the preparation, of the camp, of cooking, of glassing for game or casting for fish. The larger the choice of photographs you can offer an editor, and the better the quality of your photographs, the better your chance of selling your story. A picture is still worth 1000 words. Good photos can tell the story; the writing will just flesh it out.

Miscellaneous Notes

If you are using horses to get to wilderness areas, you will soon notice that you can get much

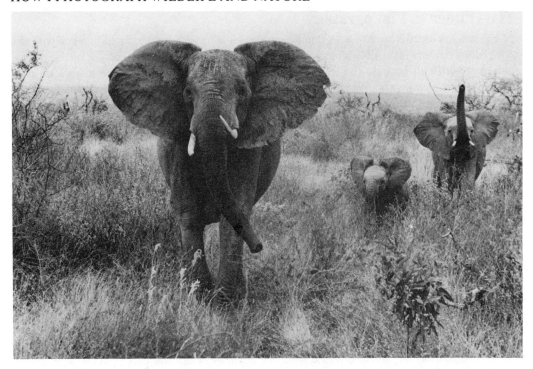

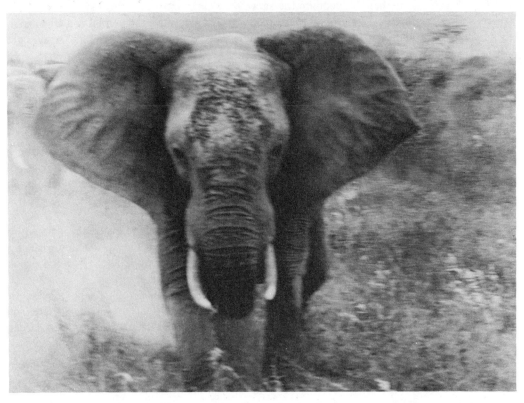

This is a dramatic sequence of a charging African elephant cow. It was taken from a Land Rover doing about 20 miles per hour. I realize that the last photos are not sharp, but then who has sharp photos taken of a charging elephant at 10 feet?

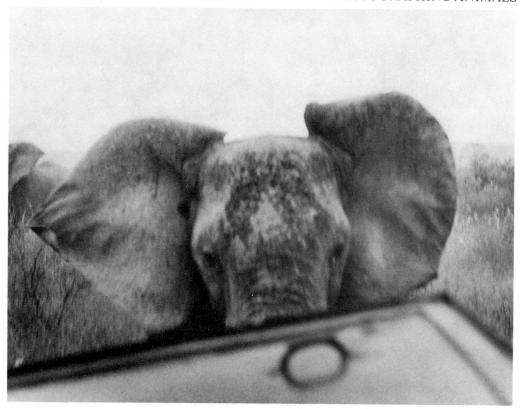

closer to the wildlife by riding than you can by walking. If the animals become suspicious of you on the horse, ride bareback and bend forward so that your body is not silhouetted in an erect position. As a kid on the farm, I often rode right in among herds of deer by lying down on the horse's back. The odor of the horse will mask your odor, and most wild creatures know that a horse won't bother them. You can also use a horse to approach an animal by walking on the opposite side of the horse from your subject. Walk near the horse's front legs so that your legs are not unduly conspicuous.

The Indians, years ago, used to stalk right in among their prey animals by covering themselves with the skins of various wild animals that the prey animal was accustomed to. Walking with a horse is the same idea.

When using a canoe for deer or moose that are feeding in a lake, stop paddling when the animal lifts its head. When the animal submerges, paddle forward three or four strokes, then stop again. Be extra careful not to hit the gunwale of your canoe with your paddle. Noise travels better underwater than it does through the air. If you were to strike your canoe with the paddle while the animal's head was submerged, the noise would send it dashing away.

Never approach a swimming bear when you are in a boat or a canoe unless you have a motor on the craft. Anyone who gets close to a swimming bear is more than likely to have the bear climb right in with him. This has happened countless times.

When photographing the young of wild animals, do not touch the little ones. Many wild animals are deathly afraid of human scent, and if you touch the young, your odor on their bodies may cause them to be abandoned by their mothers. This is as true for rabbits as it is for deer.

In national parks it is illegal to feed the animals, so the use of bait is prohibited. Usually baiting is not needed in parks anyway. Baits and scents are of tremendous importance where they are allowed, however, and they are allowed in many state parks. Another word of caution

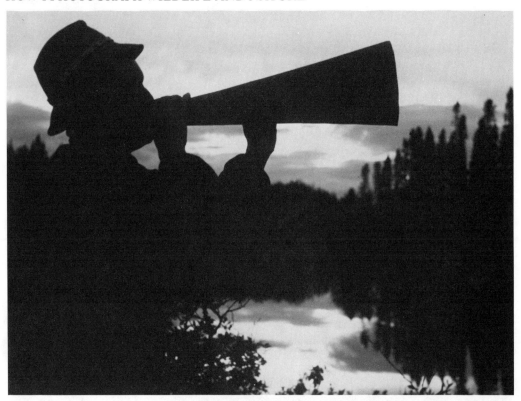

Top A dramatic sil-
houette shot of my
partner, Homer Hicks,
on my Canadian trips,
calling moose.
Bottom Support
photos, such as the
loading of the pack
animals, should be
taken.

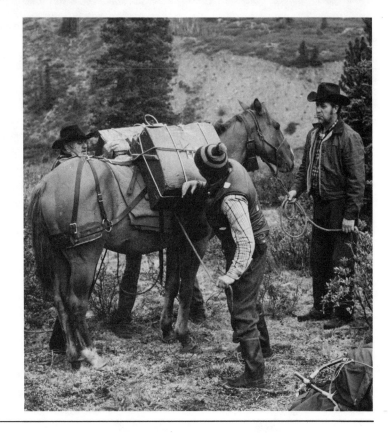

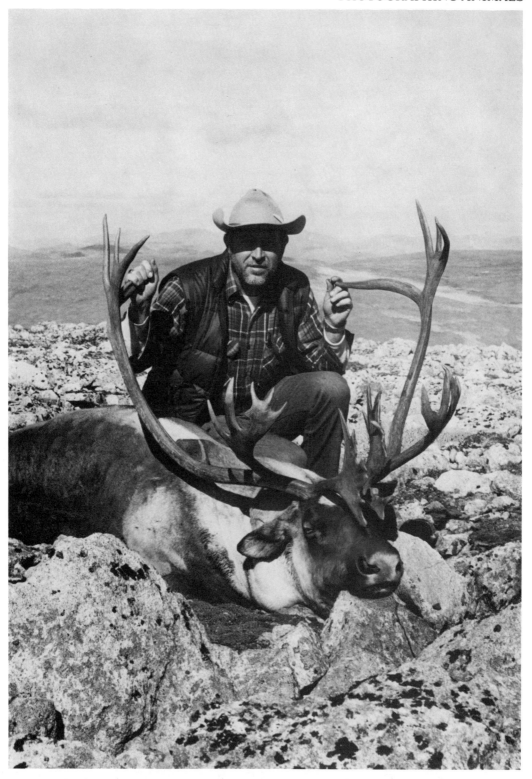

Danny Haas with a record-book moutain caribou in the Cassiar Mountains of British Columbia. By positioning the hunter farther back and lower, the caribou appears larger.

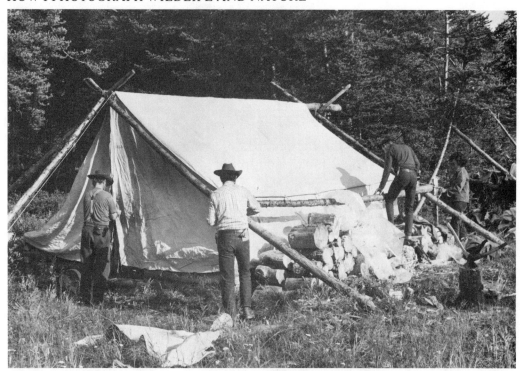

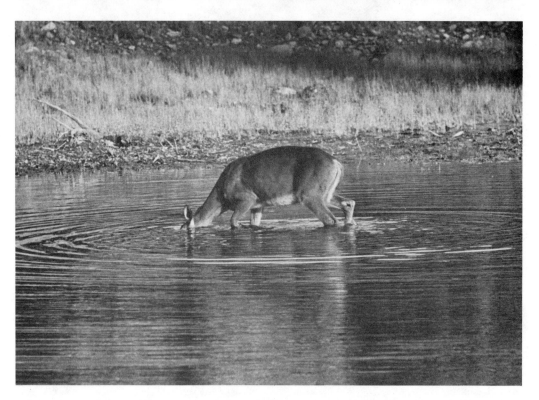

Top The photograph of the tent shows that the group was camping out in a spruce forest.
Bottom Paddle when the deer's head is submerged. Don't move when the deer raises its head to look around.

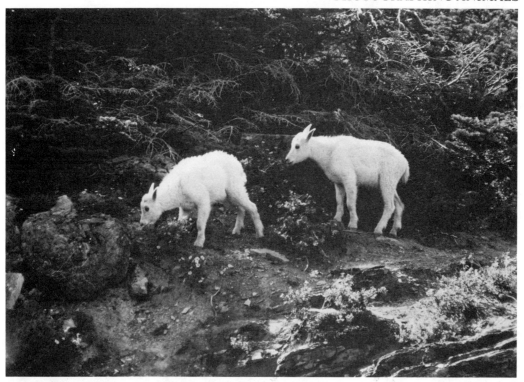

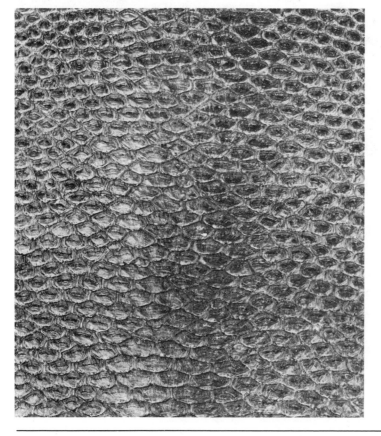

Top To photograph these mountain goat kids with backlighting, I merely took a reading from the background. *Bottom* This close-up photograph of the scales on a beaver's tail shows their similarity to a fish's scales, a snake's scales, a bird's foot, and a pine cone.

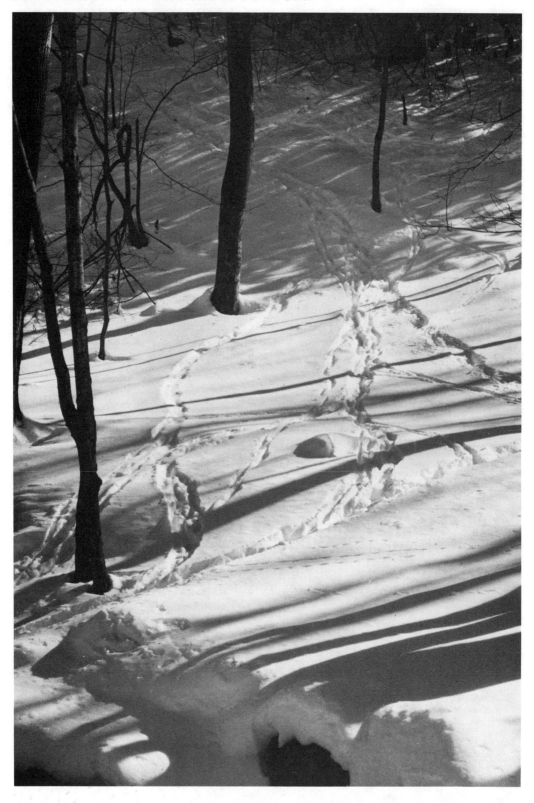

Don't miss an opportunity to take photos like this one of deer tracks.

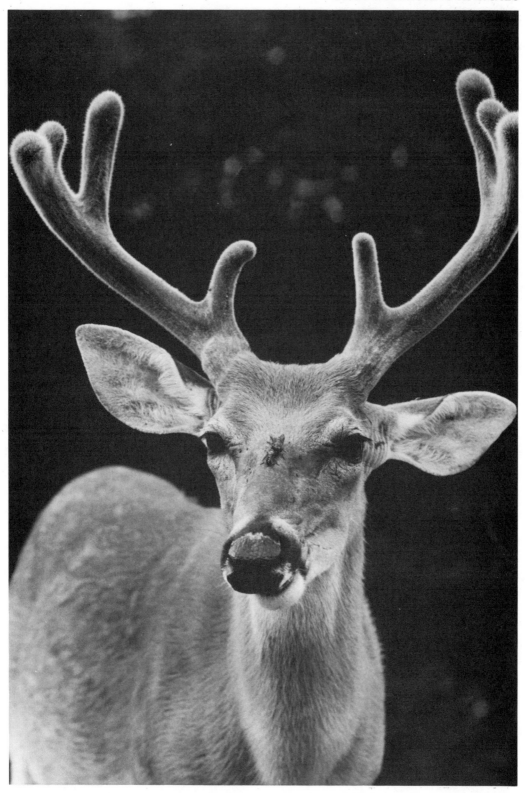

Rimlighting shows the velvet texture of this white-tailed buck's antlers growing.

is that you should not feed, even small animals, from your hand. In their eagerness to get the food, they may accidentally bite you. Any time your skin is broken with a puncture wound, you run the risk of infection.

I have talked throughout this book about having the sun behind you. For most photos, that's where the sun should be. Your color will be the brightest and your depth of field the greatest because the maximum amount of light will be falling on your subject. There are times, though, when taking photos with the sun behind your subject will produce absolutely striking photographs. Backlighted photos often show as rimlighting. One of my most commented on photographs is of backlighted mountain goats. The sun shining through their snow-white coats has created a halo effect. A lens hood should always be used to prevent stray light from hitting your lens and causing halation or flare. The hood is a must when doing backlighted photos, but if the sun is low on the horizon, it may not provide sufficient coverage. In this situation, I hold my hand or my hat between the sun and my lens, making sure that it will not be seen through the lens. This works better if you have an assistant to do the shading so that you can keep both hands on the camera.

To meter for backlighted subjects, take a reading from the general background and shoot. If you don't have time to meter, and your camera is set for the sun being behind you, simply open two and a half or three stops and then shoot. A rule of thumb is that with your camera set for the sun behind you, photos taken at right angles (90-degree angles) to the sun need one and a half stops more light; those at 180 degrees need three stops.

When doing wildlife photography, I photograph everything. Ordinarily, when I go afield, I am planning to photograph animals. If I cannot find animals, I work on birds. If there are no birds, I work on any living thing I can find, and that includes flowers.

That is the order of preference for my photography. But I want to stress that I photograph everything I encounter, even if, when I'm taking the photo, I wonder what I will ever do with it. No matter what the subject, sooner or later, some editor will want that particular shot. So I always photograph tracks, dens, feces, skeletons, feathers, parts of birds and animals, and so forth. I have a great personal interest in all this as a student of nature. And I have found that it pays off in the marketplace.

ZOO AND STUDIO PHOTOGRAPHY

*If I were ever to take a vacation I would do
just what I am doing now; photographing
wildlife.*

—L. L. Rue III

Years ago, when the National Audubon Society maintained their own photographic agency on the premises, I asked them whose photos accounted for the most sales. The person making the greatest number of sales was a full-time schoolteacher who spent every weekend and every vacation photographing every creature at every zoo that could be photographed. If foreground wire could be eliminated, it was; if the artificial background could be eliminated, it was. But even when these structures could not be removed, the photos were taken. And many of them sold. When editors needed photos, from an aardvark to a zorille, this person had it, fences and all. But the species had been photographed.

Zoos are fun to photograph, but I don't like to do it. I have taken many pictures at zoos and will probably take many more, but I never want anything man-made to appear in my photos. This is just a personal preference. It should not stop anyone else from photographing at zoos because such photography can produce good sales.

Times to Photograph at Zoos

If you are planning to photograph at a zoo, you will have to time it properly. Zoos are public places, and you want to be there when most of the public is not. Weekdays are best because during the week most parents have to work and most kids are in school. Weekends and holidays should be avoided at all costs.

Midsummer is usually the worst time of the year because the heat sends all the creatures seeking shade. Yet this is one of the best times for water animals such as sea lions, polar bears, and river otters because these creatures will be frolicking in the water to cool off.

Midwinter is usually bad because most of the creatures are in shelter, yet a new snow can give you excellent shots of bears. They don't become somnolent in zoos.

Spring and fall are usually the best times to photograph at zoos because the creatures are as invigorated as you are by the changing seasons. Fall is the breeding season for many hooved mammals, and the males are in their finest physical condition. Spring is the breeding season for most birds, and they are usually in their best plummage. You may also get the males displaying for the females and the nest-building activities. Late spring is usually a difficult time to work in any zoo because of schoolchildren's class trips. If anything, the grounds may be more crowded during the week than on weekends.

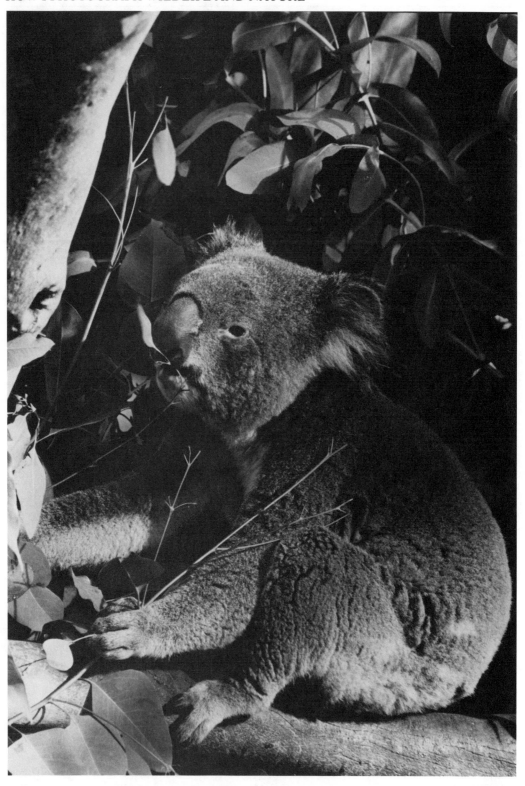

This koala was photographed at the beautiful San Diego Zoo. It is the only zoo in North America to have this marsupial. Photo by Len Rue, Jr.

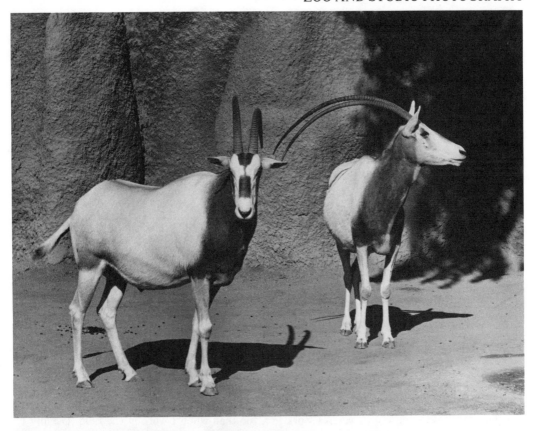

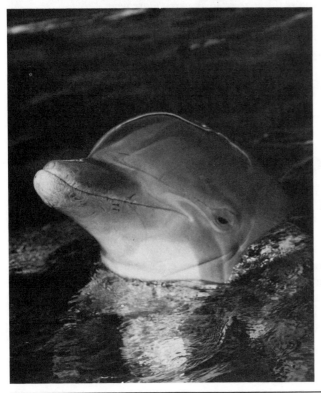

Top Scimeter-horned oryx have to be phtographed in a zoo because they were all but exterminated in the wild. Photo by Len Rue, Jr. *Bottom* The bottle-nosed dolphin is usually featured at aquariums. These dolphins are super-intelligent and can be trained to perform and work.

At any time of the year, try to get to the zoo just as they open the gates. The earlier you are there, the fewer people you will have to contend with, and the more active most wild creatures will be. Find out from the keepers the exact time each day that particular animals you are interested in are fed. Get there before feeding time because the creatures will probably be most active just before they are fed.

Delightful photographs can also be taken right after a creature has been fed. Animals usually wash themselves clean by licking with their tongues, and birds wipe off their beaks; then the animals groom while the birds preen. Prior to taking a nap, animals stretch, yawn, or scratch themselves. After they awaken, they go through the same gestures. Getting these photos means having the patience to wait for them, but the results can be well worth the wait.

For zoo photography, as well as for field photography, you have to do your homework ahead of time. You have to know the creature's location, the zoo opening time, feeding times, where the sun will be at approximately any time of the day, and so on.

Most creatures are creatures of habit. They not only have their periods of activity and are influenced by the times they are fed but they also have definite exercise patterns. Many people feel sorry for animals they see pacing their cages or compounds. The energy that the animal would ordinarily expend in hunting for, or capturing, its food is now spent pacing. Knowing this pattern can be useful when you want to take photographs. You can prefocus on a precise spot, and take your photograph when the animal passes.

Equipment for Zoo Photography

Many zoos are doing away with bars and fences and are building larger areas for compatible creatures, containing them by the use of moats. This greatly enhances such areas for photography.

I find that I carry more gear when I work in a zoo than when I work in the field. Usually I need more gear, but because of the paved paths at zoos, I can carry more gear.

I have an oversized luggage carrier, larger than the ones you see at airports. By using such a carrier I can take along a short aluminum stepladder. The ladder allows me to shoot over walls more easily and to shoot at a slight downward angle, which may eliminate a distant rear wall. A tripod should always be carried so that tight head shots can be done with long telephoto lenses. You gain by eliminating a lot of artificial background and by the shorter depth of field that goes along with using longer lenses. Zoom lenses are a blessing; they let you focus on the entire creature or just its head. And a flash gun is a must for indoor shots.

Getting Rid of Fences and Glass

I dust my lenses primarily because dust cuts down on the transmission of light, not because the dust will be seen on film. You can put a pencil in front of your lens, and if the lens is focused at infinity, an acceptable photograph can be taken. That optical fact is the basis that allows for the elimination of wire and glass.

When you have to shoot through wire, get as close to it as you can. Do not climb over protective barriers to shoot through bars or fencing. If the fence is a chain-link one or is built of a larger mesh, there is a good chance that your lens will fit through it. If the lens will not go through the wire, center the lens with the hole in the wire, and you can get by with perhaps just the slightest vignetting on the edge of the photo. Smaller mesh such as the ½-inch hardware cloth or chicken wire, has wire of a sufficiently small diameter that you can shoot right through it. Make sure that your lens is tight against the wire so that no light reflects off the wire. This reflection will cause flare enough to spoil your photos. The longer the telephone lens, the less distraction the wire will cause.

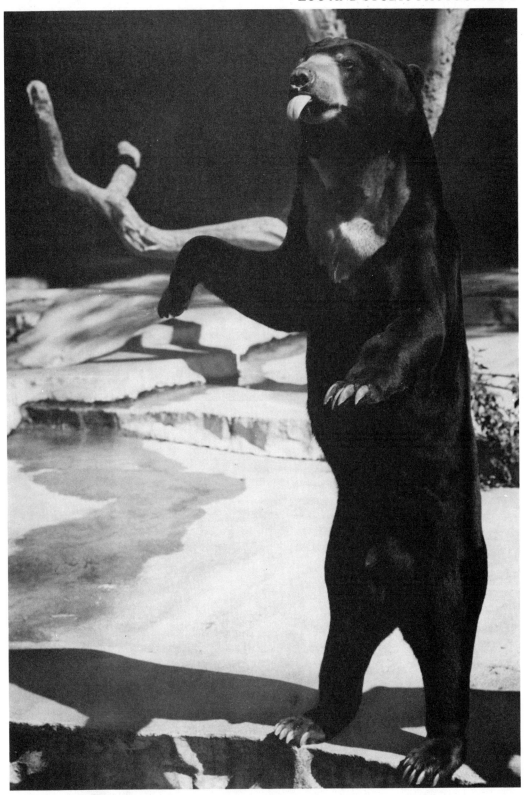

Most creatures, like this Malayan sun bear, become extremely active just before feeding time.

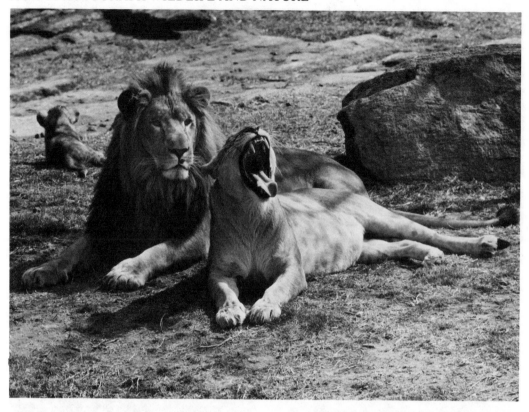

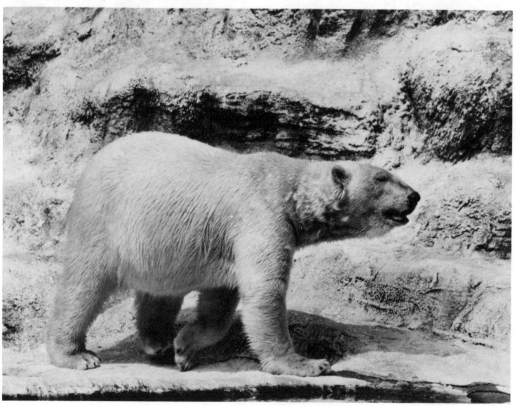

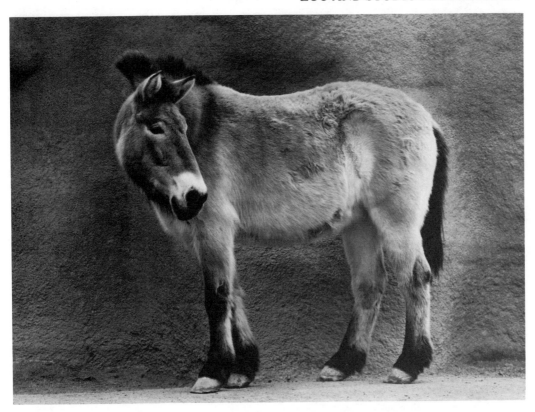

Opposite page: Top This African lioness has just eaten—note the full belly—and is yawning just before she takes a nap.
Bottom This polar bear is pacing, using up the energy it would normally expend in hunting for its food. Photo by Len Rue, Jr.

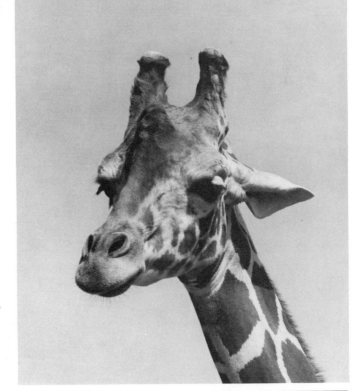

Above The Przewalski's wild horse is extinct in the wild and can be seen only in a zoo. Photo by Len Rue, Jr.
Right A long telephoto lens allowed me to photograph this reticulated giraffe's head, eliminating all signs of the zoo.

Right My son shot this wolf through a chain-link fence. It has been one of our all-time best-selling photographs. It's been used at least 50 times. Photo by Len Rue, Jr.

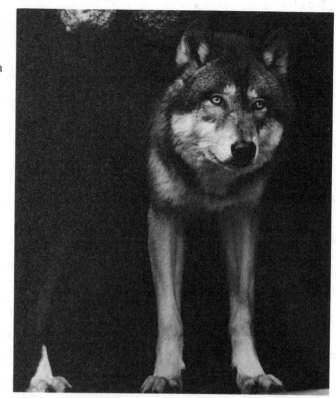

Below This beaver, swimming underwater, was photographed through glass by the methods described in the text. Photo by Irene Vandermolen

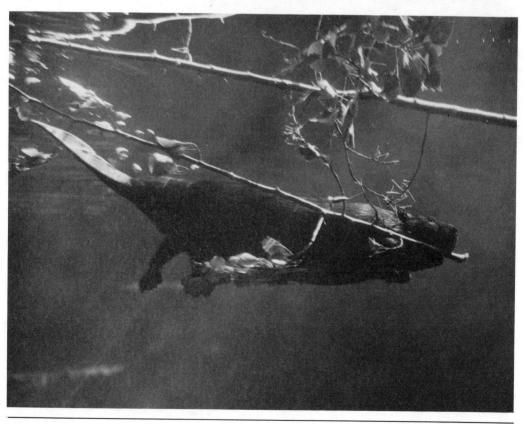

The secret to shooting through glass is to shoot through it on an angle. A reflection is possible only when you shoot straight on. If you have to shoot straight on, shoot through a large piece of black cardboard pressed over your lens. Hold your flash gun at an angle to the glass, and make sure that stray light bouncing off the glass does not light up the glass in front of your camera lens.

One of the best tricks I know to prevent such glare is to use a lightweight cardboard box that is perhaps 6 inches square. Paint the inside of the box black, and cut a hole in the center the same size as the outside diameter of your lens. Tape this box to your lens. In use, just press the box up against the glass, and you will get no reflections from your camera or flare from your flash gun or those of other people.

Many zoos have aviaries where you get in a huge oversized cage with the birds. The birds are kept in the cage by a series of gates or by jets of air. Most aviaries are climate controlled and have lush natural foliage growing inside so that the birds are in as natural a condition as possible. These areas offer great photographic opportunities but as they are poorly lighted, as they would be in natural jungle locations, the use of flash is a must.

Patience Is Needed

Many times, people who do not take photographs consider photographers to be cheating if they take pictures of creatures in captivity, in zoos, or under controlled conditions. Unless the creatures are trained to obey on command, they do what they want to do when they want to do it. It is true that having them in captivity means that you do not have to go out and find them, but it is also true that you cannot make them do what you hope they will do. To work with wild creatures takes patience whether you are photographing out-of-doors or inside.

Studio Photography

The size of your studio will be determined by the size of your subjects. Most studios are converted garages or basements or structures of similar size. Studios are usually used for photographing birds and small mammals up to the size of a fox or raccoon.

Most studios employ a small stage so that the subject can be raised at least 3 feet above the floor for ease in photographing it. Photographers simply bring in pieces of moss, clumps of grass, rocks, old logs, and the like to create a background similar to that in which the creature would normally be found.

Some photographers are really artists in creating backgrounds complete with brooks or a lake edge. They go to great lengths to get the background natural-looking, and they do so with great success. The only thing that gives away their attempt at being all-natural is their use of multiple electronic flashes.

There is only one sun. A photo taken out-of-doors under natural conditions will show only one highlight in the eye of the subject. When you see three, four, or even five highlights in a creature's eye, you know it is a studio setup. To get away from those multiple lights, some photographers use large light bars. Instead of having three or four highlights, a large square light now can be seen in the creature's eye. Even using bounce light does not give enough ambient light in a studio to allow only one major flash to be used.

There are times when two flashheads are used out-of-doors under natural conditions: one main light and one fill light. This causes two highlights. But three or more lights almost always mean a studio setup.

In photographing some of the smaller rodents it is best to work at night because this is when they ordinarily are active. Many of the little creatures, being trapped, want nothing more than to hide, and they are likely to stay hidden during daylight hours. Place the animal in the studio

Right It would be hard to tell that this short-tailed weasel was photographed in a studio if it were not for the two highlights in the eye. Photo by Irene Vandermolen.

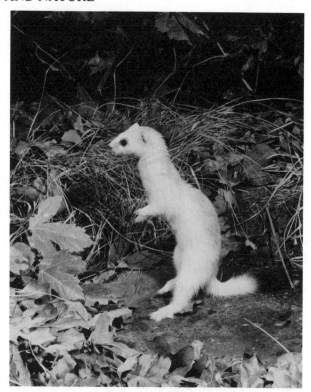

Below Ringtails are strictly nocturnal, so the black background is okay. The few simple props give this beautiful creature a natural background. Photo by Irene Vandermolen

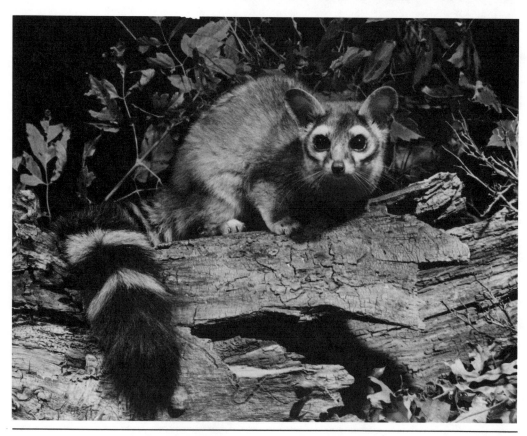

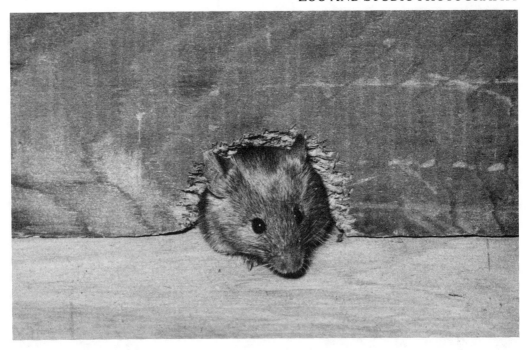

It is easier to work with this house mouse, and other small rodents, at night when they would normally be active.

and allow it to become familiar with the setup before you attempt to work. It can be baited to the center of the stage with bits of food hidden in the duff of the foreground.

Many creatures will try to hide in back corners and will have to be moved out with a long pole. A bamboo or cane fishing pole, being lightweight, is ideal. The animals do not have to be touched with the pole; often, just moving the pole into the corner will move the creatures out of it. You may have to move them a number of times, but it will not take too long before they realize that they are not molested if they come to the middle of the stage. That's where you want them.

For very small creatures, some photographers make wedge-shaped containers that have a solid back but have sides and a top made of clear plastic. The angle of the wedge shape is determined by the angle of coverage of your lens. The camera is poked through a small hole in the apex of the wedge. The top of the cage is hinged so that the specimen can be put in the cage or herded about.

The beauty of this kind of stage is that it is small enough that the interior foliage can be easily constructed or arranged. The specimen has almost no place to hide because the area covered matches your lens. The specimen can move easily and still be controlled because of the stage's small size. And the specimen cannot escape.

Lighting is usually provided by two strobes placed one on either side of the wedge. Occasionally a third strobe is used as a backlight to make the specimen stand out in contrast to its background.

How to Photograph Pets

Photographing pets can be a mighty lucrative business. Walter Chandoha is the best there is in the business; he has sold more photos of pets commercially than anyone I know, and he has written several excellent books on how to do it! It's his strong suit; it's not mine. Photograph-

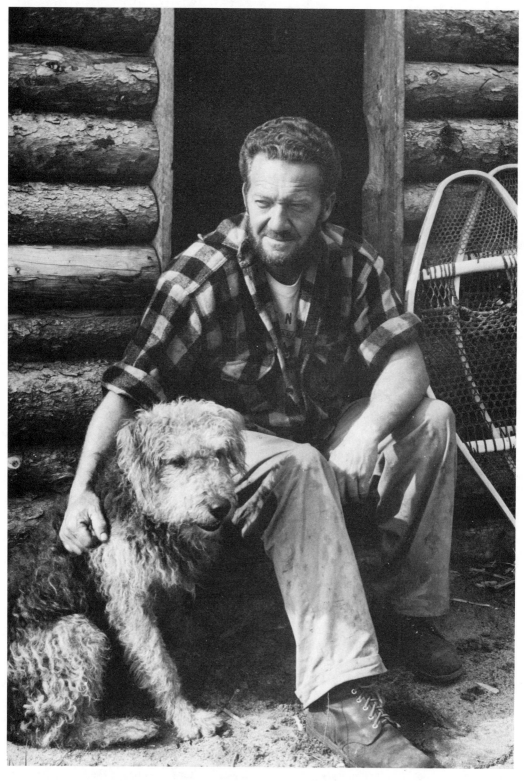

A fine portrait of both Homer Hicks and his dog, Duke. The log cabin and the snowshoes suggest a Northwoods locale. It was taken in the Canadian bush country.

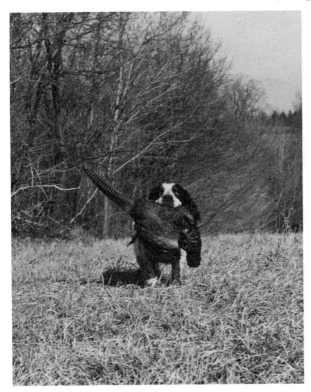

Right My springer spaniel, Freckles, retrieving a cock pheasant.

Below A proud springer spaniel mother and young.

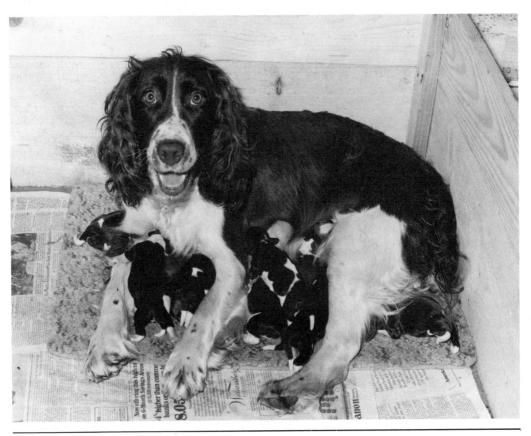

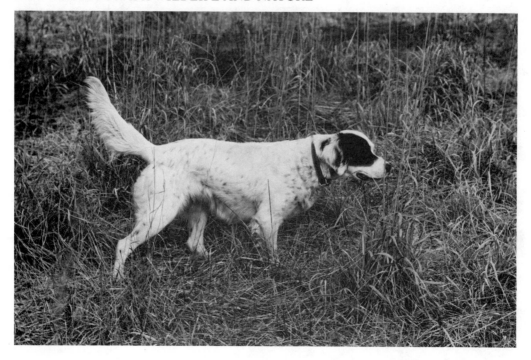

This English setter stands like a statue after having located a hiding pheasant. The dog will not move until it is given the command to move.

ing domestic animals has just never turned me on. I would and do advise any young person starting out in photography to take photos of pets if they like working with animals. Probably as much money can be made having a pet portrait studio as having one for humans. I don't say that the pets are easier to photograph, but you do get less verbal flack from your subjects. If you can take professional-quality pet photos, you can easily get commercial prices. More pet photos command more dollars and are more in demand than are most wildlife photographs.

Coaxing or cajoling cuddly domestic creatures to pose is too much like posing people for their portraits. I don't do that either. I do photograph pets when they are of the working breeds doing their thing out-of-doors. Again, it pays to know your subject. For years I raised springer spaniels, and they were like members of my family. I knew what they would do under certain circumstances and could anticipate their acitons and reactions. Springers are retrievers. Some of the best photos I've taken were when they were bringing back a downed bird.

The black labrador retriever is probably the most popular dog in America today. A few years ago it was the beagle. Black and Chesapeake "Labs," and the golden Labrador, are all excellent retrievers and love to be in the water. They are big, powerful, and full of action—and they will use any excuse to go swimming. They will retrieve, retrieve, retrieve. Get them going into action as they leave the shore or boat. Get them swimming back carrying the duck. For a more formal portrait, have them sit with the duck laid out in front of them.

Setters, pointers, and Brittanies are excellent field dogs that will "go on point" when they locate their quarry. This pointing is as good an example of controlled tension as you are ever likely to find. The dogs are so eager, so tense that only their training prevents them from dashing in on the bird. Whereas you need a fast shutter speed to capture the action of retrievers, you can use a regular speed on pointers.

Try all the different angles. If the dogs are being posed for a portrait I like to shoot at or below eye level. If the dogs are working, I usually shoot at a slightly downward angle. I like to include the hunter and the dog's quarry, if at all possible.

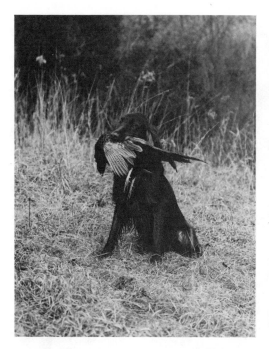
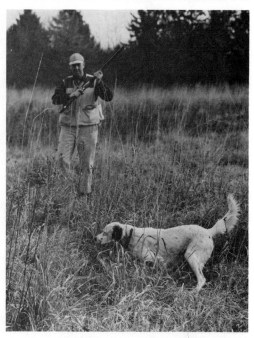

Left This Irish setter is very proud of itself, and well it should be. It has just made a fine retrieve on a downed pheasant.
Right When possible, include the hunter with his dog. Note the effective use of the "third lines" for composition in this photo.

Knowing that rabbits almost always run in circles, if they are run slowly, means that both the rabbit and the dog may come past a particular spot again. This knowledge allows you to get your exposure set and the distance focused. A fast dog will cause a rabbit to hole up; this is why bassets and beagles are favorites for hunting rabbits. Keep your dog on a leash until a rabbit has been started, then focus on the path the rabbit took, have someone release the dog and get pictures of it barreling by on the trail. With most pet photography I can cover almost any situation with a 70 to 210 mm or similar zoom lens.

If you know a dog trainer, that can be a tremendous source of dog photos. The trainer works the dogs every day, so all you have to do is tag along. As various commands and actions are repeated, you will know what to expect. The trainer can set up most situations for you.

Although you will not be allowed to work close when dogs are actually competing in field trials, you should try to get to the trials a couple of days before the show. Usually the best dogs are competing, and trainers try to get to the field-trial area several days before the main event so that their dogs can become familiar with the terrain. Most trainers are more than willing to cooperate with photographers, especially if they get a few photos in return.

To photograph the dogs in action in a duck blind, you will probably have to use a faster film than ordinary. The best duck and goose hunting is done on the worst days. Most action takes place right after dawn when the light is low. To get good action shots with good lighting, you usually have to either set up the situation or work with a trainer working the dogs.

To get the dogs to be at their most alert, make sudden noises, loud noises, blow on a whistle, or get someone to shoot off a gun in the distance. There is nothing like a shot being fired to get the attention of a good gun dog. If you are going to reward the dog for being good, remember a small tidbit is as well received as a large one, and it leaves the dog hungry for more.

Fill light is often used to lighten up a dark dog against a drab background. Regular flash has to be used to get photographs of a coon dog at work because the raccoons are nocturnal.

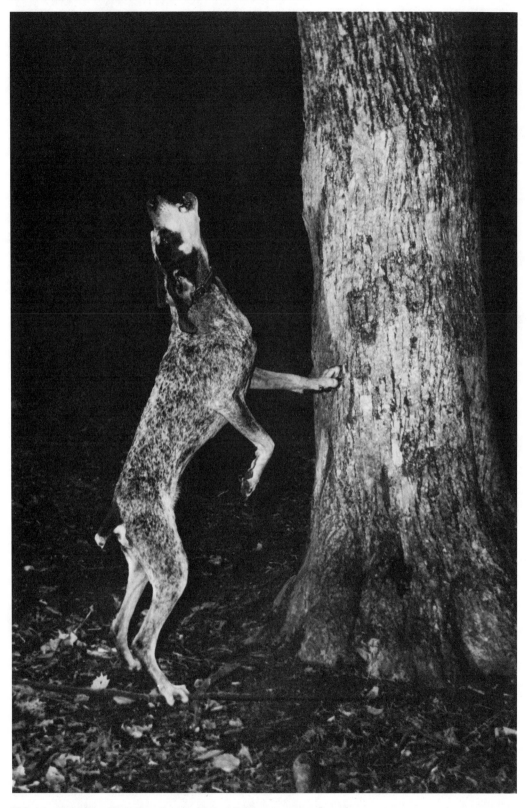

This bluetick hound is telling the world that it has a raccoon treed.

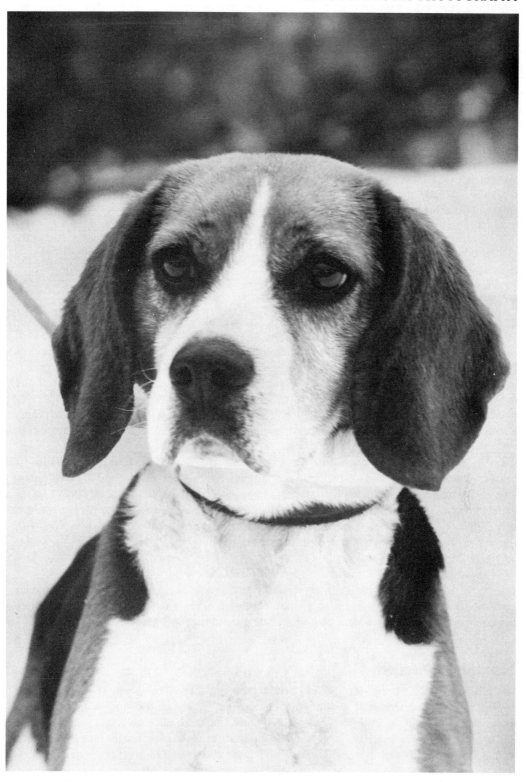

A few years ago, the beagle was the most popular dog in the United States. This portrait clearly shows the dog's great appeal.

UNDERWATER PHOTOGRAPHY

*We are really all underwater creatures having
spent the first nine months of our lives in
amniotic fluids.*

—L. L. Rue III

There is a brand new, exciting world waiting for you underwater. To neglect it is to miss out on what life there is on seventh-eighths of the world's surface. It is a world of freedom from gravity where you can soar, float, dive, and roll about as nowhere else except outer space. I love being in the water, I feel so at home there. I am also cognizant of the dangers there.

I became interested in diving back in 1959-60. A friend of mine was a certified scuba instructor, and he taught me the proper procedures. No one should attempt to use aqualungs without first having professional instruction.

In the early 1960s I took some of the first, if not the first, underwater photographs of beavers. I was writing a book on beavers, and my tank and wetsuit allowed me to go underwater to make observations and do photographs. I know exactly what a beaver does when it swims underwater because I was there. I was also able to dispel the myth that a beaver's top speed is only 2 miles an hour. Writers who continually echoed that speed hadn't been swimming with the beaver. If you really want to see a beaver move, just dive down and grab him by the tail; it will do better than 7 miles an hour.

Twenty-five years and five major ear operations later, I have put aside my air tanks and have to be satisfied with snorkeling. I can comfortably go down to 20 feet or so, but I can no longer equalize the pressure in my ears at greater depths. I haven't really had to give up much because a good part of underwater photography is done in the top 20 feet.

Equipment Needed

In addition to your bathing suit, you will need a face mask, a snorkel, a pair of flippers, and if the water is cold, some sort of wetsuit. In an emergency I have used two pairs of long winter underwear to prevent the rapid exchange of body heat that cold water causes.

I prefer a large-size face mask that has bent sides to the front plate because it gives me side vision. There are now self-draining snorkels, so you do not have to blow all the water from the tube when you come to the surface. If you are going to spend some time over fairly deep water, I would also recommend that you have a large inflated tube with a net bottom in it that can be anchored over your diving location. This is handy to use if you need a rest, it gives you a place

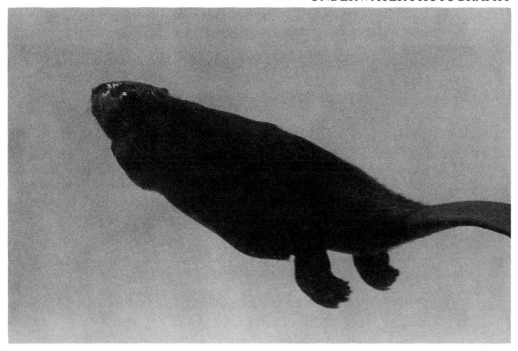

One of the first photos taken of a beaver swimming underwater.

to put your gear, and it marks your location so that you aren't run over by a speedboat. I have used several underwater rigs to keep my cameras dry. When I did the beaver photos, I was using an Alpa 35 mm camera in a Mar-vel waterproof housing. I used a Weston meter in a plastic case. I would have to dive down; take a meter reading; come up; set the camera's shutter speed, f stop, and distance; and put the camera in the underwater housing. I usually used the 24 mm lens so that my depth of field was considerable, and critical focusing was not that important for black and white films. I did have external housing knobs to trip the shutter and advance the film.

Water has a tendency to magnify objects, and there is refraction or a bending of anything entering from the surface, be it light rays or a solid object. Things just are not where they seem to be underwater.

Rangefinders are not used very often underwater because of the water's magnification. Usually, the distance is estimated. What you see and estimate with your eye is also what the lens sees and records. If actual measurement from the subject to the camera is done, then 25 percent of that distance must be subtracted before you set the distance on the camera to allow for the water's magnification.

Because of this magnification, the 35 mm is considered the normal lens; the 28 mm is even more popular. These shorter than normal lenses allow for a much greater depth of field, minimizing errors in distance estimation.

A special lens can be placed over the 28 mm, 35 mm, and 80 mm lenses for close-up photography. This lens is used with a wire-framing device so that exact focusing is precise.

Soft camera housings were once available, but they just were not as satisfactory as the rigid cases. Today I use a Nikonos, which has to be the most commonly used and certainly one of the least expensive ways to take underwater photographs.

The Nikonos is a completely waterproof camera sealed with lubricated rings. It is well designed, and you can do all the basic camera functions—setting your f stop and shutter speed, focusing, releasing the shutter, and winding the film—while submerged.

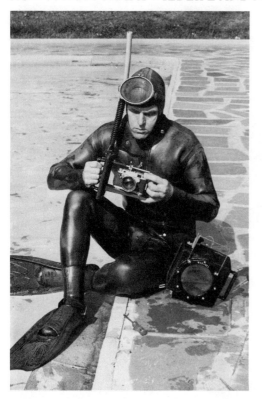

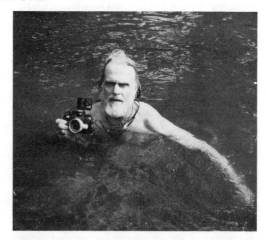

Above L. L. Rue III with Nikonos IV.

Left L. L. Rue III using wetsuit, snorkel, flippers, a 35 mm camera and a Mar-Vel underwater camera housing.

My newest Nikonos IV can be set for automatic shutter exposure control. After you set the camera for the proper ASA-ISO number, you then set the lens aperture that you want, and depress the shutter release knob halfway. If the scene has enough brightness coming through your lens aperture, a light glows inside the viewfinder. If the light blinks, there is not enough light to take the photo. The lens aperture should be opened one stop at a time till the light glows and then the picture taken will be properly exposed. If the light continues to blink after the lens is wide open, you have to use a faster film or have to use flash. This system does away with having to use an external exposure meter.

The Nikonos comes with a 35 mm lens that focuses down to about 3 feet. This basic outfit also can be used above water in wet situations, such as when rafting, water skiing, or when out in rainstorms. Auxiliary plastic viewfinders act as a sportsfinder and are calibrated for the several lenses available for this camera.

The 28 mm lens has a greater depth of field than the 35 mm lens, but can be used only underwater. It is the preferred lens for most underwater work. I do not like "fisheye" lenses at any time, and the 15 mm can be used only underwater. The 80 mm works equally well underwater or on dry land. This again makes the Nikonos a very versatile camera for above water, bad weather situations, or water sports photography.

Water absorbs light. Particles of silt and a microscopic plankton further absorb, scatter, or prevent light from penetrating to any great depth. Distances below 15 feet require a light. Almost no one uses flashbulbs today because of the high cost per shot and the time and trouble that carrying, changing, and retrieving the bulbs entails. The bulbs pack a more powerful punch of light than do most electronic flash guns. Nevertheless, the electronic flash is used almost exclusively today.

Several new cameras are available that can be used around water, above or beneath the surface. The Minolta Weathermatic, the Alfon All Weather, and the Fuji All Weather cameras are all designed to be used above the surface under rainy or snowy conditions or when you

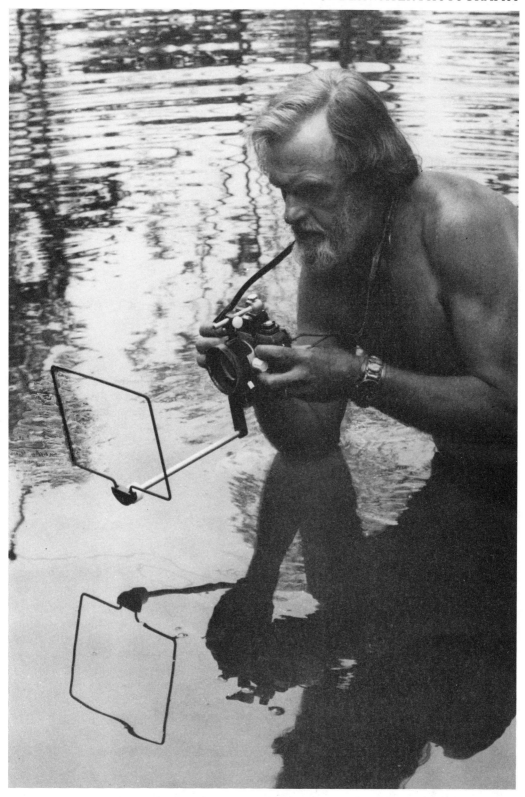

A wire framing device for precise focusing with the close-up lens.

are water skiing, sailing, or running rafts in rough water. These cameras can be used underwater if you do not go deeper than 10 or 12 feet. The Fuji is a full-frame 35 mm; the Minolta and Alfon take 110 film.

The Hanimex Amphibian, the Sea & Sea Pocket Marine, and the Vivitar 85AW are also 110 format cameras, but they can be used underwater to depths of 150 feet, with the Vivitar good for 300 feet.

The Formaplex, the Hanimex 35mm Amphibian, the Sea & Sea Motor Marine, and the Ricoh ADI are of the 35 mm format and are good for depths of 98 to 230 feet, according to the model.

Ikelite has always produced good, rigid cases that sustain pressures down to 300 feet. They even have a case that fits the new disc cameras. The Ewa Marine is a soft case that fits a large number of cameras. It features a molded glove that is a part of the case and allows you to focus, change f and speed stops, push the release button, and advance the film. These will keep your gear dry down to 100 feet.

All-weather and underwater cameras and cases depend on a rubber O-ring to keep the water out. These rubber gaskets must be carefully checked for dirt and cracks before each usage. Then the thinnest film of O-ring grease must be applied and the ring seated properly before the case is closed. If cared for properly, these cameras will keep the water out. After using any of these cameras in salt water, they must be washed off, externally, with fresh water before being allowed to dry.

Photographing Underwater

The ideal time to photograph underwater is when the sun is as high in the sky as is possible, say from 10:00 A.M. to 2:00 P.M. This allows for the deepest penetration of light. Remember, when light rays enter the water at an angle, they are bent so that they refract in different directions. A cloudless sky is preferred, although high, thin clouds offer good diffusion with little light loss.

The faster the film speed, the greater depth of field, whether above or below the water. This is one of the few times I use an Ektachrome film, and I prefer the Ektachrome 400 over the 200. Or, if you want to stay with the chromes, I much prefer the Fuji 100 and then use an electronic flash, no matter what the depth.

If you are working in shallow water and the bottom has good, white sand, the reflections may allow you to shoot without flash.

Water not only drastically reduces your visibility, but what you can see also depends upon the turbidity. Suspended particles not only cut down visibility, but may also cause reflections from either the sunlight or your flash unit. There is no way you can cut out the sun's reflections, but by shooting your flash a foot or more away above the camera's lens, you can lessen flash reflection.

Colors change drastically as the water, acting as a filter, absorbs various wavelengths of the spectrum. Red coloration is lost at depths of 10 to 12 feet, orange at 20 to 35 feet, and yellow at 60 feet. At depths beyond 15 feet you have to use flash to ensure enough light for a proper exposure; and flash is a must if you want to record your subjects in true colors. Occasionally you may even have to add a red filter to your lens or over your electronic flash.

Remember, as you go deeper you continually lose more light through water absorption. It is the same as losing light when shooting in a dark forest. If you are using an automatic electronic flash that has a light sensor governing the light's output, you are all right. If you are using a manual flash, you will have to open up the lens aperture corresponding to your depth and the light loss incurred.

Plan to photograph on as calm a day as possible. Wave action makes it all but impossible to remain in one position. I was snorkeling off Marchena Island in the Galapagos in 1978. The

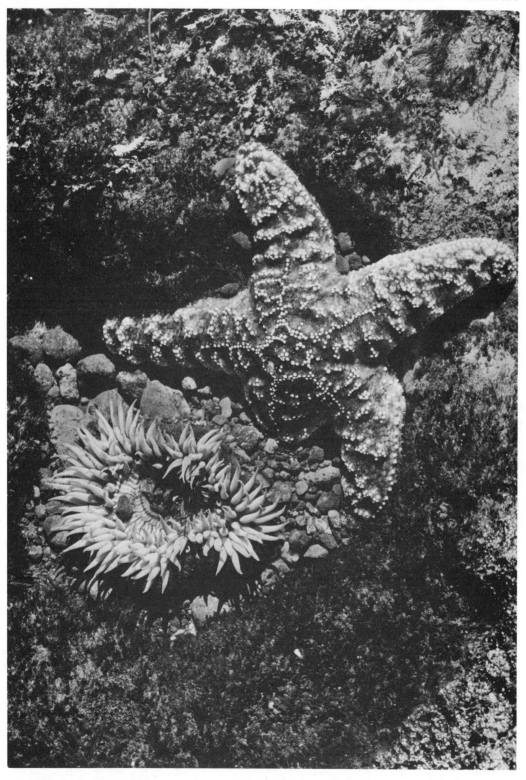

Sea anemone and starfish in a shallow tidal pool. Photo by Len Rue, Jr.

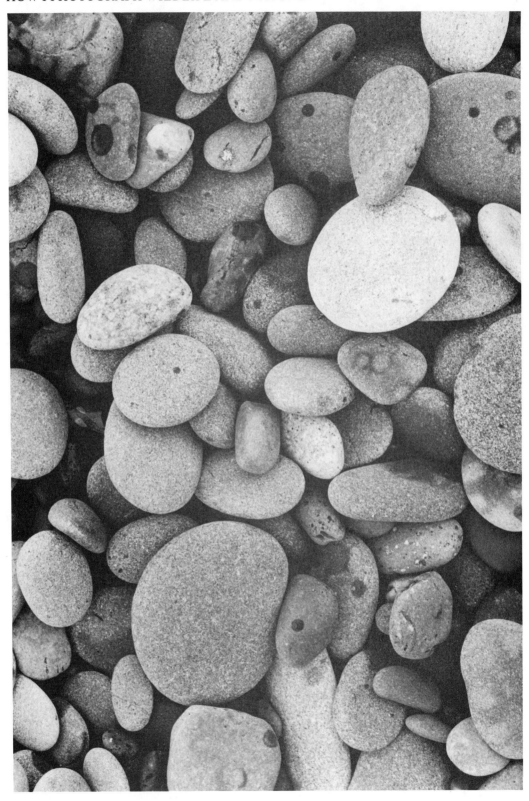

Beach pebbles. Photo by Len Rue, Jr.

fish life was unbelievable; they were there by the thousands. Photography was out of the question because the rip tides were so strong that everything, the fish included, were in constant motion. And because of rock formations, the currents were split and diversified. I never got in sync with the fish.

Do not forget yourself and attempt to change lenses or film underwater. You have to come to the surface and dry off your equipment and yourself before changing film. Don't drip salt water on the camera's interior; dry off first.

Any equipment used in salt water has to be washed off with fresh water before you put it away.

Precautions

You should not do underwater photography alone. You can become so intent on doing the photography that you may not be aware of danger. You should not dive with an aqualung alone, either, with or without a camera.

I like to wear a heavy glove on my left hand in case I have to reach out to touch something. Coral is often exceptionally sharp. Many swimmers cut by coral do not realize they have been cut till they get ashore and find that they are bleeding. Some corals cause painful infections.

Unless you have been doing a lot of swimming with fins, wear regular socks under your fins. The socks will prevent the fins' straps from chafing your ankles.

Many spiny fish and sea urchins have poisonous spines for protection; they should not be touched. Jellyfish seem to be cyclic; their numbers are so high in some years, in some areas, that it is not safe to be in the water unless you have on a wetsuit that will prevent body contact. Poison from a jellyfish can cause anything from a burning sensation to intense pain. Some people who have touched jellyfish have drowned after going into anaphylactic shock.

Barracudas are usually more curious than dangerous. They are more dangerous to spear fishermen than photographers because of the attraction of the fish blood.

Shark attacks are either increasing or the attacks are getting better coverage by the media. We hear of many more cases of people being attacked than we did just a few years ago. According to statistics, there are over 250 species of sharks throughout the world with an estimated population well in excess of 5 billion! Most species of sharks do not attack humans, but some do. At the first appearance of a shark, get out of the water. There has been only one authenticated shark attack in the Galapagos, but when a shark appeared in the bay where we were swimming, we got out of the water at once.

Sharks feed either along the bottom or near the surface of the water. They are particularly attracted to the blood of speared fish, so if you are photographing a spear fisherman, bear that in mind. The normal splashing that a swimmer makes on the water's surface also attracts sharks. If you are some distance from shore when a shark is sighted, swim 6 to 10 feet beneath the surface, coming up just for air.

The ocean is a fascinating place to photograph, but it can be deadly. Treat the ocean with the respect it deserves.

SELLING YOUR PHOTOS

*You cannot make a good living just selling
wildlife photographs; you also have to write
and lecture with them.*
—Allan D. Cruickshank

Although I am the most published wildlife photographer in North America, perhaps in the world, I endorse Allan Cruickshank's statement wholeheartedly. He gave me this advice in a personal letter dated June 17, 1950, when he was the most published bird photographer in the country, and I was just getting started. It is the advice I pass on today to anyone who asks me about wildlife photography. I am quick to add, however, as Allan did: Do not give up on wildlife photography. It can add new and exciting dimensions to your life. Forewarned is forearmed. You have been warned, and I have written this book to help arm you. If you approach wildlife photography realistically, it can produce considerable income. The amount depends on your knowledge of wildlife, your skill as a photographer, the time you are able to spend doing photography, the protection of your rights, the researching of your markets, and the time you spend trying to sell your work.

Skill in wildlife photography may help you get a job, or it may prove to be an important adjunct to your present job. Almost every job in the biological sciences will be helped by a knowledge of wildlife photography. A biologist who is a good photographer will always be hired before one who does not know how to use a camera. Although some states' fish and game or environmental resources departments have an official wildlife photographer on staff, many do not. Even those that have a staff photographer often find that it is cheaper to buy work from freelance wildlife photographers than to send their staff man out to do the job from scratch. The bulk of the wildlife photography produced in this country is done by people with steady jobs who freelance on the side.

I hate all aspects of business, yet I must be a businessman if I want to make a living. Every hour spent at a desk, and I have spent months at one, writing this book, is an hour that I cannot spend out-of-doors. Everyone envies me because they think I spend all my time out-of-doors, photographing wildlife. That is the first and greatest fallacy about wildlife photography. The time actually spent photographing wildlife is the icing on the cake; it is the smallest of my time expenditures.

It is also a little-known fact that for every day spent out-of-doors doing photography, you will spend one day looking through your photographs, selecting, rejecting, stamping, coding, captioning, encasing in plastic, querying editors, shipping, filing, and so on. That's if you shoot color. If you shoot black and white, the time spent will be much greater because there are so

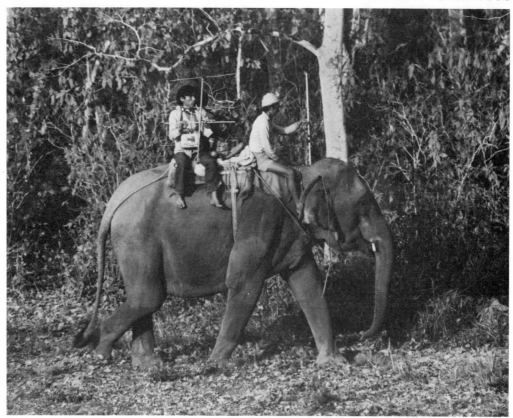

Bioligists radio-monitoring tigers in the jungles of Nepal. It was by using elephants that we got our best rhino photos. Photo by Irene Vandermolen

many more processes or steps involved. Even though I employ a darkroom technician to print the photos, one woman to dry the photos and another to caption the photos, and I have a secretary to handle filing and shipping, black and white photographs require more of my time than color does. And black and white photos do not sell as well, or pay as well, as color.

Why bother with black and white? Because many magazines, newspapers, and books cannot afford to buy or cannot use color. I have sold to every major and most every secondary publication in this country, and throughout most of the world, that uses nature or wildlife photography. Top-grade magazines pay top-grade prices, but my entire business has been built on the idea that if I take care of enough of the little guys, they will take care of me.

For years my darkroom turned out over 100,000 8″ X 10″ black and white prints a year. The exorbitant cost of paper has now forced me to cut production to about 60,000 prints a year. I am currently servicing about 100 publishers and clients each year on a regular basis. Twenty-seven of the states' fish, game, and environmental protection agencies use my photos. When people say they see my photos everywhere, my answer is that they should. I work long hours every day, seven days a week, either taking photographs, processing them, or promoting them.

I am truly blessed. I am one of those fortunate people who love the work they do; most people don't feel that way. Photography has made this possible. I never take a vacation because I always end up taking wildlife photos. Yet my life cannot be considered a constant vacation, as some claim, because I work hard. My goal, and I think everyone should constantly set realistic goals, is to be able to spend even more time photographing wildlife. As I tell everyone, when it comes to my production of wildlife photos, "You ain't seen nothing yet."

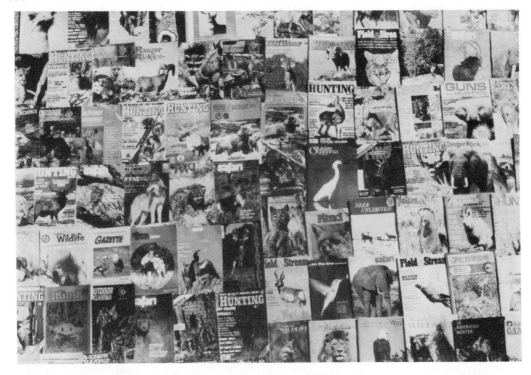

I have sold over a thousand magazine covers; I had five in one day.

Protecting Your Film

Every photograph is the result of an expenditure of considerable time, effort, and money. Maximum protection should be given to your photos from the time that you purchase the film.

Buy your film in as large a quantity as you can afford to ensure that it is all from the same emulsion batch. There are slight differences in every batch, although they may be too slight to make a difference.

Film has a shelf life of about 12 months. After film has been "aged" for 2 months by the manufacturer to stabilize any color shifting, it is shipped to the dealer. I would not shoot any color film that listed more than one year till the time of that film's expiration date. Any film with more than one year has not been aged properly and the film will have a green cast when processed. A test should be done on each batch of film so that you will know exactly what it will do. Then store the unopened film in a refrigerator or freezer, and it will remain in good condition for years. Remove the film, and allow it to thaw for at least 24 hours before you intend to use it. Do not store film in the cold if you have removed it from the canister, or you will get condensation marks on the film.

Never leave film where it will be subjected to intense heat, such as in the back window of your car. You can carry film in a styrofoam ice chest with or without a coolant. Always load and unload film in the shade, or if that's not possible, at least shaded by your body.

Always process film as soon as possible after exposure. I have absolutely nothing against independent film processing labs; I just don't use their services. I always recommend that you have the film manufacturer process its own film. There is enough of a discrepancy in the quality of the work turned out by the manufacturer's various processing plants. I have found, as have many other professionals, that Kodak's labs in Rochester, New York, and Fairlawn, New Jersey, do the best job with their films. My results with Fuji film are best when the film is processed in their lab in Anaheim, California.

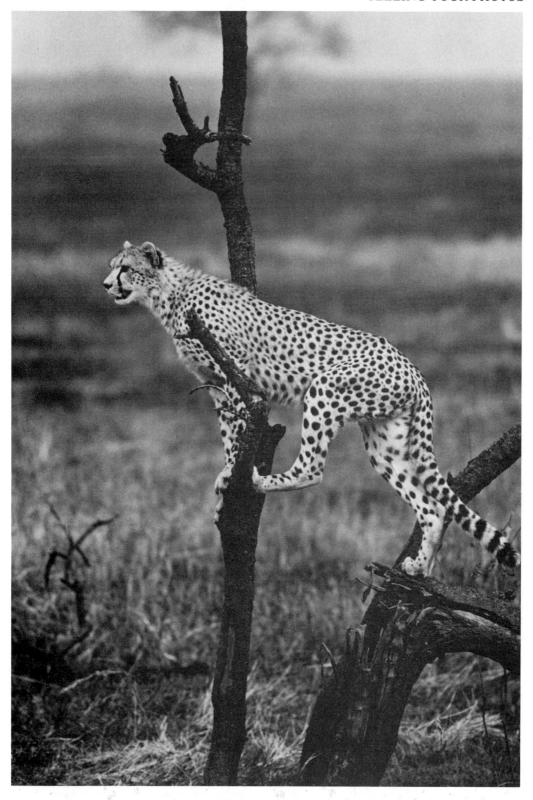

I feel privileged to have photographed cheetah in the wild.

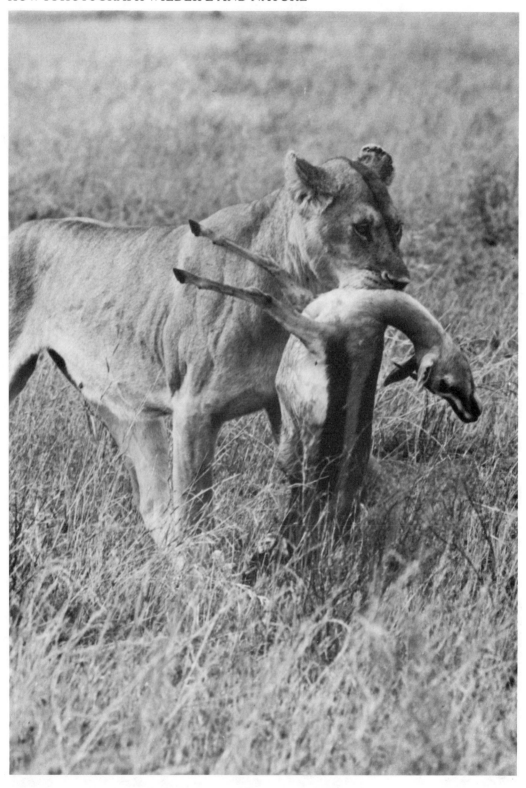

When I'm overseas, I airmail small batches of film home periodically for testing both film and cameras. I wouldn't want to miss photos like this lioness carrying a gazelle.

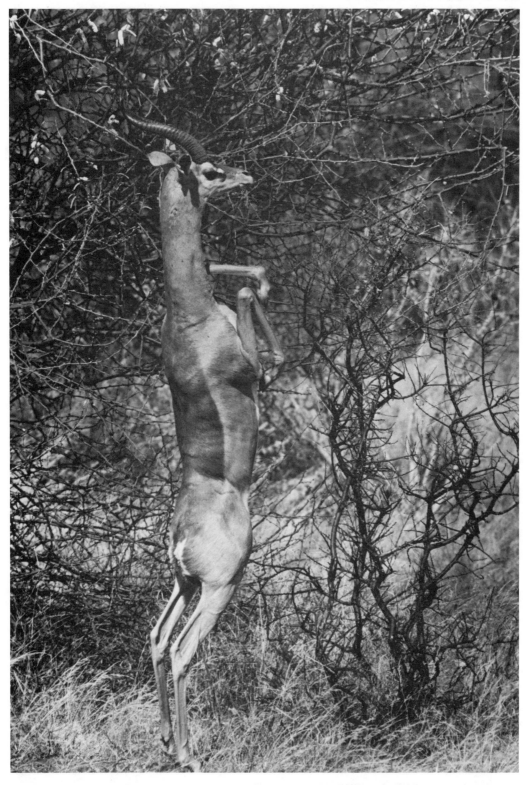

Northern Kenya, where I photographed this male gerenuk feeding, is hot and dry. I kept my film insulated in blankets in the shade during the heat of the day.

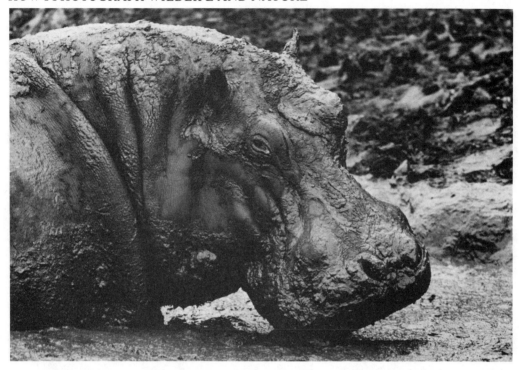

Humidity was a problem when I was photographing hippos in Uganda.

If you are going to travel overseas, I suggest you buy and test your film here at home, before you go, and take the film with you. All too often you will not be able to buy your favorite film overseas, or the film may be outdated. I can guarantee that buying film overseas will be far more expensive. Most of the developing countries do not have film processing plants, and so you will have no way to test the film after you shoot it. On any extended trip I periodically airmail film back home. My secretary previews it and sends me a report and often one or two transparencies. The results not only run a check on the film but also on the performance of the cameras.

Thank God, and I do, I have not had any problem with X-ray machines spoiling my film. I get to the airport early and have the film and my cameras inspected by hand instead of being sent through the machines. Lead-lined bags will protect your film against X-rays, but I carry too much film to use the bags. Be sure to ascertain the regulations on film and cameras of the countries you intend to visit before you go. Some countries have restrictions on cameras and film. Call the country's consulate in New York City or Washington, D.C.

If you are going to use film in the field under extremely cold weather conditions, carry the film in your pants' pockets where it can be warmed by the heat from your legs. When temperatures get down below zero, film becomes brittle and will shatter like glass. As you use the film, keep replacing it with rolls from an outside pocket.

If you are doing photography under extremely dry atmospheric conditions, you must be careful when rewinding the finished film back into the container. Rapid rewinding creates static electricity, which can produce streaks on the film. Although this has less likelihood of happening when the film is wound back by hand, it can easily occur when using a motor drive for rewinding the film. Often the streaks are mistakenly thought to be scratches made on the film by a rough spot on the camera's film pressure plate.

To prevent the pressure plate from actually scratching the film, the plate should be cleaned

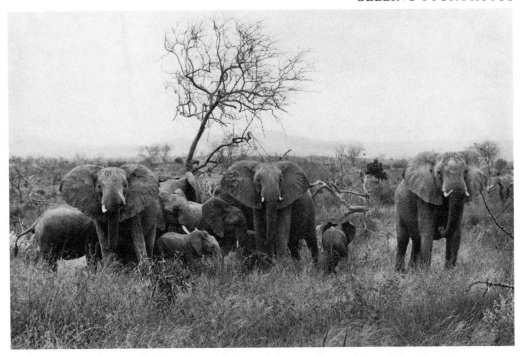

The "one-time use" proviso has allowed me to sell this elephant herd to five different major publishers.

with a camel's hair brush. The inside of the camera body should be blown clean with air periodically.

When working in the desert, I have never had trouble with heat affecting my film. I carry my film in a large styrofoam cooler. As it is usually cold in the desert after dark, I leave the lid off the cooler all night and allow both film and container to cool down. By putting the lid back on at dawn, the film is kept fairly cool all day. The styrofoam chests are white, which also reflects heat away during the daytime.

In the tropics, or any other area of high humidity, both your film and your cameras should be protected from moisture by being in watertight cases that have a package of silica gel enclosed. The gel will remove the moisture inside the cases. Periodically, the gel can be dried in the sun or in an oven. Without these precautions, fungus will grow very rapidly on both the film and your equipment.

Protecting Your Cameras

Before leaving the country, make a list of the serial numbers of the camera gear that you are taking with you and give it to the customs officials. They will often accept a Xeroxed copy of your insurance policy listing the items. Without such a listing, on your return you may be asked to pay an import tax on any equipment that looks new if you cannot prove you purchased it before you left this country.

Always carry your basic cameras and lenses on the plane with you to be sure that they will get off the plane when you do. Make sure that the camera and lenses you carry, as well as the spares that you ship as baggage, are well padded. The Lowe Pro sack that I carry on planes is well padded and fits under the seat nicely. The foam inserts in Pelican cases are very good for the gear I ship as luggage. This is particularly important because the vibrations of a plane's jet engines will cause screws to loosen in both cameras and lenses.

LEONARD RUE ENTERPRISES
R. D. No. 3, Box 31
Blairstown, N. J. 07825
Phone: (201) 362-6616
    or (201) 475-2952

ONE-TIME U.S. REPRODUCTION RIGHTS ONLY
OTHER RIGHTS NEGOTIATED
USE:

FEE:

Date Shipped To:

MARK 9:23 "I BELIEVE"

Photos not held for final selection must be returned on or before

IMPORTANT ➤
Please Read Reverse Side Carefully

*SIGN PINK COPY TO SIGNIFY RECEIPT OF THE PHOTOGRAPHS AND RETURN TO LEONARD RUE ENTERPRISES AT ONCE.

Total Number of Photographs

35mm	2-1/4	4x5	8x10

Number	Subject of Photograph	Number	Subject of Photograph

*We acknowledge receipt of all of the above listed photographs, and agree to all of the above terms as well as to the terms set forth on the reverse side hereof.

Signed

LEONARD RUE ENTERPRISES

Credit Line Must Read LEONARD LEE RUE III, or the Photographer's Name Stated on Back of the Photo.

TERMS OF SUBMISSION AND SALE:

All photographs (said term includes black and white photographs as well as color transparencies) are submitted to you for the length of time specified on the front side. After said date the rejects must be returned to us although any photographs still under consideration may be held until the final decision is made, providing you let us know the approximate date of the decision. Failure to return the rejects and to let us know what photographs are being held for further consideration makes you liable of a holding charge of $1.00 per week per photograph. Upon submission to you, all photographs are held at your risk against loss, theft or damage, until received back by Leonard Rue Enterprises.

For our mutual protection, you are to return the photographs to us in the following manner:

Color transparencies via registered mail, insured.

To assure accurate billing, you are to advise us in writing which photographs you have selected by specifying the title and the number of each photograph as it appears on the reverse side hereof. You are to return the rejected photographs, if any, on or before the date specified on the front hereof, and you are to return all photos selected by you for reproduction within a reasonable time after publication.

If you fail to return the photographs submitted to you on or before the expiration of the original or agreed extended holding period, as the case may be, such failure to return within two weeks after our written demand for return of the photographs shall constitute your agreement to a sale of one-time reproduction rights, and an invoice will be rendered to you by us for the full quoted price of such rights plus holding fee to date. The holding fee will continue to accrue until full payment of such invoice is made.

Color transparencies damaged, lost, or not returned immediately after the color plates are made, or within six months after date of invoice, will be billed for at three times the price specified for one-time reproduction.

Money due us that is not paid within 60 days of rendered bill will have annual percentage rate of 18% added on monthly basis of 1½%.

Upon our receipt of your written advice of selection and confirmation of acceptance of prices and terms quoted, you will acquire one-time U.S. reproduction rights to the photographs selected by you. You will also acquire one-time reproduction rights to the photographs for which an invoice was rendered to you by reason of your failure to return such photographs upon written demand, as set forth in the preceding paragraph. The right to reproduce a photo does not give the purchaser any other rights to the original photo.

No rights granted to you by us may be disposed of by you to others without prior written consent from us.

If the photograph selected by you and invoiced to you for use in a book or other publication, a separate reproduction fee must be negotiated and paid for each subsequent edition, revised edition, foreign edition or foreign language edition, advertising material or any other reproduction whatsoever.

All prices are doubled if credit line is omitted. Credit line should read, "Leonard Lee Rue III." or the photographer's name stated on back of photo. Where credit line cannot be used, consideration will be given to exceptions in special cases.

Leonard Lee Rue III is the owner of the photographs submitted, and holds the copyright therein.

LEONARD RUE ENTERPRISES

Do not leave your camera where it will be in a confined area exposed to sunlight, such as inside a locked car in the summer. Cameras, being black, readily absorb heat and can cook your film. If possible, don't leave the camera lying in the sunshine for any extended period.

If you are using several cameras at one time, do not place the unused camera on its back with an uncapped lens pointing up. The sun shining through the lens is magnified and can burn holes through a cloth focal plane shutter and ruin the film.

On packhorse trips into the back country, make sure that your cameras are in their plastic Pelican cases or in strong wooden panniers. Do not put your cameras in soft leather saddlebags. I have had horses deliberately lie down and roll to get rid of anything and everything they have on their backs. Be particularly careful of even the horse you are riding when you stop for a break or to let the horses rest because many will try to roll at that time. Inadvertently, the packhorses often smash into trees or jutting rock ledges.

I deliberately paint my camera bags and cases with camouflage. I do this so that they are not noticed by the wildlife in the field or the wild life on the streets. My gear does not look worth the trouble of stealing.

Protecting Your Rights

Every photograph I take, be it black and white or color, is stamped with my name, address, copyright seal, and code number; it says "one-time use only," is captioned, and the color transparencies are encased in Kimac plastic sleeves before anything leaves my home. Your photographs should be protected in the same manner.

Your photographs do not have to be filed with the Copyright Office for you to be protected. For years, the moment you stamped that copyright seal in place, that showed your ownership and your intent to file, if needed. Under the new law, the moment you expose the film to light, you are the owner of that film unless you are working for a salary, and in that case, whoever pays your salary owns the copyright. However, you must still stamp the copyright seal and the year date and your name to be fully protected. Exceptional photos should be filed with the Copyright Office. Copyrighted material can now be protected for 75 years. Let no photograph out without a copyright seal: ©.

Before you ship any photograph, you should query the editor of the publication to see if he or she is interested in seeing the subject you have photographed. An editor who expresses an interest in your work will probably assume the responsibility of return postage and handling. If you submit without a prior query, make sure you enclose a self-addressed return envelope stamped with enough postage to get your work back. Many editors do not have the time to look at unqueried work, and they are not under any obligation to return it to you. Photographs that are solicited by editors or publishers will be returned to you at their expense.

So, you have made your query, and the editor wants to see your work. Don't ship it out until you have some sort of a shipping sheet, spelling out the terms of the agreement, the agreed-upon price, the photo usage, and the length of time the editor can hold the work before it must be returned.

Rather than go through all the details, I'm reprinting a copy of my shipping sheets. Make sure that you send the client two copies so that one copy can be signed and returned to you.

I would suggest that you always ship your photographs by a carrier that requires an acceptance signature when the package is delivered.

Pricing Your Work

One of the fastest ways of learning the hard, cold facts of life concerning wildlife photography is when you attempt to set the price that is to be paid for your photographs.

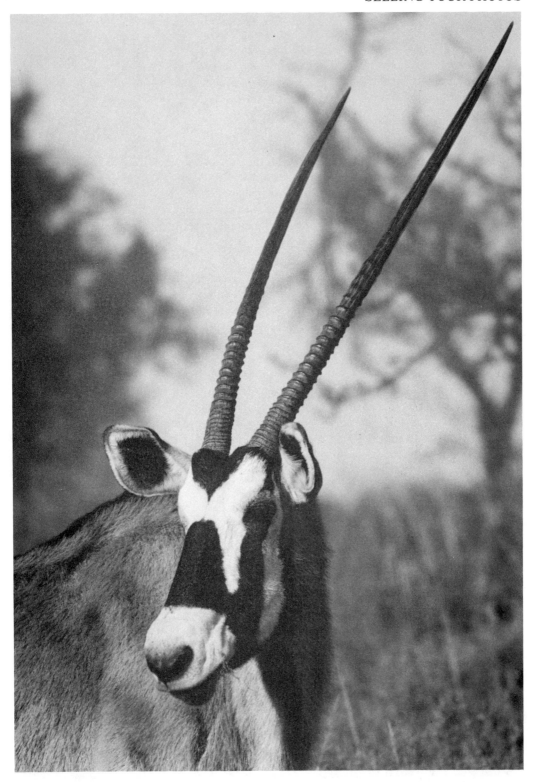

Although this is a great photo of a South African gemsbok, photos of African game do not sell well in this country.

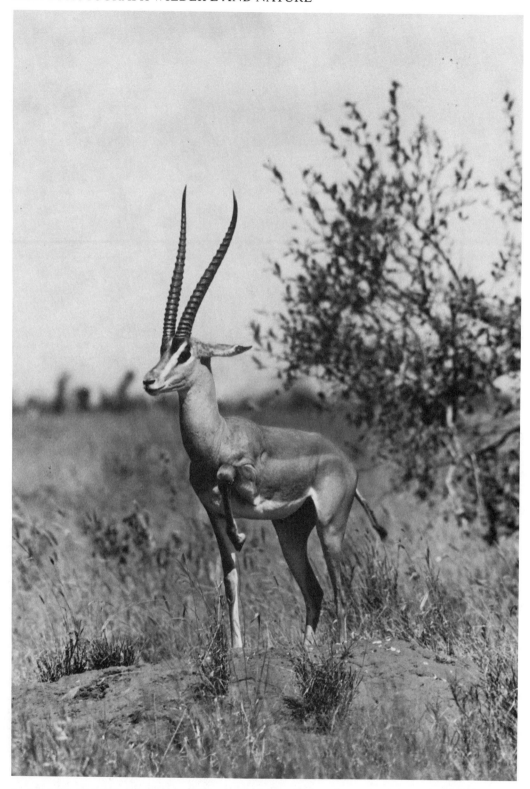

A photographic agent can be selling my pictures of a Peter's gazelle while I'm out in the field photographing something else.

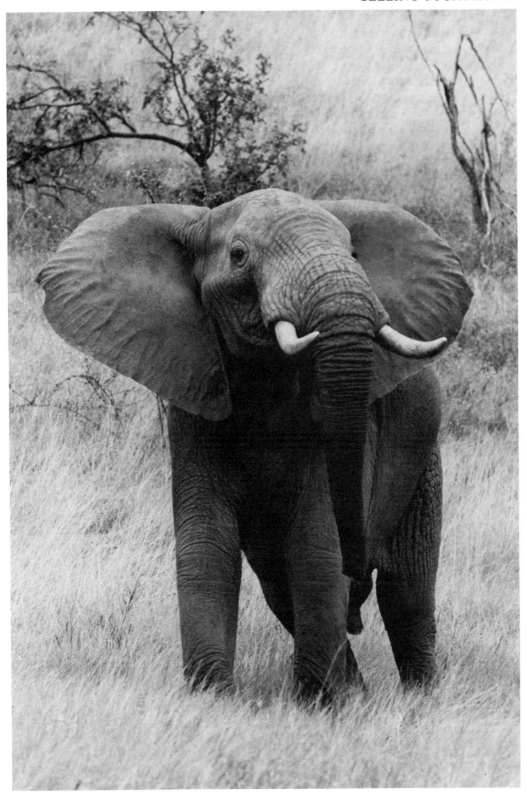

This photo of an African bull elephant has sold a number of times.

HOW I PHOTOGRAPH WILDLIFE AND NATURE

Prices paid for photographs are based on how the photographs are to be used. Generally, work used in advertising commands the highest prices. Magazine covers are in second place. Calendar photographs rank about third. Rates of payment of photographs sold to various magazines are generally based on the magazine's circulation. The larger magazines pay the highest rates. The most prestigious magazines do not necessarily pay the highest prices; only large-circulation magazines can usually afford really high prices.

Many publications have a hard-and-fast set of prices that they pay for different uses. The only recourse the photographer has in such a situation is the right to refuse to sell his work. I absolutely refuse to deal with some publications because their price structure is too low to make it worthwhile.

Such publications often depend on donated photographs, and the quality of their magazines is abysmal. It is amazing how many beginning photographers are willing to donate their work, good work, just to see their name in print. These same photographers later wonder why they have such a difficult time getting a decent price for their work.

Book publishers are more prone to be open to negotiations than magazine publishers are.

Pricing rates are getting much more complex today as you offer U.S.A. rights; North American rights; English-speaking world rights; entire world rights; $\frac{1}{8}$, $\frac{1}{4}$, $\frac{1}{2}$, $\frac{3}{4}$, full-page, and double-page rights; exclusive rights; first-time rights; and on and on.

The best guide to pricing is the American Society of Magazine Photographers Guidelines. But don't think that you will be paid these prices for nature work. You won't. These prices are based on advertising rates—the cream of the crop. It's what we would all like to get, but won't. Still, the prices can be used as a guide. There are far more photographers doing nature work than there are in advertising.

Very few assignments are given out to wildlife photographers. It is far simpler for editors to put out a call for photos and be guaranteed all the photos they could possibly want to see than to pay a photographer to go to a particular spot and hope that all the conditions are right so that all the pictures that are needed can be gotten. There is always a market for the exceptional photograph, the outstanding photograph, but the general wildlife market is saturated.

By all means, get a photographic agent if you can and if you are producing enough work to make it worthwhile. While some agents split the fee 60/40 in favor of the photographer, most of them split it 50/50. I realize that it is my time, my equipment, my travel expenses, and at times, my life that produce these photos, and the agent takes 50 percent of the sales. Still, while I am out in the field, the agent is back there selling and perhaps earning enough for me to stay in the field. The agent has high rental overhead and salaries and business expenses to pay that must come out of his 50 percent. The better my photography, the better my sales.

Several good books are devoted to selling photographs. I list them and the address of the American Society of Magazine Photographers in the appendix.

BIBLIOGRAPHY

Angel, Heather. *The Book of Nature Photography.* New York: Knopf, 1982.

Bauer, Erwin and Peggy. *Photographing the West. A State-by-State Guide.* Flagstaff, Ariz.: Northland Press, 1980.

Chandoha, Walter. *How to Photograph Cats, Dogs, and Other Animals.* New York: Crown, 1973.

Eastman Kodak. *The Joy of Photography.* Special Portfolios by Gordon Parks and Ernst Haas. Reading, Mass.: Addison-Wesley, 1979.

Eisendrath, David B. *Modern Photography's Dictionary of Camera Gremlins.* Des Moines, Iowa: Modern Photography, n.d.

Feininger, Andreas. *Feininger on Photography.* New York: Crown, 1949.

Freeman, Michael. *The Complete Book of Wildlife & Nature Photography.* New York: Simon and Schuster, 1981.

Jacobs, Lou, Jr. *Amphoto Guide to Selling Photographs: Rates and Rights.* New York: American Photographic, 1979.

Kinne, Russ. *The Complete Book of Nature Photography.* Introduction by Roger Tory Peterson. New York: American Photographic, 1962.

Logan, Larry L. *The Professional Photographer's Handbook*, 1st ed. Los Angeles: Logan Design Group, 1980.

Roche, John P. and Mary A. *Photographing Your Flowers. A Practical Guide for Indoor and Outdoor Use.* New York: Greenberg, 1954. Toronto, Canada: Ambassador Books, 1954.

Roth, Charles E. *The Wildlife Observer's Guidebook.* Englewood Cliffs, N.J.: Prentice-Hall, 1982.

Rue, Leonard Lee, III. *Complete Guide to Game Animals. A Field Guide to North American Species.* New York: Outdoor Life Books-Times Mirror, 1968.

Rue, Leonard Lee, III. *The Deer of North America.* New York: Crown, 1978.

Rue, Leonard Lee, III. *Furbearing Animals of North America.* New York: Crown, 1981.

Rue, Leonard Lee, III. *Pictorial Guide to Mammals of North America.* New York: Crowell, 1967.

Rue, Leonard Lee, III. *Tracks and Tracking, Reading Signs.* Photographs by the author, illustrations by Jim Arnosky. Forthcoming.*

Shiras, George, III. *Hunting Wild Life With Camera and Flashlight.* Vols. 1 and 2. Washington, D.C.: National Geographic Society, 1898.

Wobbe, Harve B. *A New Approach to Pictorial Composition.* East Orange, N.J.: Arvelen Publishers, 1941.

Wooters, John, and Smith, Jerry T. *Wildlife Images A Complete Guide to Outdoor Photography.* Los Angeles: Petersen Publishing, 1981.

*Personally autographed copies are available through Leonard Rue Enterprises, R.D. 3 Box 31, Blairstown, N.J. 07825.

Recommended References for Basic Background Information and Identification of Species:

Audubon Society. *Field Guide to North American Butterflies*. New York: Knopf, 1981.

Audubon Society. *Field Guide to North American Insects and Spiders*. New York: Knopf, 1980.

Audubon Society. *Field Guide to North American Reptiles and Amphibians*. New York: Knopf, 1979.

Borror, Donald J., and White, Richard E. *A Field Guide to the Insects of America North of Mexico*. Boston: Houghton Mifflin, 1970.

Carrier, Rick and Barbara. *Dive: The Complete Book of Skin Diving*. Newly revised by Charles Berlitz. New York: Funk & Wagnalls, 1973.

Palmer, E. Laurence. *Fieldbook of Natural History*, 2d ed. Revised by H. Seymour Fowler. New York: McGraw-Hill, 1975.

Peterson, Roger Tory. *A Field Guide to the Birds East of the Rockies*. Boston: Houghton Mifflin, 1980.

Reader's Digest. *North American Wildlife*. Pleasantville, N.Y.: Reader's Digest Association, 1982.

Robbins, Chandler S.; Bruun, Bertel; and Zim, Herbert S. *A Guide to Field Identification: Birds of North America*. New York: Western, 1966.

Vinning, Frank. *Guidebook of Wild Flowers of North America*. New York: Western, 1984.

SUPPLIERS OF SERVICES & EQUIPMENT

(Bob) Allen Sportswear
P.O. Box 477
Des Moines, IA 50302

American Society of Magazine
Photographers (ASMP)
205 Lexington Avenue
New York, NY 10016

Baker Tree Stands
P.O. Box 1003
Valdosta, GA 31601

Ben Rogers Lee Turkey Calls
Coffeeville, AL 36524

Burnham Brothers
P.O. Box 43
Marble Falls, TX 78654

Cabela's Outfitters
812 13th Avenue
Sidney, NE 69160

Coleman Company
P.O. Box 1762
Wichita, KS 67201

Danner Boots
5188 S.E. International Way
Milwaukie, OR 97222

Early Winters
110 Prefontaine Place South
Seattle, WA 98104

Edwal Correct-A-Chrome Kit
Edwal Scientific Products Division
Falcon Safety Products, Inc.
1065 Bristol Road
Mountainside, NJ 07092

E. Leitz, Inc.
Link Drive
Rockleigh, NJ 07647

Gitzo Tripods
c/o Karl Heitz
P.O. Box 427
Woodside, NY 11377

Gokey Boot Company
84 South Wabasha Street
St. Paul, MN 55107

Gregg Dale
c/o Dale Instruments
P.O. Box 5222
Arlington, VA 22205

(Bob) Hinman Outfitters
1217 West Glen
Peoria, IL 61614

Katadyn Water Filter
c/o Provisions Unlimited
RFD 1
Oakland, ME 04963

Kelty Pack Company·
1801 Victory Boulevard
Glendale, CA 91201

Kimac Plastic Photo Sleeves
478 Long Hill Road
Guilford, CT 06437

Leonard Rue Deer Scents
c/o Hunter's Pro-Pack Ltd.
P.O. Box 362
Edinburg, VA 22824

Leonard Rue's Photographic Equipment
P.O. Box 85
Blairstown, NJ 07825

L.L. Bean, Inc.
Freeport, ME 04033

Lowe Pro Packs
Lowe Alpine Systems
802 South Public Road
Lafayette, CO 80026

Made-To-Order
Pam & Dan Bacon
44 Main Street
Clinton, NJ 08809

Martin Tree Steps
1742 Brown Road
Hephzibah, GA 30815

Old Town Canoes
Old Town, ME 04468

Orvis Company
Manchester, VT 05254

Pelican Cases
c/o Pelican Products
23763 Madison Street
Torrance, CA 90505

Perfection Diaphragm Turkey Calls
P.O. Box 164
Stephenson, VA 22656

Photographer's Markets
c/o Writer's Digest
9933 Alliance Road
Cincinnati, OH 45242

Photographic Society of America
2005 Walnut Street
Philadelphia, PA 19103

Randall Made Knives
P.O. Box 1988
Orlando, FL 32802

Seat Vest
Albert McMillan
P.O. Box 530
Carthage, MS 39051

Space Blanket
Metallized Products
37 East Street
Winchester, MA 01890

Super Yelper Turkey Calls
Richard Shively
Route 2 Box 236
Stephens City, VA 22655

Thermarest Mattress
c/o Cascade Designs, Inc.
Seattle, WA 98100

Trebark Camouflage
c/o Bowing Enterprises, Inc.
P.O. Box 6076
Arlington, VA 22206

Turkey Calls
c/o Penn's Woods Products, Inc.
19 West Pittsburgh Street
Delmont, PA 15626

Winona Sportswear, Inc.
904 East Second Street
Winona, MN 55987

International Health Care
Service
525 East 68th Street
New York, NY 10021

INDEX

World Almanac Publications
Order Form

Quantity	ISBN	Title/Author	Unit Price	Total
	31655-X	Abracadabra! Magic and Other Tricks/Lewis	$5.95/$7.95 in Canada	
	32836-1	Africa Review 1986/Green	$24.95/$33.95 in Canada	
	32834-5	Asia & Pacific Review 1986/Green	$24.95/$33.95 in Canada	
	32632-6	Ask Shagg™/Guren	$4.95/$6.50 in Canada	
	32189-8	Big Book of Kids' Lists, The/Choron	$8.95/$11.95 in Canada	
	31033-0	Civil War Almanac, The/Bowman	$10.95/$14.75 in Canada	
	31503-0	Collector's Guide to New England, The/Bowles and Bowles	$7.95/$10.95 in Canada	
	31651-7	Complete Dr. Salk: An A-to-Z Guide to Raising Your Child, The/Salk	$8.95/$11.50 in Canada	
	32662-8	Confidence Quotient: 10 Steps to Conquer Self-Doubt, The/ Gellman and Gage	$7.95/$10.75 in Canada	
	32627-X	Cut Your Own Taxes and Save˙ 1986/Metz and Kess	$3.95	
	31628-2	Dieter's Almanac, The/Berland	$7.95/$10.25 in Canada	
	32835-3	Europe Review 1986/Green	$24.95/$33.95 in Canada	
	32190-1	Fire! Prevention: Protection: Escape/Cantor	$3.95/$4.95 in Canada	
	32192-8	For the Record: Women in Sports/Markel and Brooks	$8.95/$11.95 in Canada	
	32624-5	How I Photograph Wildlife and Nature/Rue	$9.95/$13.50 in Canada	
	31709-2	How to Talk Money/Crowe	$7.95/$10.25 in Canada	
	32629-6	I Do: How to Choose Your Mate and Have a Happy Marriage/ Eysenck and Kelly	$8.95	
	32660-1	Kids' World Almanac of Records and Facts, The/ McLoone-Basta and Siegel	$4.95	
	32837-X	Latin America & Caribbean Review 1986/Green	$24.95/$33.95 in Canada	
	32838-8	Middle East Review 1986/Green	$24.95/$33.95 in Canada	
	31652-5	Moonlighting with Your Personal Computer/Waxman	$7.95/$10.75 in Canada	
	32193-6	National Directory of Addresses and Telephone Numbers˙,The/Sites	$24.95/$33.95 in Canada	
	31034-9	Omni Future Almanac, The/Weil	$8.95/$11.95 in Canada	
	32623-7	Pop Sixties: A Personal and Irreverent Guide, The/Edelstein	$8.95/$11.95 in Canada	
	32624-5	Singles Almanac, The/Ullman	$8.95/$11.95 in Canada	
	31492-1	Social Security and You: What's New, What's True/Kingson	$2.95	
	0-915106-19-1	Synopsis of the Law of Libel and the Right of Privacy/Sanford	$1.95	
		Twentieth Century: An Almanac, The/Ferrell		
	31708-4	Hardcover	$24.95/$33.95 in Canada	
	32630-X	Paperback	$12.95/$17.50 in Canada	
	32631-8	Vietnam War: An Almanac, The/Bowman	$24.95/$33.95 in Canada	
	32188-X	Where to Sell Anything and Everything/Hyman	$8.95/$11.95 in Canada	
	32659-8	World Almanac˙ & Book of Facts 1986, The/Lane	$5.95/$6.95 in Canada	
	32661-X	World Almanac Book of Inventions˙, The/Giscard d'Estaing	$10.95/$14.75 in Canada	
	29775-X	World Almanac Book of World War II, The/Young	$10.95/$14.75 in Canada	
	0-911818-97-9	World Almanac Consumer Information Kit 1986, The	$2.50	
	32187-1	World Almanac Executive Appointment Book 1986, The	$17.95/$24.95 in Canada	
	32628-8	World Almanac Guide to Natural Foods, The/Ross	$8.95/$11.95 in Canada	
	32194-4	World Almanac's Puzzlink™/Considine	$2.95/$3.95 in Canada	
	32626-1	World Almanac's Puzzlink™ 2/Considine	$2.95/$3.95 in Canada	
	31654-1	World Almanac Real Puzzle™ Book, The/Rubin	$2.95/$3.95 in Canada	
	32191-X	World Almanac Real Puzzle™ Book 2, The/Rubin	$2.95/$3.95 in Canada	
	32625-3	World Almanac Real Puzzle™ Book 3, The/Rubin	$2.95/$3.95 in Canada	
		World of Information: see individual titles		

Mail order form to: **World Almanac Publications**
P.O. Box 984
Cincinnati, Ohio 45201

Orders must be prepaid by one of the following methods:
☐ Check or Money Order for _____ attached
☐ Bill my charge card (Add $5.00 processing charge for orders under $20.00)

Order Total_____

Ohio residents add 5.5% sales tax_____

Shipping and Handling:_____
(Add $2.50 for every purchase up to $50.00, and $1.00 for every $10.00 thereafter)

TOTAL PAYMENT_____

Visa Account # _____ Exp. Date

Master Card Account # _____ Exp. Date

Interbank # _____ Exp. Date

Authorized Signature

Ship to:
Name_____
Street address_____
City/State/Zip Code_____
Special Instructions:_____

All orders will be shipped UPS unless otherwise instructed.
We cannot ship C.O.D.